AF575248

Life's
too short
for bad photos,
these choices
really matter

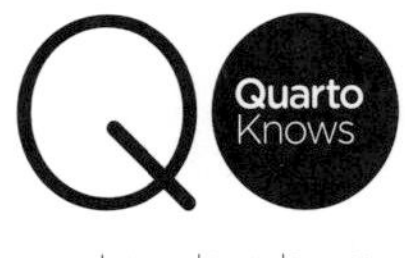

First published in 2021 by Ivy Press,
an imprint of The Quarto Group.
The Old Brewery, 6 Blundell Street
London, N7 9BH,
United Kingdom
T (0)20 7700 6700
www.QuartoKnows.com

A catalogue record for this book is available from the British Library.

ISBN: 978-0-7112-5604-0

10 9 8 7 6 5 4 3 2 1

Design by Eoghan O'Brien

Printed in China

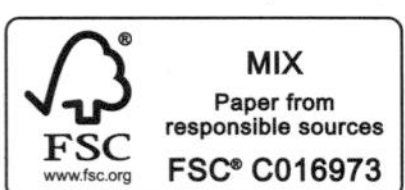

Gemma Padley

LOOK AT THIS *IF YOU LOVE* GREAT PHOTOGRAPHY

A critical curation of
100 essential images

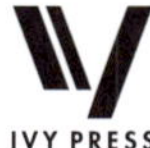

IVY PRESS

CONTENTS

INTRODUCTION

When I was invited to write a book featuring one hundred photos that people must see, I couldn't wait to get started. One hundred photos of any genre, from any period in history? I didn't need to be asked twice. And then the enormity of the task sunk in; how on earth could I pick only a hundred photographs? What criteria should I choose? Lots of photography compendiums exist already, how could I make this book stand out from the rest?

It all started with the curation. The way the images would be grouped and ordered was paramount. A chronological approach is tried and tested but didn't, I felt, leave much room for creativity. Likewise, using a genre-first structure would work fine but who needs another book extolling the virtues of street photography, fashion and documentary in turn? I began thinking about the kinds of questions, thoughts and feelings looking at my favourite images elicited – why has the person taking the picture photographed their subject like that? What is *really* going on in the picture? How does this image make me feel? I began to realize that my approach should not be to try and offer a guide to one hundred noteworthy images as I saw them, but to embrace the unanswered (and in many cases unanswerable) questions that photography opens up. Not just the 'hows,' but the 'whys' too.

As I began searching for images, certain themes started to appear. Drawn to images that were in many ways unconventional, that didn't fit the mould, I saw that a chapter on 'rule-breaking' images was starting to take shape. Perhaps this would be a good place to start: to showcase images that aren't what one expects photographs to be; photographs that shouldn't work but somehow do. And what better way to bring the collection to a close, to point to photography's uniqueness and agency, than by featuring images that reveal what the human eye on its own cannot see?

Over the following pages are photographs that readers will recognize by both famous visionaries and exciting young talents. A mixture of both the lesser known, and those that have become ingrained in our collective consciousness, such as the tragic image of toddler Alan Kurdi washed up on a Turkish beach. We are inundated with images but how often do we stop and really look at photographs and in doing so appreciate the enduring power of photography? This collection invites readers to pause and contemplate one hundred photographs made during the last 160 years that cut through the visual noise.

Please note: Some of the imagery in this book (especially chapter 3) is of a particularly sensitive nature. These photos don't make easy viewing, but serve as important reminders of what is happening in our world.

User Guide

The chapters in this book have been uniquely curated to offer an intriguing juxtaposition of works; and every entry comes packed with extra recommendations to take your appreciation to the next level. Here's a breakdown of what you can expect.

The Links

+ GOOGLE THESE

Other great images by the same photographer; or on occasion, works with similar thematic links by other photographers.

+ DISCOVER THIS

An interesting fact about the photograph.

+ READ THIS

Books, biographies and articles to gaze upon and further your knowledge.

+ WATCH THIS

Movies, documentaries, online interviews or talks worth investigating.

+ LISTEN TO THIS

Podcasts and interviews to find out more about the photographer and their work.

+ LIKE THIS? TRY THESE

If you like what you see, look up these three other photographers with similar works or influences.

The Chapters

Breaking the Rules (10–31)

The main subject might be obscured, the composition unusual or the image blurry, but this adds to rather than takes away from the strength of the photograph.

Photos That Make You Look Twice (32–53)

This chapter features images that trigger a double-take reaction. At a glance they appear to be straightforward, easy to fathom, but all is not as it seems. A second look reveals there is more to these images than first appears.

A Punch in the Gut (54–73)

These are images that spotlight terrible suffering caused by war, migration, racial inequality and poaching as seen through the lenses of photojournalists and documentary photographers across the world.

Reflecting on Who We Are (74–95)

Neither a single image nor small selection of images such as this can answer the question 'what does it mean to be human?' But what these images hope to do is provoke questions about the nature of human endeavour and the trials and tribulations of being alive.

Flirting with Other Art Forms (96–115)

Photography does not exist in a vacuum; it has always rubbed up against other media, whether it's painting, sculpture, collage, performance art or installation. These images are a celebration of photography's relationships with other visual arts.

Photos That Could Be Dreams (116–35)

Once believed to be a medium of indisputable truth, photography is inextricably bound up with fiction, fantasy, dreamworlds and illusion. The images in this chapter may have their roots in the real but evoke dreamlike states or alternative realities.

Reappraising the Everyday (136–55)

These are images that appear uninteresting, unremarkable. On a first look they beg the question, why did the photographer photograph *that*? The images that follow are in fact quite extraordinary because of their apparent ordinariness.

Colour is King (156–77)

This chapter is a celebration of colour in photography, a collection of images where the photographer's use of colour 'makes' the image.

A Wonderful World (178–99)

The images in this chapter reveal how photography has been used to capture, champion and preserve the natural world, from idyllic countryside scenes to dramatic vistas and changing landscapes.

Capturing What the Eye Can't See (200–19)

Photography is celebrated for its ability to 'stop' time, and, as the images in this chapter show, in doing so it allows us to see things we wouldn't otherwise be able to see.

CHAPTER

1 BREAKING THE RULES

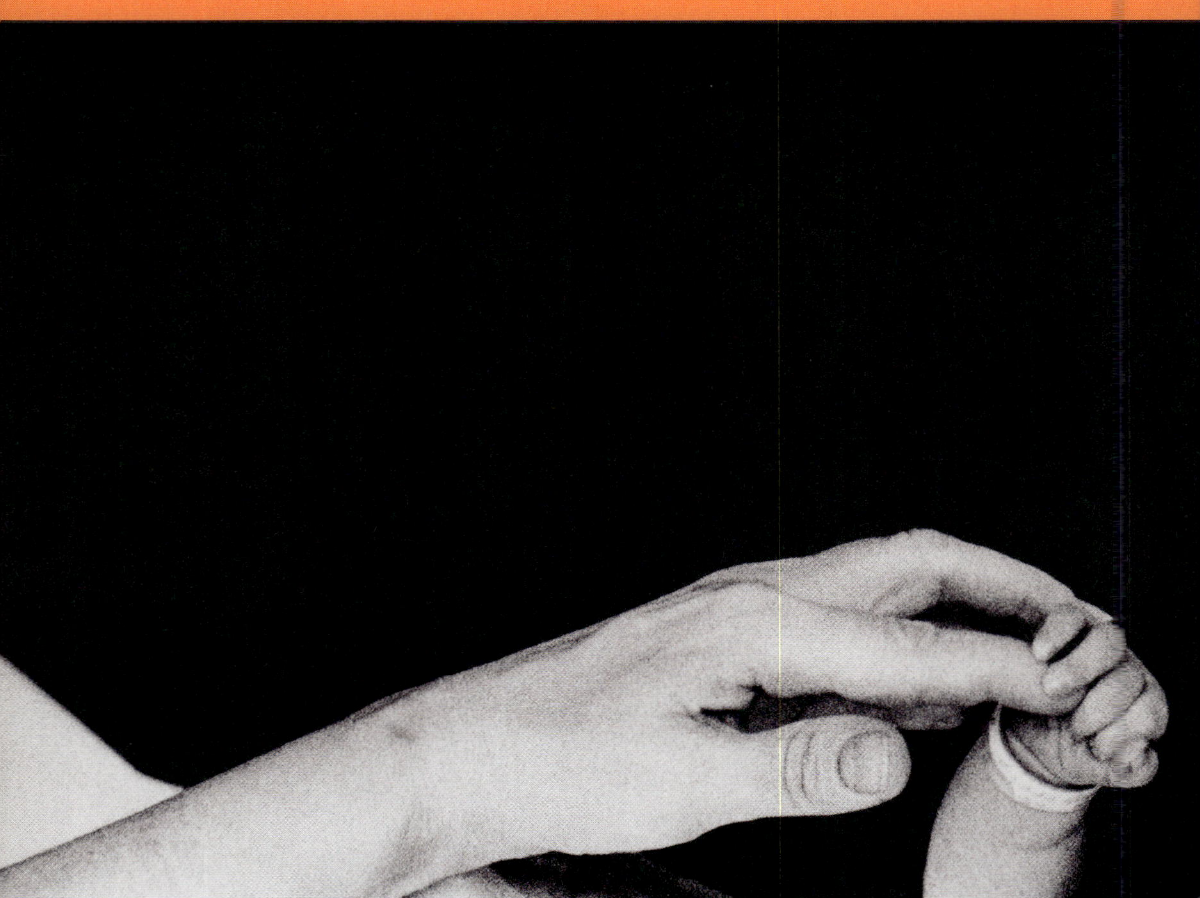

 Eve Arnold—A Mother Holds Her Child's Hand, Port Jefferson, Long Island, New York, USA

Eve Arnold

A Mother Holds Her Child's Hand, Port Jefferson, Long Island, New York, USA

1959

This is a photograph of few elements, yet what impact it has, what emotional resonance it holds. When the photograph was published in the 16 November 1959 issue of *LIFE* magazine as part of a photo essay about the first five minutes of a baby's life, the image was accompanied by the caption: 'Mother and son in an eternal pose'.

Here is the embodiment of mother-child love. The bond, the closeness between newborn and mother, could not be plainer. It is the universality of the picture, the timelessness, which contributes to the image's clout and longevity, meaning it still resonates in the 21st century. The other images from the story shot in a New York hospital by the photojournalist Eve Arnold – at this point just two years into her membership of the esteemed Magnum Photos agency – record the events of the baby's (Steven's) first moments in a more matter-of-fact, reportage style. Yet this image has an unparalleled immediacy and potency. Perhaps it is because Arnold captures what love can be in an understated, unforced way, demonstrating how love can look in a photograph. The slightly irregular framing lends the image a wonderful naturalness, and the black empty space of the background amplifies the emotion of the moment.

Arnold, who died at the age of ninety-nine, was known for her ability to catch intimate moments up close. She was a photographer of celebrities but also photographed ordinary folk and those who had been delivered a less fortunate hand in life with the same honesty. There is a rawness to her candid portraits of stars such as Marilyn Monroe that is also evident in this image. The subject matter is different, but the delivery – the capturing of the tiniest flicker of emotion, subtly executed – is similar. Arnold had an interest in cinema and shot stills on film sets during her long career. The cinematic closeness with which she photographs here is unsurprising. By giving just enough of a glimpse of her subjects she creates an image that tells us everything you need to know about new life. Only Arnold could tell so much through only the hands of a mother and baby.

+ PHOTOGRAPHER BIO
American, 1912–2012

+ GOOGLE THESE
Marlene Dietrich at the Recording Studios of Columbia Records, New York City, USA (1952), *Ear Girl in a Brothel in the Red-light District, Havana, Cuba* (1954), *Marilyn Monroe on the Set of* The Misfits (1960), *Malcolm X, Chicago, Illinois, USA* (1961)

– WATCH THIS
The documentary 'Marilyn Monroe and Photographer Eve Arnold', which can be found on the Marilyn Monroe History YouTube channel.

Like This? Try These

→ Margaret Bourke-White

→ Jane Bown

→ Dorothea Lange

John Hilliard

Off Screen (3), Large Study

1999

A blank projector screen dominates this photograph while onlookers, perhaps in a restaurant or bar, gaze at something behind it that we the viewers cannot see. Our curiosity is immediately awakened but so too is our frustration at being unable to see what the protagonists are looking at.

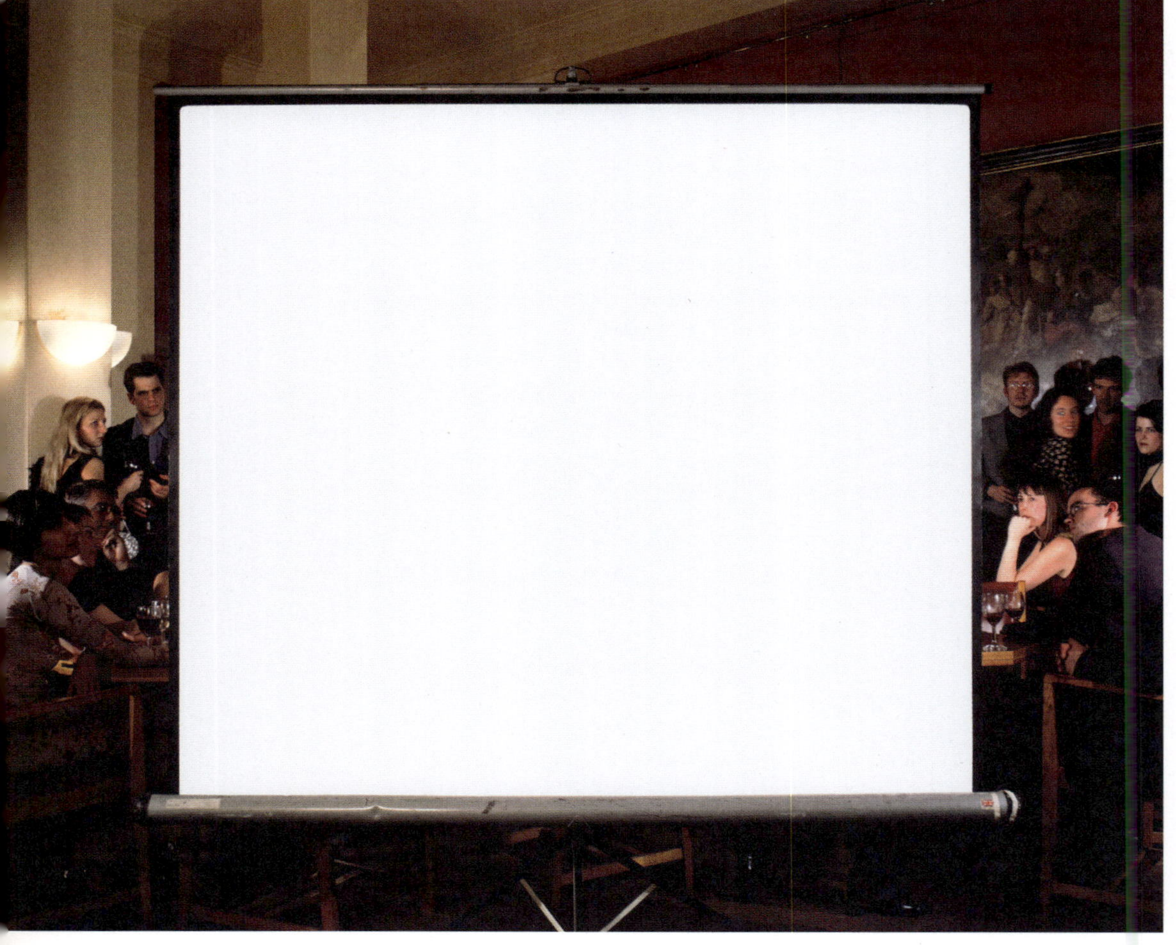

The image prompts many questions: who are these people? What are they doing? What is the projector for? Why has the photographer decided to photograph from this viewpoint when clearly it prevents us from seeing what is going on? Surely the point of a photograph is to show its subject clearly? That is not the case here. Or is it? John Hilliard's conceptual masterpiece provokes more questions than it offers answers, but, while frustrating to some, his illusory artwork is a clever comment on photography itself. The subject is photography – or rather, a photograph's ability to faithfully represent whatever is in the frame.

Hilliard has spent most of his long career questioning photography as a medium, pondering its purpose, asking what it has the potential to do and what it actually does. His methods of exploration have been diverse. Hilliard has used a camera to record its own condition, and played with photography's core elements of time, light and motion. He has even interfered with the photographic space as with this image: a blank screen takes the place of the expected subject. By placing a screen at the very point where the action is expected to be, Hilliard boldly disrupts notions of what a photograph should be and do. The screen acts as a literal barrier, forcing our attention to the edges of the frame to try to make sense of what we are seeing. At the same time, this is an invitation to fill the void with our own thoughts and ideas. Hilliard reminds us that what a photograph means is not easy to decipher and that very ambiguity, as infuriating as it might be, is what makes photography so devilishly delightful.

+ PHOTOGRAPHER BIO
British, b. 1945

+ GOOGLE THESE
Camera Recording its Own Condition, (7 Apertures, 10 Speeds, 2 Mirrors) (1971), *Sixty Seconds of Light* (1970)

+ WATCH THIS
Visit Tate.org.uk and search for 'Tateshots John Hilliard' to see Hilliard discussing his practice.

Like This? Try These

- → Keith Arnatt
- → John Baldessari
- → Dóra Maurer

Shōji Ueda

Cloud

1940

One of the first things people are taught when composing photos is to avoid placing the subject in the centre of the frame. Received wisdom says it does not make for a strong composition. In this photograph, master Japanese photographer Shōji Ueda breaks this fundamental photographic rule.

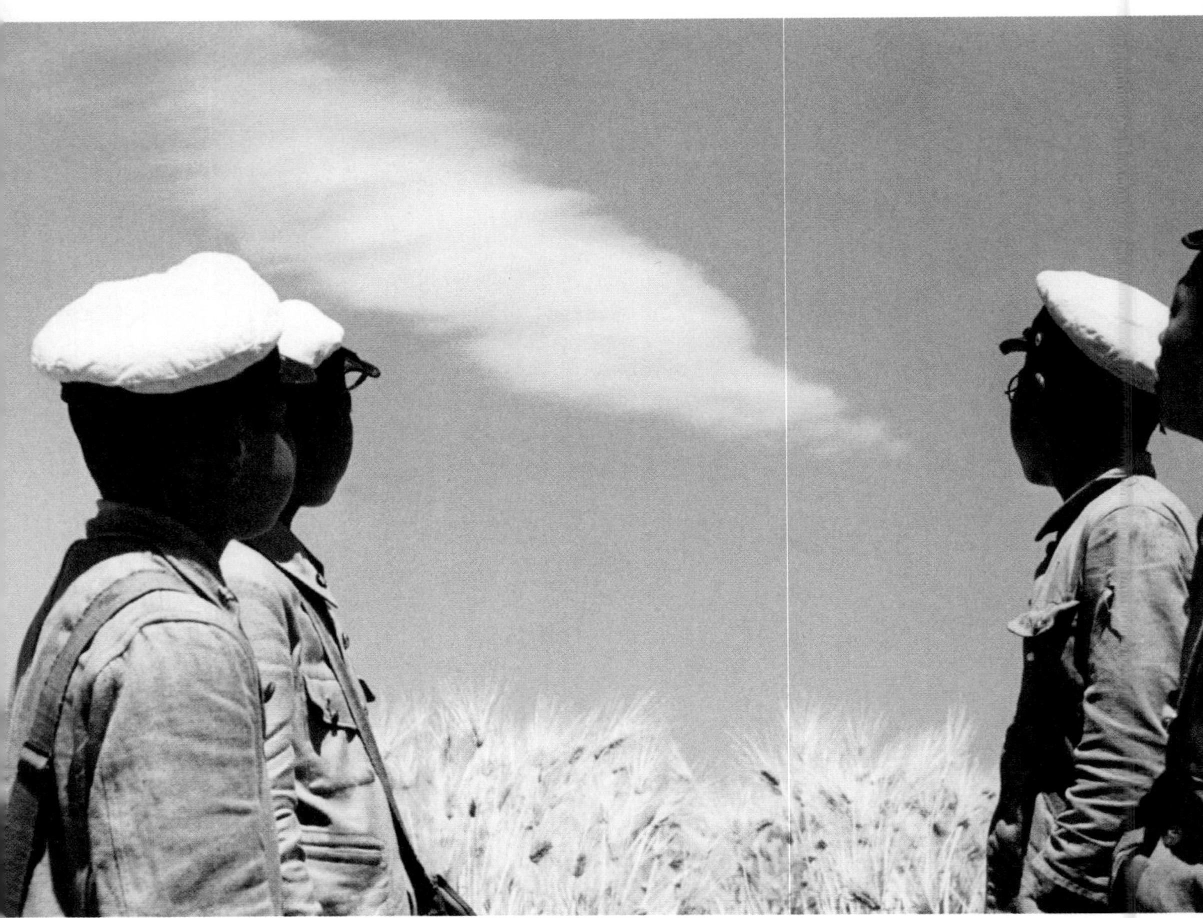

Ueda does not place something in the centre but leaves it empty save for a wisp of cloud that tapers off into the distance like a puff of cigar smoke. Conversely, it is also possible to say that Ueda has broken a cardinal rule by placing his subject in the middle of the frame if his subject is the nothingness of the sky that opens out before our eyes or an invisible object the people are staring at. Either way, Ueda is knowingly playing with photographic convention. He is unapologetically breaking the rules for brilliant effect.

Ueda was a photographer who had a penchant for surrealism and enjoyed experimenting with photography's capacity for capturing surreal sights in the everyday. We can see this at work in many of his photographs – where a distant mountain becomes a hat on a boy's head, the heads of embracing schoolgirls are entwined in the most unnatural way, or boiler suits hung out to dry appear like floating headless torsos.

He was fascinated by, and deeply fond of, the landscape around his home in Tottori on the coast of Japan, namely the beautiful, if sometimes stark, sand dunes. He photographed the dunes often, exploring how the human figure and landscape might be brought together in photographic space. The people in this photograph are used as a deliberate device to draw the viewer's eye up to the great nothingness beyond. What are they looking at? We want to look too. Once Ueda's slant towards the surreal is acknowledged, the emptiness he depicts seems full – it is bursting with possibility – and the centre is the only place it could be.

+ PHOTOGRAPHER BIO
Japanese, 1913–2000

+ GOOGLE THESE
My Wife on the Dunes (c. 1950), *Warabegoyomi (Children the Year Around)* (1955–1970), *Kogitsune Tanjō (Appearance of a Fox Cub)* (1948)

+ READ THIS
Shōji Ueda (2015) by Toshiyuki Horie.

Like This? Try These

- → Ken Domon
- → Ikkō Narahara
- → Akiko Takizawa

Hannah Price

Hasan, West Philly

2009

Who is the subject of this photograph? Is it the man who confronts the camera's gaze head on? Or the woman who appears to be sitting on his knee, whose face is cut off by the edge of the frame, her body out of focus? Is it the photographer we cannot see, but whose presence we sense? Or is it you, the viewer, who is looking at this photograph, making conscious and unconscious assumptions about this man and this woman?

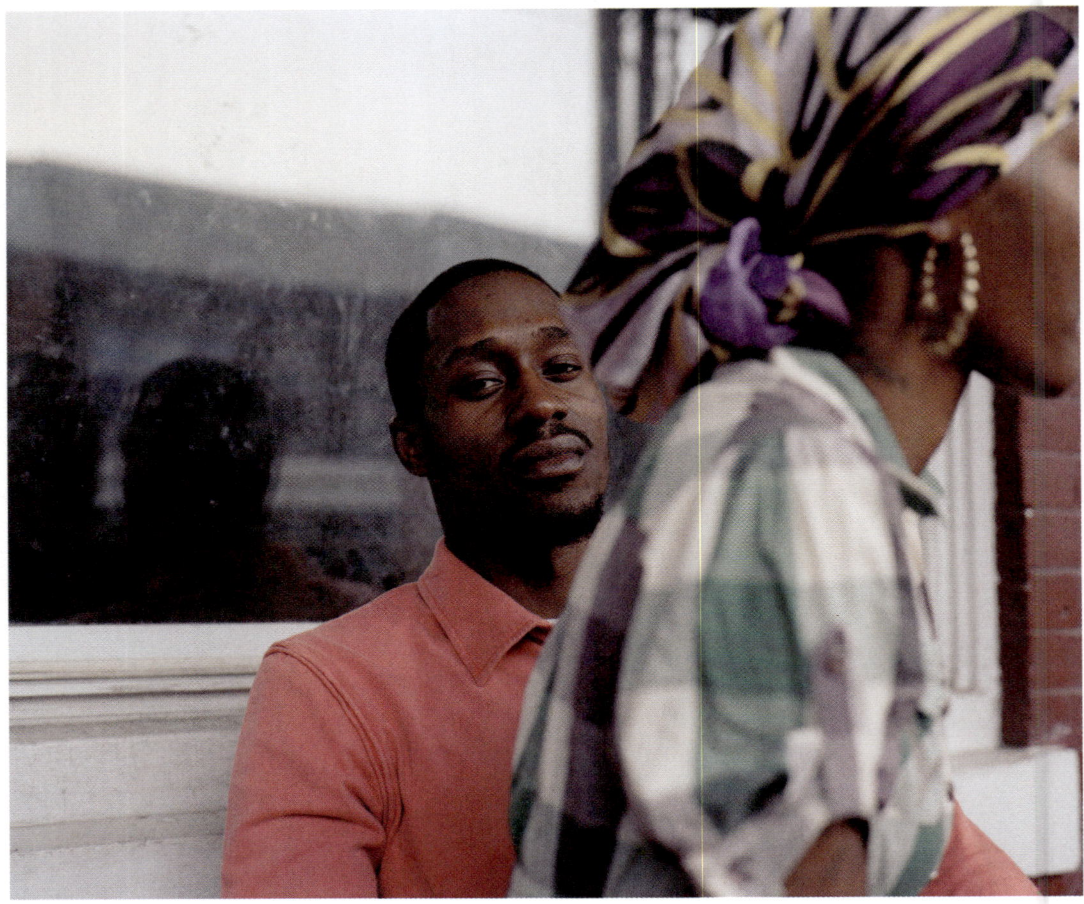

Photography, or rather the act of reading a photograph, is a tricky business. What each of us brings to a photograph as viewers is just as important as what the photographer conveys and what the photographed, be it a person, people, inanimate object or landscape, gives away. Equally difficult is to say what a photograph is about, since there is never one clear answer. A photograph can be about many things at the same time, or different things at different times, or different things to different people. Or perhaps nothing at all. The act of looking at and in turn reading a photograph throws up all kinds of questions and challenges that must be negotiated if we are to get any closer to telling anything at all.

In the case of this intimate photograph by photographer and filmmaker Hannah Price, there are no straightforward ways to read the image. This has much to with the way she has photographed the scene and its protagonists: the presence of the woman just off centre disrupts the flow of the relationship between the man and the viewer as mediated by Price. She dominates much of the frame, but we know even less about who she is than we do her companion because we are unable to make eye contact. She is merely passing through, it seems, and yet she is an important part of the picture.

We all make assumptions about the people we encounter, whether that's in a photograph or in our daily lives. Part of what Price wants to do through her images, which frequently tackle issues of race politics and the construction of identity, is to challenge those preconceptions and perceptions, to go beyond the surface. By overturning the conventions of photographic portraiture, our expectations of what a portrait should be, Price makes the viewer sit up and take note, and from there the journey into the photograph and all that it might mean, begins.

+ PHOTOGRAPHER BIO
American, b. 1986

+ GOOGLE THESE
City of Brotherly Love (2009–12), *Cursed by Night* (2012–13), *Kayla & Zane* (2018)

+ READ THIS
The article 'Hannah Price on Identity, Projections and Distortions' on the Magnum Photos website, magnumphotos.com.

Like This? Try These

→ Khalik Allah

→ Colby Deal

→ Ming Smith

Matt Black

Farmworker Camp, Alpaugh, California

2013

Photography has a knack of telling so much by showing so little, and Matt Black's image of an unidentified little girl is an example of this. By stripping back his environmental portrait to its sparsest elements, Black conversely creates an even more visually powerful and emotionally charged photograph.

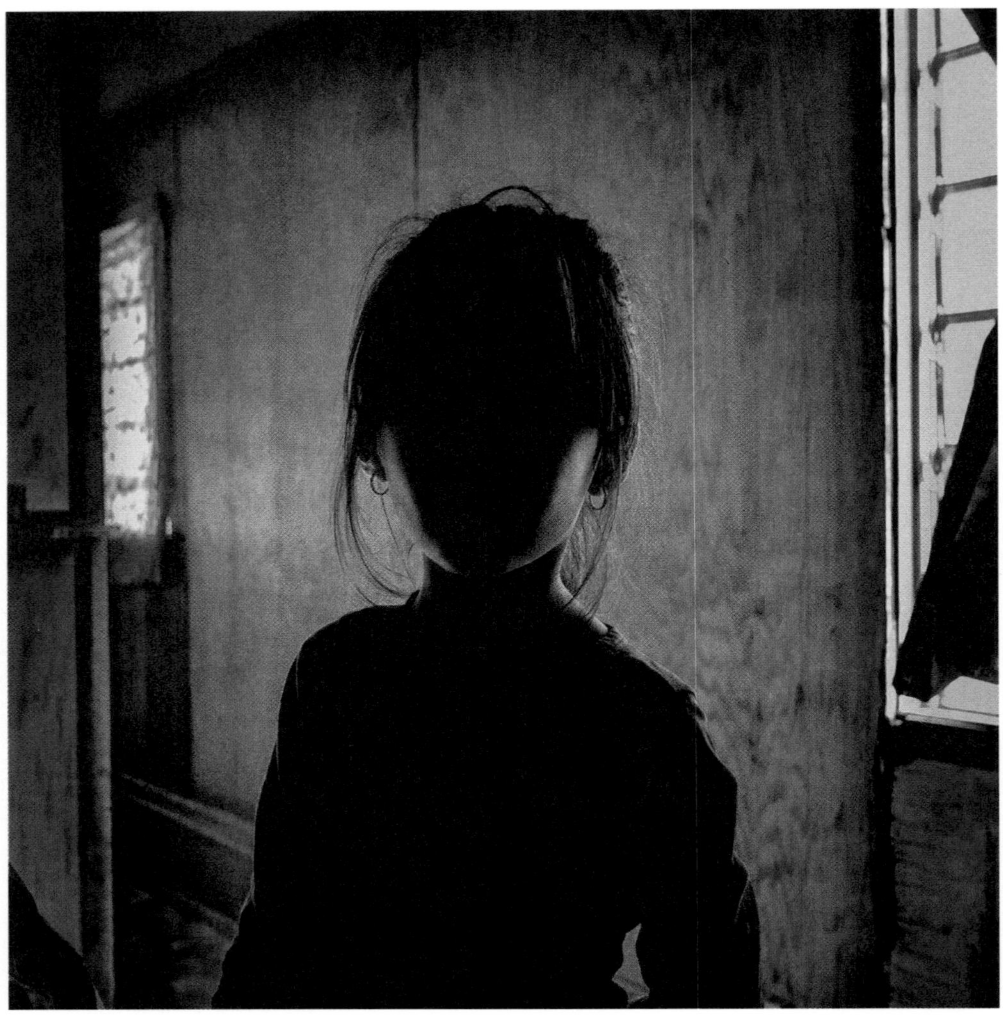

He has removed from the image most of what we would normally use to read a person, most obviously the girl's eyes and her expression, creating a deep void literally and metaphorically, but in doing so forces us to seek out other visual clues in order to build a picture of what might be going on. The plywood wall in the background and bare setting suggest a modest homestead – one could be forgiven for thinking this is an image taken in Depression-era America – but otherwise the girl's surroundings give little away. We must instead turn to the child herself. Despite being in shadow, she cuts a striking figure. She has an air of confidence and self-assuredly meets the photographer's searching lens.

Black made this portrait in the town of Alpaugh in the agricultural region of Central Valley, California. It's an area Black knows well – he grew up there in the 1970s and 1980s. More than half the population of Alpaugh, a farming community, lives in poverty and life for many is unbearably hard.

Much of Black's work has focused on marginalized communities across the United States, but he does not paint a picture of complete hopelessness in this photograph. Yes, the use of black and white accentuates the starkness of the scene and lends a heavy air, but there is a sense of resilience too, of hope, even, suggested not least by the presence of light, which gently illuminates the dark interior. The anonymous girl rises up out of the frame, in one sense symbolizing all those who are impoverished in this region but serving too as a symbol of courage in the face of adversity. Poverty is made visible in Black's photograph – we are made to literally confront it head on – even if, on the face of it, the photographer's intention seems to be to obscure rather than show.

+ PHOTOGRAPHER BIO
American, b. 1970

+ GOOGLE THESE
Kingdom of Dust (2013–14), *American Geography* (2014–20).

+ LISTEN TO THIS
Matt Black talks about his work in 'America From The Bottom: Documenting Poverty Across The Country' on NPR, at npr.org.

Like This? Try These

- Walker Evans
- Trent Parke
- Alessandra Sanguinetti

Olivia Arthur

Watching TV at Home

2009

We might look at this photograph and assume something is wrong with it. A flash must have gone off, the photograph must be an outtake. Yet how wrong it would be to suppose that some kind of technical mishap or error of judgment has taken place. The light is an integral part of the picture and its inclusion is intentional on the part of the photographer.

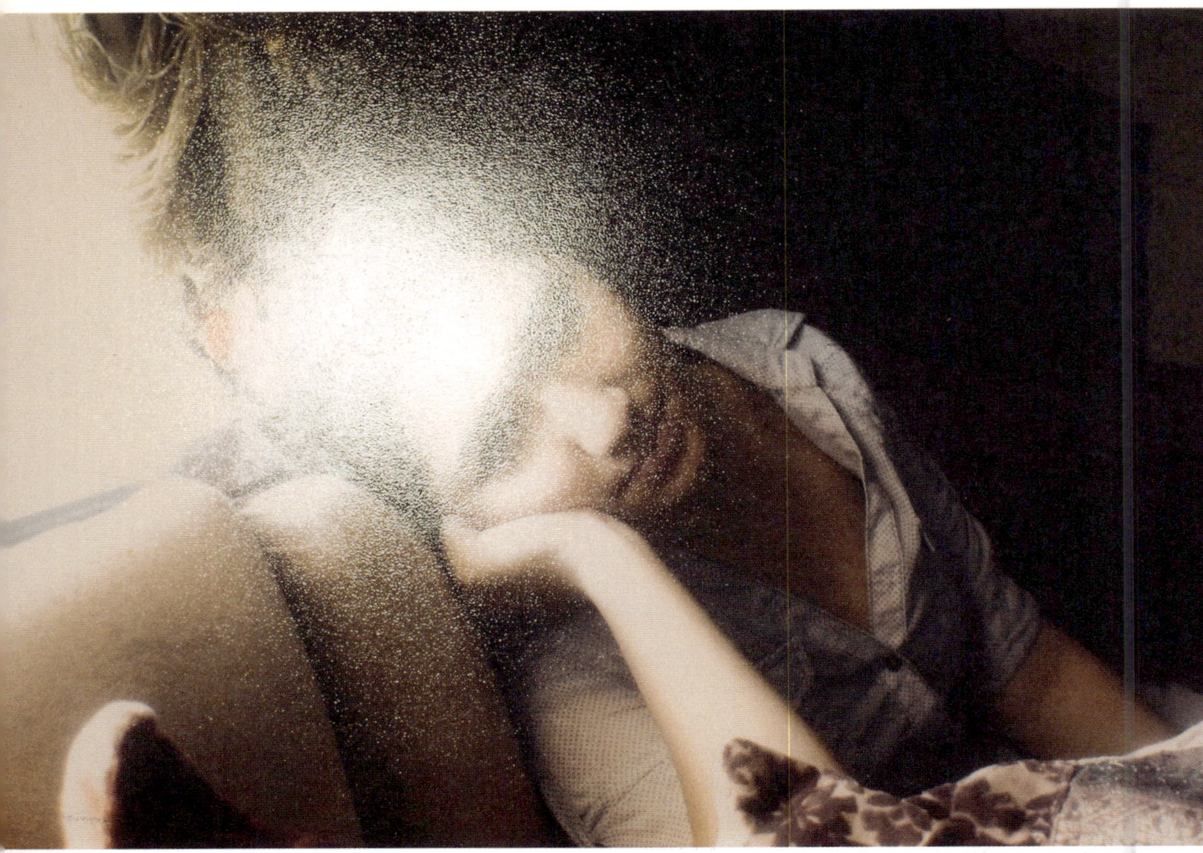

Olivia Arthur made this portrait as part of *Jeddah Diary*. Published as a book in 2012, it tells an intimate story of the lives of young women in Jeddah in Saudi Arabia. The work permits the viewer to glimpse happenings not usually seen, let alone photographed by a Westerner or witnessed by Western audiences – secret partying, drinking, flirting, kissing and general hanging out in a culture that is known as deeply conservative. As such, Arthur had to be mindful of showing the girls' faces. Some would only agree to be photographed if they could wear their abayas while others were happy to have their picture taken as long as they could not be identified. In some cases, when she had recorded a private moment and was then asked not to show it, Arthur decided to re-photograph small prints she had made of the photographs under a bright light, which reflected off the surface, utterly transforming the original photographs in the process. Patches of light at once emanate from the photographs and appear sprayed on.

The partial or total covering of eyes or faces in photography, disrupting the gaze of both subject and viewer, has a long and colourful history, but in this image it has a distinct purpose – to protect the young woman's identity. For Arthur, the technique also represented her experience in Jeddah, a place of complexities and contradictions where, she has said, it is not always clear what 'you're allowed to see and what you're not'. It is paradoxical that a patch of blinding bright light obscures the subject yet draws the viewer's attention so compellingly in an image that tells so much by revealing so little.

Like This? Try These

- → Tasneem Alsultan
- → Giulia Frigieri
- → Shirin Neshat

+ PHOTOGRAPHER BIO

British, b. 1980

+ GOOGLE THESE

The Middle Distance (2006–2007), *Magnum Retold: Olivia Arthur's Children of Europe* (2017)

+ WATCH THIS

'Olivia Arthur: The Secret Lives of Saudi Women on Through the Lens' at bbc.com/culture.

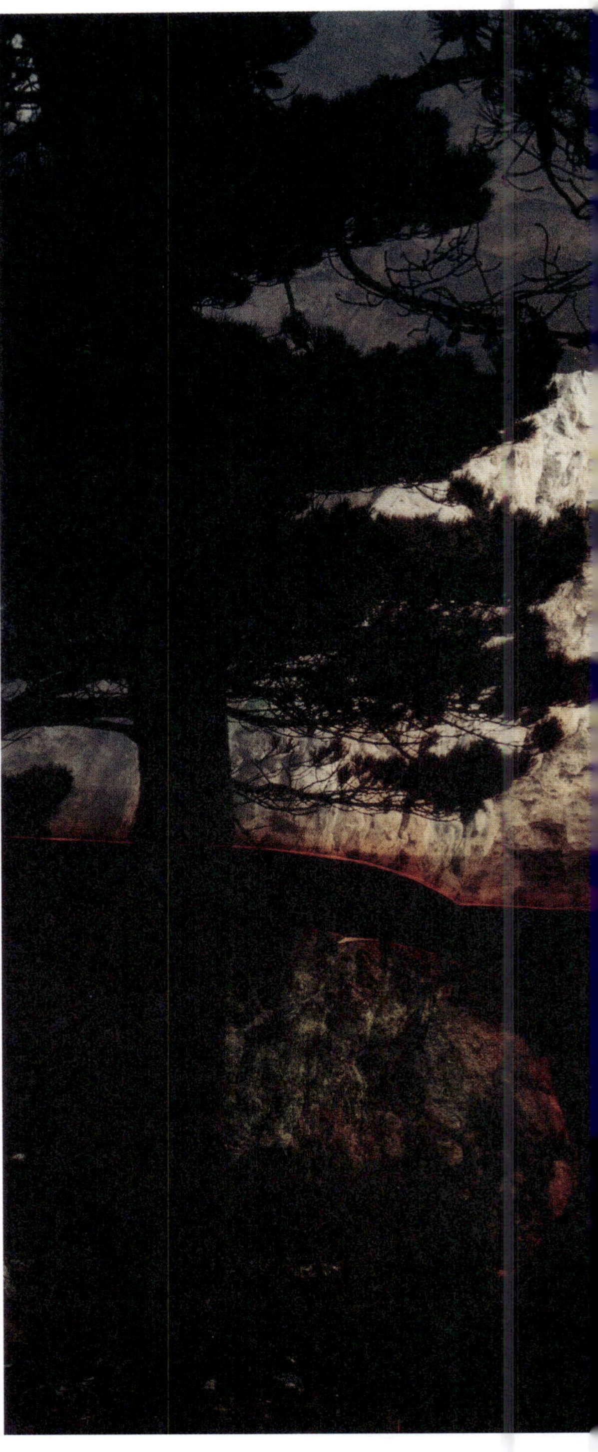

Dafna Talmor

Untitled (1212–2)

2013

To look at an image by Dafna Talmor is to fall deep into a rabbit warren of possible meanings. It is like stepping through a looking glass into a world of untold possibilities. Talmor quotes French philosopher Michel Foucault's idea of the mirror as 'an unreal, virtual space that opens up behind the surface', which is at the heart of her photographs that paradoxically depict spaces that are both real and imaginary at the same time.

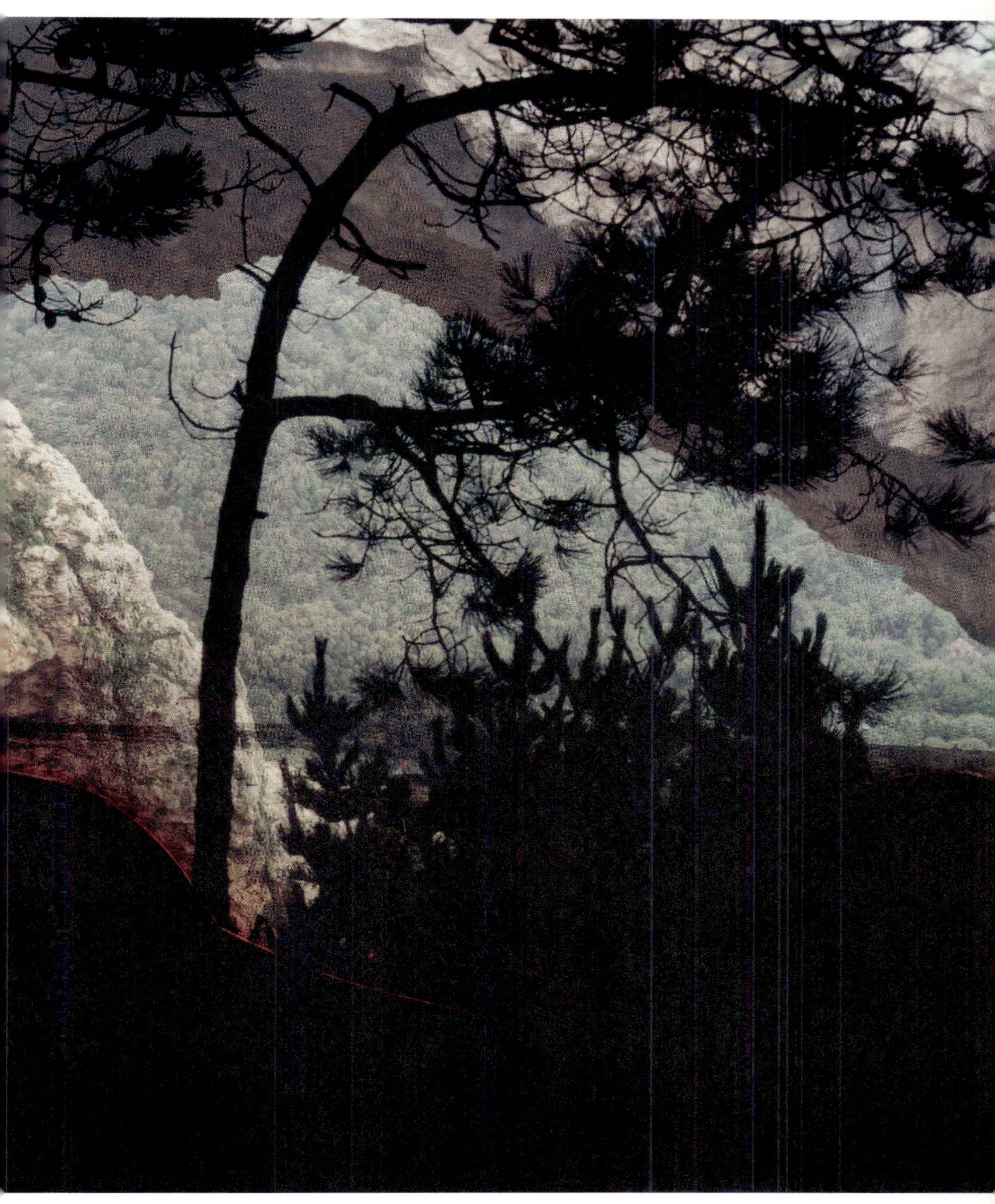

+ PHOTOGRAPHER BIO
Israeli-British, b. 1974

+ GOOGLE THIS
Constructed Landscapes Volume II (2014–)

+ READ THIS
Constructed Landscapes (2020) by Dafna Talmor.

What you're looking at are two colour negatives of different places that have been cut and reassembled, or 'sliced and spliced' to use Talmor's phrase, to create a hybrid space that could be anywhere but is in fact nowhere. The new collaged or 'constructed' landscape referred to in the title of the series, *Constructed Landscapes Volume I* (2013–), only exists in the photograph.

For years, Talmor photographed the landscapes she passed through: in Israel where she was born, in Venezuela where she grew up, in the UK where she has made her home and in the USA where her sister lives. This was out of a desire to record those places but when she returned home, she packed the negatives away and was unsure what to do with them. 'It dawned on me that perhaps the way I could make use of them was by making interventions directly onto the negatives,' she explains. 'The fact that they were "failures" or "disappointments" meant I wasn't precious about cutting them up. People generally find that to be such an extreme act – there is something so sacred about the negative – but I didn't feel that way. There was a kind of exhilaration about finding a purpose for material that I felt had no purpose.'

Referencing early pictorialist techniques of combination printing, and modernist experiments such as collage and multiple exposures, but also acknowledging the irreversibility of manual intervention in an age where digital master files can be easily replicated and preserved, Talmor's work is multilayered both literally and figuratively. In an image where space, memory and time are blurred, we look through to a place, an idyll or utopia, that is always just out of reach.

Like This? Try These

- → Chrystel Lebas
- → Corinne Silva
- → Esther Teichmann

Alice Mann

Dr Van Der Ross Drummies, Cape Town, South Africa

2017

+ PHOTOGRAPHER BIO
South African, b. 1991

+ GOOGLE THESE
Khanyi's Dance (2019), *Maximum Effect (La Sape D'Europe)* (2016)

+ WATCH THIS
Alice Mann talks about *Drummies* on the It's Nice That (Nicer Tuesdays) YouTube channel.

Some photographs are full of joy and Alice Mann's sprightly, uplifting image of young female drum majorettes, known as 'drummies' in South Africa, is one of them.

Its irrepressible energy and lightness of spirit are palpable the moment you set eyes on the photograph. The way the girls are holding their arms, their easy smiles and the ease with which they move together as a group make the image sing and soar.

The photograph belongs to a series by the young, London-based South African photographer that tells a story of female empowerment, pride, self-belief and hope. Drummies is a competitive sport that first appeared in South Africa in the 1970s. Although its popularity has waned in recent years there are still significant numbers of girls who not only partake but take it very seriously indeed. The training can be intense and requires a huge amount of discipline, but those who do it feel a great sense of achievement. A real transformation occurs when the girls put on their uniforms, Mann says: 'They hold themselves differently.'

As with all of her work, Mann endeavours to work collaboratively, her ethos being one of conveying positivity and ensuring her subjects feel a sense of authorship and agency. We really get that here in an image that beautifully balances spontaneity with a curious feeling that the girls are performing happily for the camera. The compelling sense of movement aside, what gives the photograph its intensity is the closeness of the photographer to her subject and the intimacy that affords. Furthermore, Mann's use of colour – all slightly desaturated, faux-faded powdery pinks, pastel purples, blues and greens that nod to an implicit nostalgia or an idealized – almost utopian – view of femininity – is exquisite. Her biggest coup though comes as a result of daring to make something of the edges of the frame and refusing to be bound by those limits. In framing the image so that her subjects are split with their fingers and toes chopped off, Mann breaks all the rules but captures a perfect, breathless, exuberant slice of life that feels as if it is happening in the here and now.

Like This? Try These

→ Catherine Hyland

→ Tyler Mitchell

→ Cian Oba-Smith

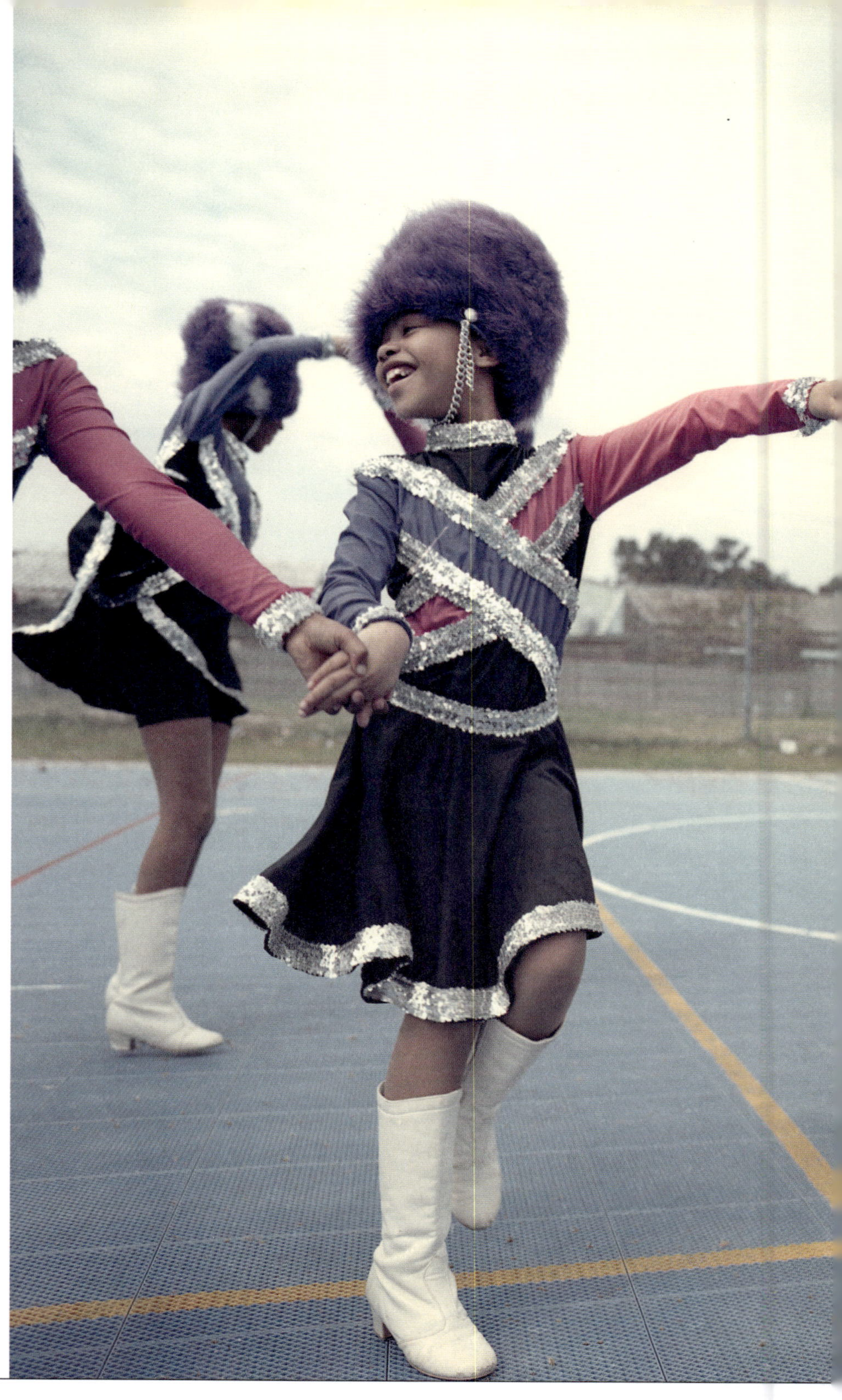

 Alice Mann—Dr Van Der Ross Drummies, Cape Town, South Africa

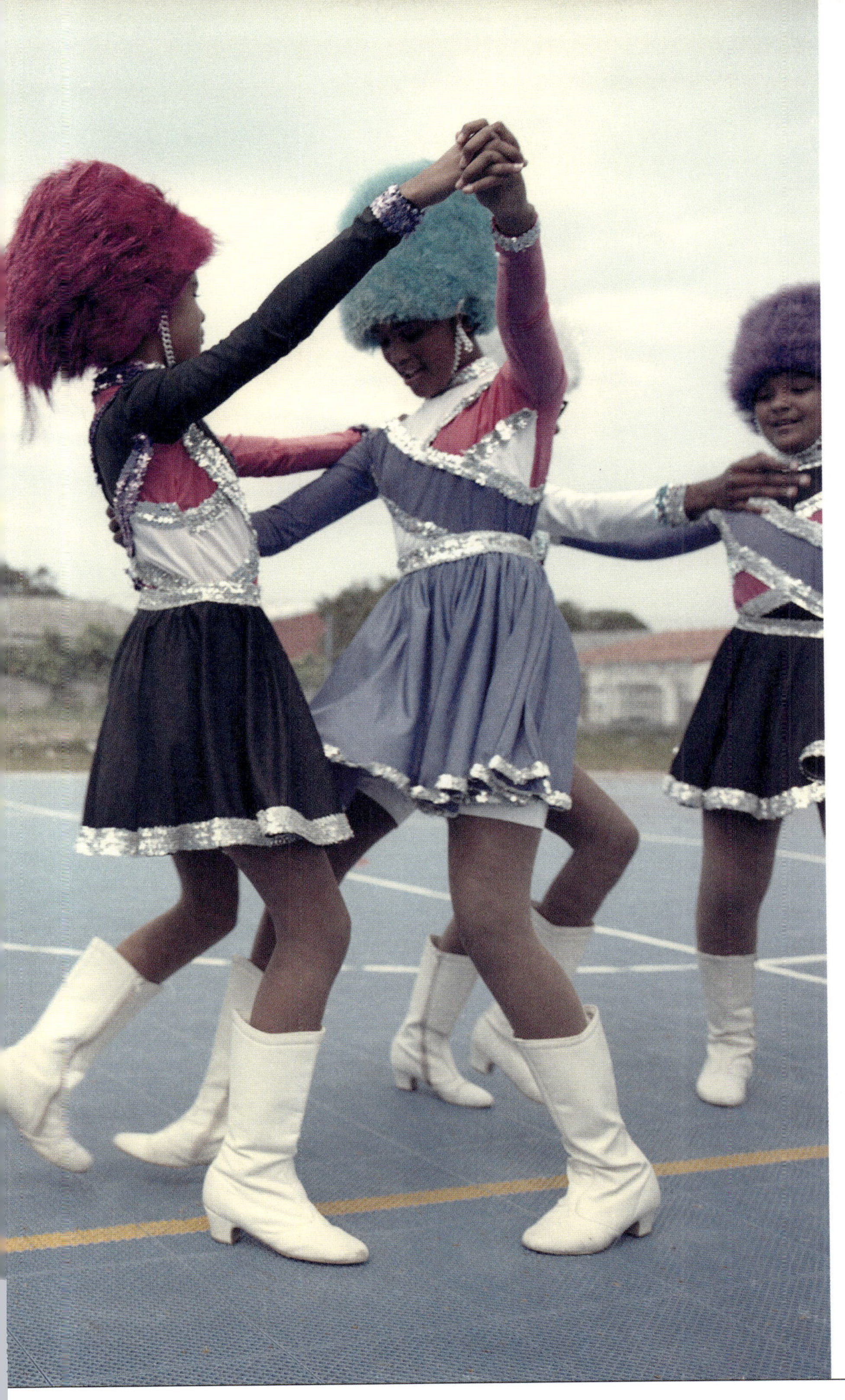

Ernst Haas

Mardi Gras Costume, New Orleans

1978

What appears to be a woman wears a fancy hat tied with a ribbon. A bright pearl necklace is at her throat and there are frills aplenty. Because she is turned away from us, her face is unseen, so we must work harder to read the image. Yet it is generally accepted that portrait photographs show a person's face and not the back of their head, so you would be forgiven for passing this photo by or, if you did stop and look, for asking what merit it has or wondering if it was taken in error.

Never one to follow traditional notions of what one should and should not do when it comes to any photograph, let alone a portrait, Ernst Haas created an image that captures the essence of a moment in perfect colour. Known for his exquisite use of natural light and experimentations in colour photography, Haas was a master of seeing the unseeable: those barely there, in-between moments that vanish as quickly as they appear. Haas made photographic poems where light and colour are the subjects in and of themselves rather than merely the means with which to make an image. Indeed, Haas, who has been described as possessing 'the eye of a painter and the soul of a poet' once said he 'was searching for a composition in which colour became much more than just a coloured black and white picture.'

He made it his life's mission to explore the meaning of colour in photography. Here, with his image of a person dressed up for the Mardi Gras in New Orleans, he does just that: the photograph works precisely and only because it is in colour; the brilliant white of the silky ribbon is in perfect balance with the red ruffle, linked by a string of shiny pearls and a frilled loop. In black and white with hues rendered in various shades of grey it would likely be unremarkable at best, a muddled mess at worst. However, on examination of the meticulous detail Haas chooses to present to us, it is evident that this is no incidental photograph but one that has all the hallmarks of a truly remarkable image, even if, or rather because, it defies convention.

+ PHOTOGRAPHER BIO
Austrian-American, 1921–86

+ GOOGLE THIS
Pool Reflections. Lights from a Neon Sign and a Stained-glass Window, Reflected in a Swimming Pool, California, USA, July 1977 (1977) *TV And Shadows. A Television Set by a Window, California* (c. 1975)

+ READ THIS
Ernst Haas: Color Correction (2011) by Phillip Prodger.

Like This? Try These

→ Werner Bischof

→ Harry Gruyaert

→ Saul Leiter

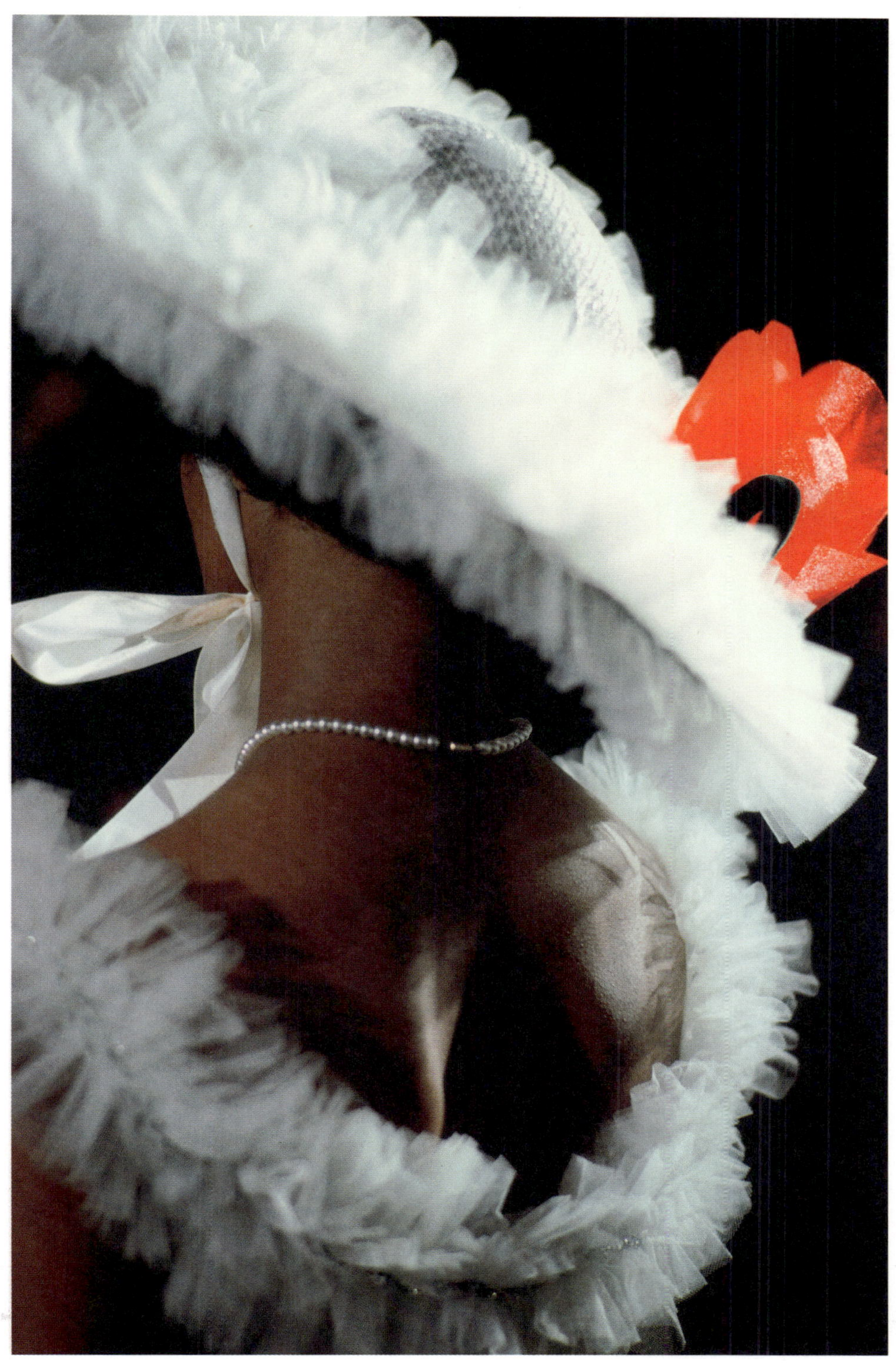

Jack Davison

Untitled

2017

+ PHOTOGRAPHER BIO
British, b. 1990

+ GOOGLE THESE
26 States (2013), *Great Performers/L.A. Noir* (2016), *Stranger than Paradise* (2016)

+ READ THIS
Photographs (2019) by Jack Davison.

With his instinctive, experimental style, British photographer Jack Davison has a knack for finding the surreal in the everyday.

In Davison's photographs, things are frequently not what they seem. Strange juxtapositions abound, and shadows, reflections and blur are among his favourite photographic tools. His colour photographs are either drenched in rich hues or awash with desaturated colours, while the sometimes high-contrast black and white shots play with light and shade in arresting ways.

Davison was born and raised in rural Essex and then moved to London. He picked up a camera at the age of fifteen and has been taking pictures ever since. Entirely self-taught, his subjects are typically people he notices when out and about, friends or family, and incidental moments that catch his eye, as appears to be the case here. He has said: 'I always love photographs that come out of nowhere – from an unexpected space.'

Many of Davison's images seem chanced upon. It is as though they are moments hidden in plain sight that only he can see. In just a few years, he has built up an impressive editorial and commercial portfolio, with *The New York Times Magazine*, *British Vogue*, Hermès, Margaret Howell and Burberry among his clients.

Hands and eyes are frequent motifs in Davison's work. He also combines shapes and forms to create compositions that are carefully composed yet also retain a sense of spontaneity and playfulness. This image is a good example of how Davison likes to work. By bringing seemingly disparate elements together in the frame he turns an inconsequential scene into something worth viewing. The viewer notices the moon-like disc, which appears to be held by a shadowy hand, as though it is a ball. A sculptural metal structure and its shadow, the backbone of the picture, prop it up or seek to contain it. At a glance, this is a puzzling picture that plays with two- and three-dimensional space in a way that should not make sense but does. It is an image the viewer can enjoy for its quirky aesthetic, a slice of visual poetry amid the drab everyday.

Like This? Try These

- → Chieska Fortune
- → Ralph Gibson
- → Saul Leiter

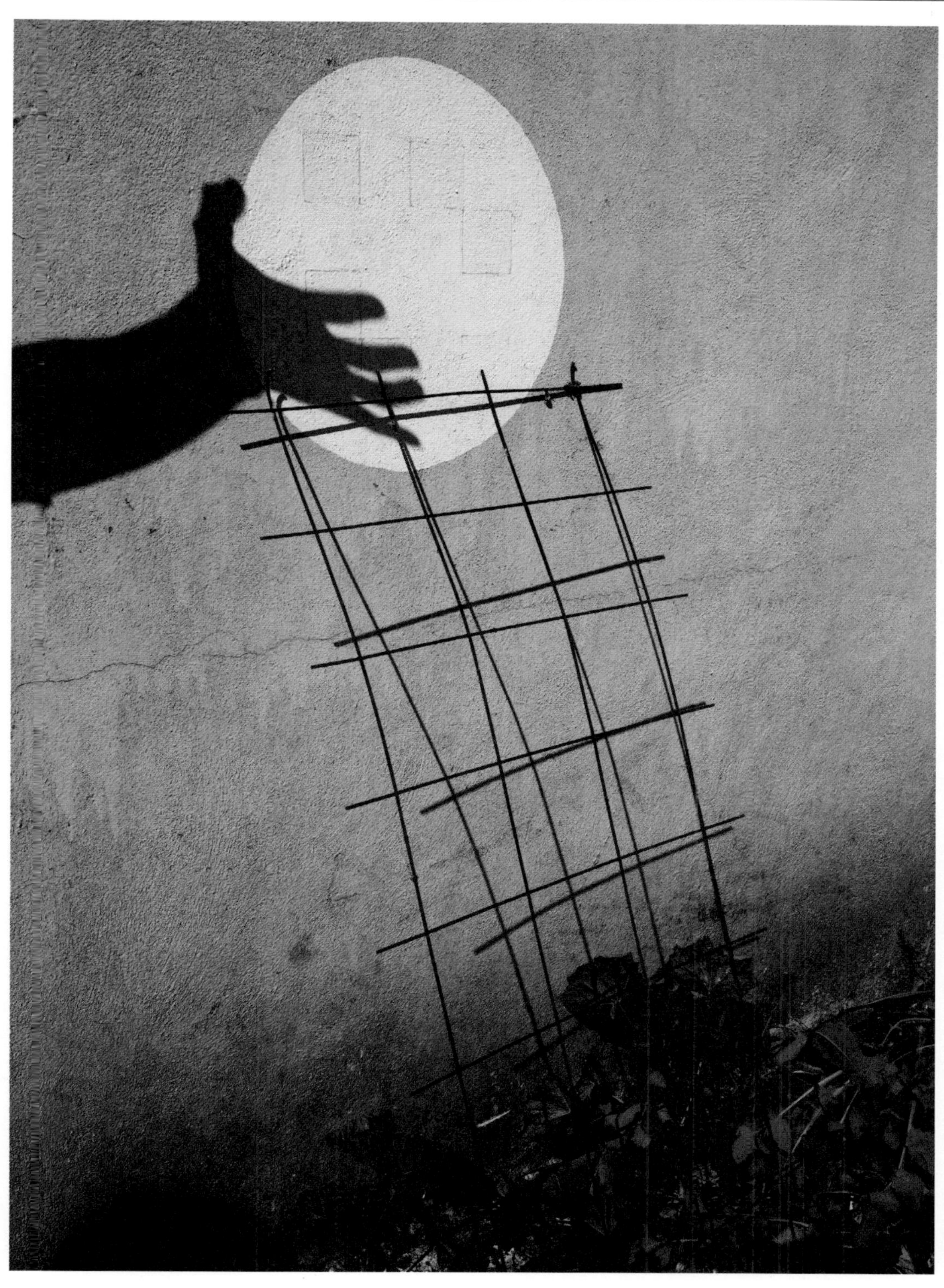

CHAPTER

2 PHOTOS THAT MAKE YOU LOOK TWICE

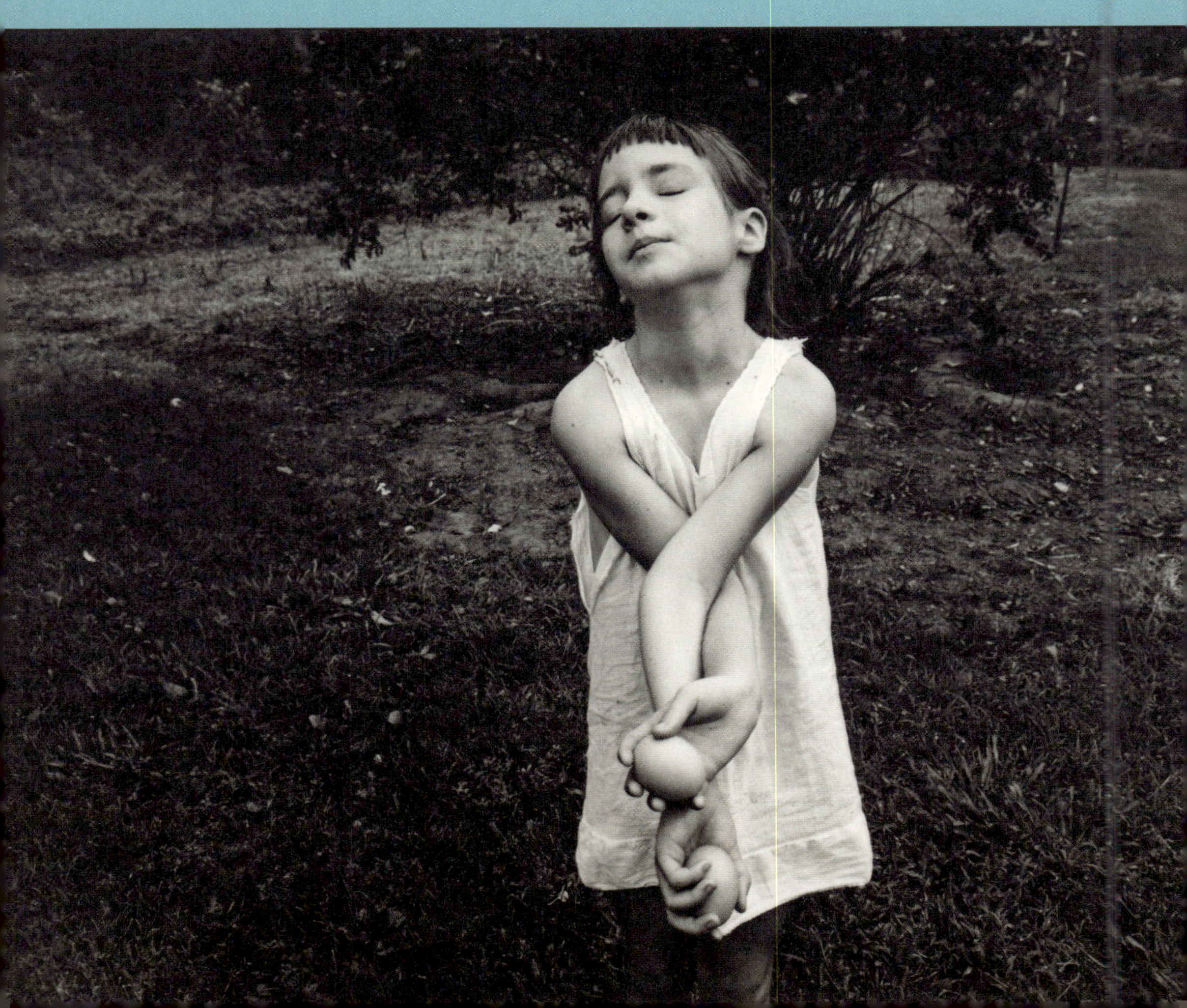

Emmet Gowin

Nancy, Danville, Virginia

1969

What do you see when you look at this photograph? A young girl with her eyes closed in a rural setting, arms entwined, eggs in her palms. But look again and you will see that this is a picture that tricks and teases in a playful way.

The child is Nancy, the niece of photographer Emmet Gowin's wife, Edith, pictured in Danville, Virginia, in 1969. At a glance, the photo appears to be a snapshot, a candid, off-the-cuff shot of a child playing. What Gowin captures however, is an air of mystery. The viewer senses there is something odd about the image. Nancy's arms look unnatural and peculiar, they appear to be elongated giving the image an air of 'strange impossibility' to quote Gowin. Her closed eyes suggest she is mentally somewhere far away. What is she doing? What is she feeling and thinking? The photograph raises many questions and leaves the viewer to search for answers. It is an intriguing image because it provokes such questions and captivates the viewer because it suggests rather than depicts absolutely.

Gowin is best known for the intimate images he took of his family from the 1960s onwards, in particular of his wife. He is a master of suggestion, creating images that teeter on the edge of unreality, which hint at something otherworldly yet remain firmly of this world in their resolute honesty. This image in particular with its almost luminescent sculptural figure and dark, imposing background, invites the viewer to study it more closely, to look deeper. Its puzzling, unfathomable beauty never becomes tired. Its lively composition appears simultaneously constructed and entirely spontaneous. Gowin has said: 'Constantin Brâncuși [sculptor, painter, photographer and a founding figure of modernism] once said that simplicity was complexity resolved and this photograph somehow embodies a quality of complexity resolved.' That, perhaps, is all you need to know.

+ PHOTOGRAPHER BIO
American, b. 1941

+ GOOGLE THESE
Edith, Danville, Virginia (1963), *Edith, Chincoteague, Virginia* (1967), *Nancy and Dwayne, Danville, Virginia* (1970)

+ WATCH THIS
Emmet Gowin: A Life in Photography on the Aperture Foundation YouTube channel.

Like This? Try These

→ Harry Callahan

→ Sally Mann

→ Mary Ellen Mark

Phil Chang

Replacement Ink for Epson Printers (Black 172203) on Epson Premium Luster Paper

2014

Is this a photograph and can you call Phil Chang a photographer? The answers to these deliberately provocative and difficult questions depend on what we understand a photograph and a photographer to be, and those cannot be easily defined.

Strictly speaking, Chang's artwork made by applying inkjet printer ink to inkjet paper with a sponge is not a photograph since he has not used a camera. Nonetheless, while his work might be firmly rooted in the more conceptual side of photography, it can be considered photographic. This is because it asks us to consider photography's intrinsic properties and character and those of related technological processes such as digital printing. With this image from his series *Works on Paper* (2013–) Chang explores what it means to make a photographic print and where the hand of the artist might lie in an age of digital reproducibility. Chang's piece is a stroke of genius in that he uses the inkjet process, a mainstay of contemporary photographic digital printing, as both material and subject, while ironically referencing abstract painting in the process. Curator and writer Charlotte Cotton points out that in doing so Chang renders the artwork as 'neither painterly nor obviously photographic', instead it sits between the two.

Chang confronts photography head on and strips it back to its purest elements, encouraging us to look at the photographic process with fresh eyes. This is photography laid bare: it is as direct and pure an experience with the medium of photography as you can get. Chang's work is a welcome disruption or jolt in an age of digital overload, ease of availability and disposability. At a time in which we have forgotten to pause and look, it quietly and unpretentiously calls upon us to see anew.

+ PHOTOGRAPHER BIO
American, b. 1974

+ GOOGLE THESE
Replacement Ink for Epson Printers (Cyan, Red, and Yellow 243001) on Canson• PhotoSatin Premium RC Paper (2015), *Untitled (Purple Monochrome 02)* (2015)

+ SEE THIS
Phil Chang's work and interviews at the M+B gallery site: mbart.com.

Like This? Try These

- → Jessica Eaton
- → Taisuke Koyama
- → Hannah Whitaker

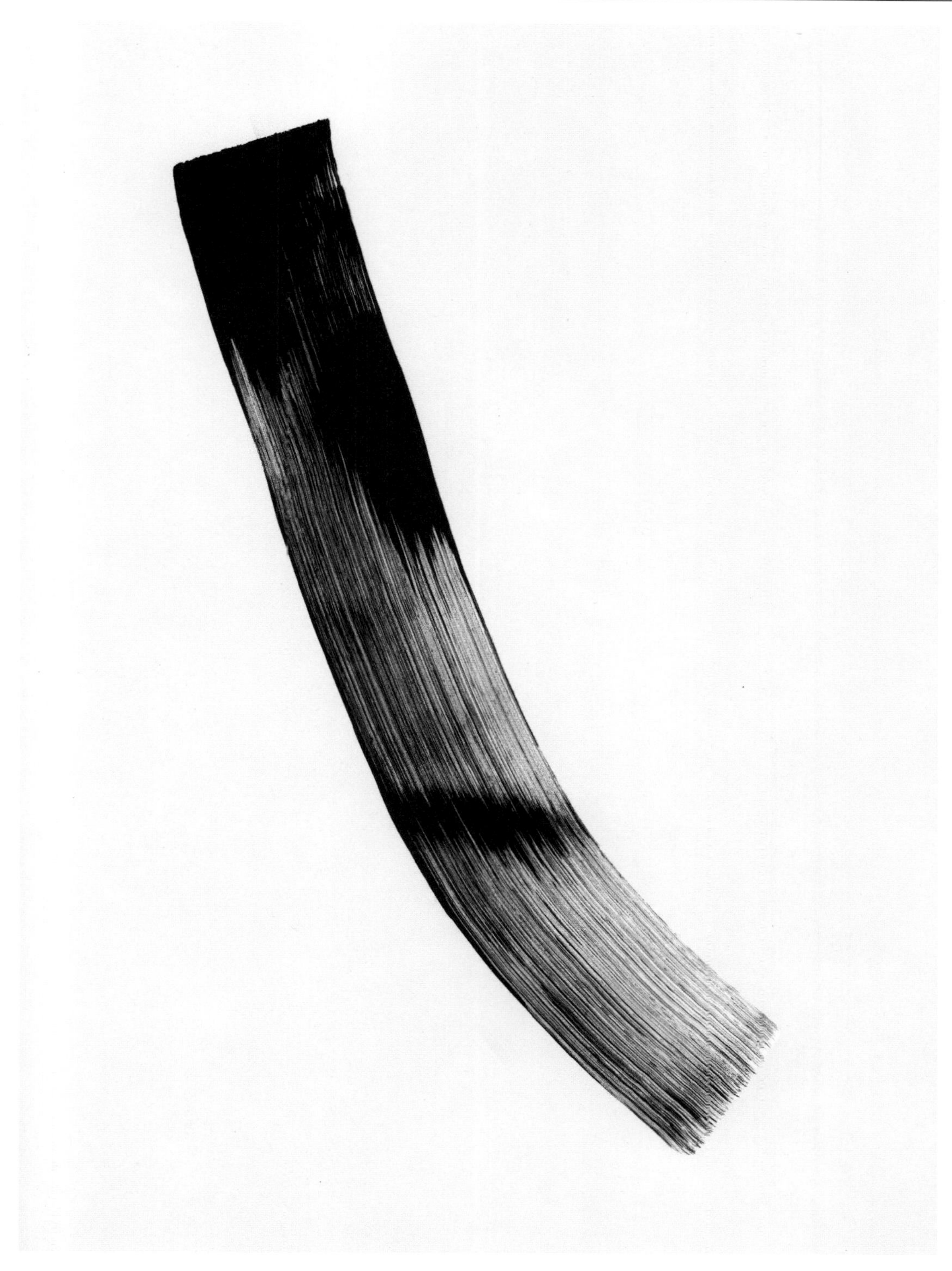

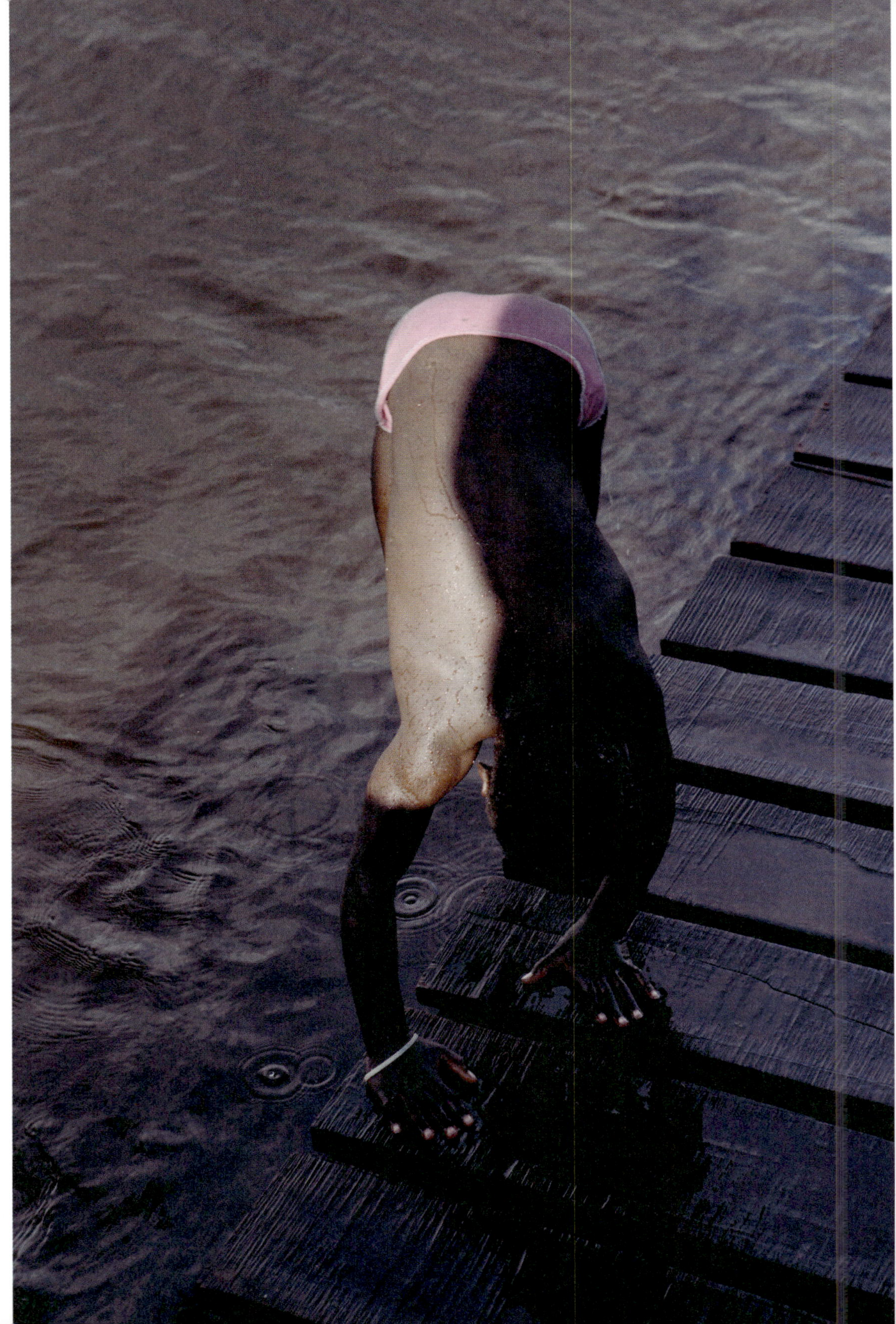

Viviane Sassen

Sling, Suriname

2013

+ **PHOTOGRAPHER BIO**
Dutch, b. 1972

+ **GOOGLE THESE**
Pikin Slee (2014), *Of Mud and Lotus* (2017)

+ **READ THIS**
Viviane Sassen: In and Out of Fashion (2013) by Charlotte Cotton and Nanda van den Berg.

There is something utterly mesmerizing about Viviane Sassen's images, which unsettle as much as they intrigue. Dismiss them as little more than playful combinations of jumbled, abstract forms at your peril. There is nothing accidental or *ad hoc* about a Sassen image.

Sling, Suriname may look simple but there is far more going on than you might initially suppose. Everything is in its right place. What can we discern on a first look? A girl or boy – we cannot be certain – is doing an awkward handstand on what looks to be a jetty. They are in bright sun and partially in shadow, perhaps that of the photographer given Sassen is known for putting herself in her images by using her shadow.

The image belongs to the photographer's series, *Pikin Slee* (2014) named after a rainforest village on the Upper Suriname River in Suriname, a former Dutch colony on the north-eastern coast of South America. The people who live there are mostly members of the Saramacca tribe whose ancestors, the Maroons, fled from Dutch plantations in the eighteenth century. Sassen went to Suriname in 2012 in search of a 'simpler way of looking' and was struck by the beauty she uncovered in the everyday. The pictures she made there are typical of her work. Like this one, they reveal a preoccupation with form, light and shadow. Abstracted figures become almost sculptural in her work and the interplay between light and shadow – devices to reveal and obscure – is a recurrent motif and part of her visual signature.

Sassen's are images that are not about something specific but that hint at a feeling, a mood. She throws us off here by eliminating all other points of reference: the camera is angled downwards so that gently rippling water fills the frame giving us no choice but to focus our attention on the figure whoever he or she may be. Sassen's images link the worlds of dreams and real life inextricably, they are spaces where illusion, visual trickery and abstraction play out. They are thought provoking but, more importantly, they implore us to emote.

Like This? Try These

→ Jack Davison

→ Erik Madigan Heck

→ Aïda Muluneh

Jeff Wall

Picture for Women

1979

Canadian artist Jeff Wall's early masterpiece *Picture for Women* remains as perplexing today as it was when it was first released into the world more than forty years ago, but that does not mean we should not keep looking at it and wondering what it is about. The fun lies in the thinking.

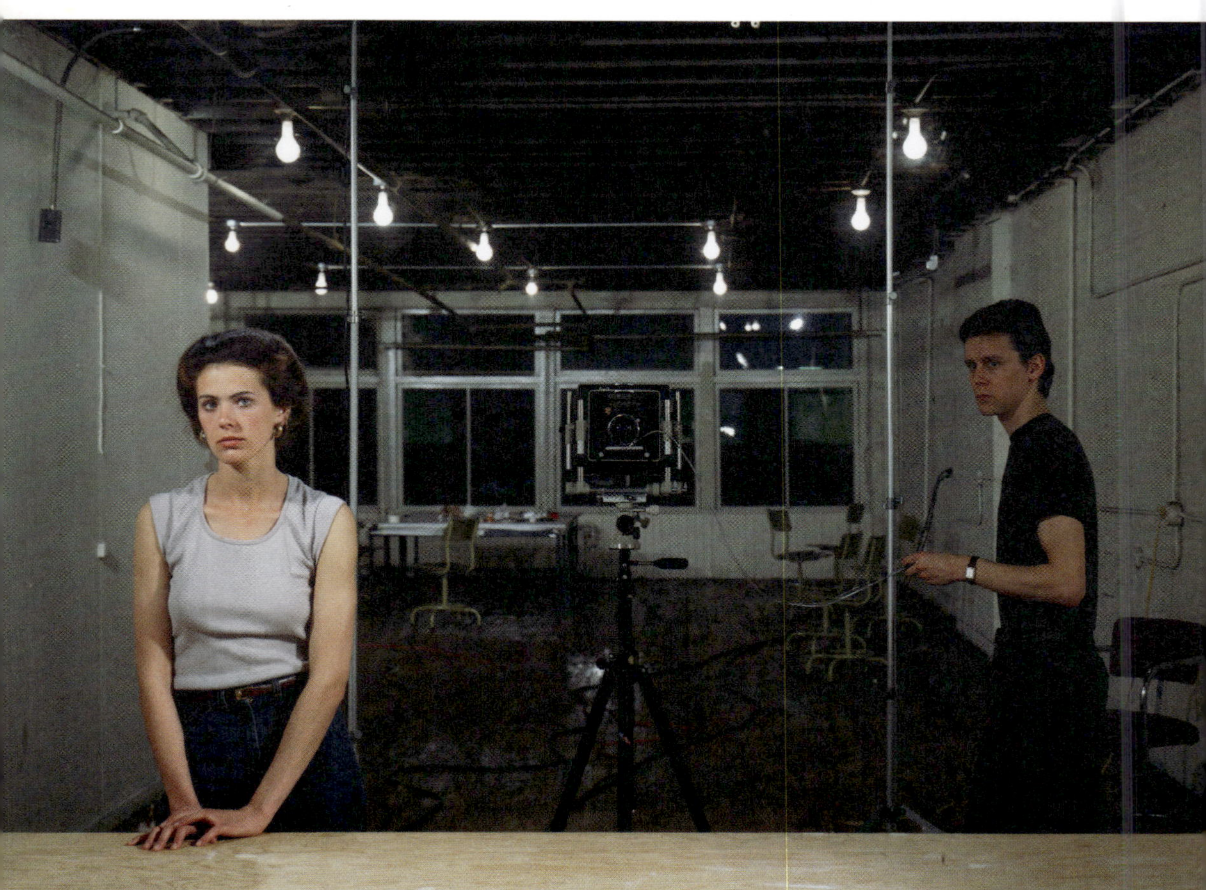

Picture for Women is about looking and being looked at although what we think we are looking at is not as straightforward as we might first suppose. Credited with marking photography's transition as an art form from the printed page to the gallery wall, the work is a reimagining of *Un Bar aux Folies-Bergère* (*A Bar at the Folies-Bergère*, 1882) by Édouard Manet. Like the painting that inspired it, *Picture for Women* has sparked much discussion as to what it might mean on show. The photograph is presented as a large-scale, light-box transparency and touches on several key themes that Wall explores in his later work, including the role of the spectator and photography's relationship to classical painting.

Wall is an art critic and a professor as well as a photographer. He is well versed in art history and one of the most well-known creators of staged photographs or tableaux, an approach inherited from history painting and narrative art. Each work is the product of meticulous preparation and collaboration, and Wall uses the term 'cinematographic' to describe these important aspects of his process. Indeed, as British writer, curator, artist and teacher David Campany points out in his book *Jeff Wall: Picture for Women* (2011), cinema influenced Wall's work from the beginning, evidenced here through the dynamic *mise en scène*, subjects' positions and sense of spectacle. Much has been made of the assumption that we are looking at a mirror reflection and what this might mean in terms of discussions around spectatorship, the gaze (the protagonists', ours and the artist's) and pictorial space. However, Campany posits that it may not have been shot in a mirror at all since there is nothing that confirms the presence of a mirror, such as visible doubling. We are led to believe this is a mirror image because of the way the scene is set and lit, and assume it is the camera we can see that took the picture, although we cannot be sure. Yet it is not the quest for answers that should occupy our thoughts, but rather the questions Wall suggests we ask about photography itself.

+ PHOTOGRAPHER BIO
Canadian, b. 1946

+ GOOGLE THESE
The Destroyed Room (1978), *Mimic* (1982), *A Sudden Gust of Wind* (after Hokusai) (1993), *After 'Invisible Man' by Ralph Ellison, the Prologue* (2000)

+ READ THIS
'The Domain of Occurrence: Jeff Wall in conversation with David Campany' at davidcampany.com.

Like This? Try These

→ Gregory Crewdson

→ Thomas Demand

→ Hannah Starkey

Elliott Erwitt

New York, New York

1974

In photography, as with most art forms or indeed anything in life, there is a fine line between the humorous, the witty, and that which is not in the slightest bit funny. In other words, creating images that are both convincing and humorous is not an easy task.

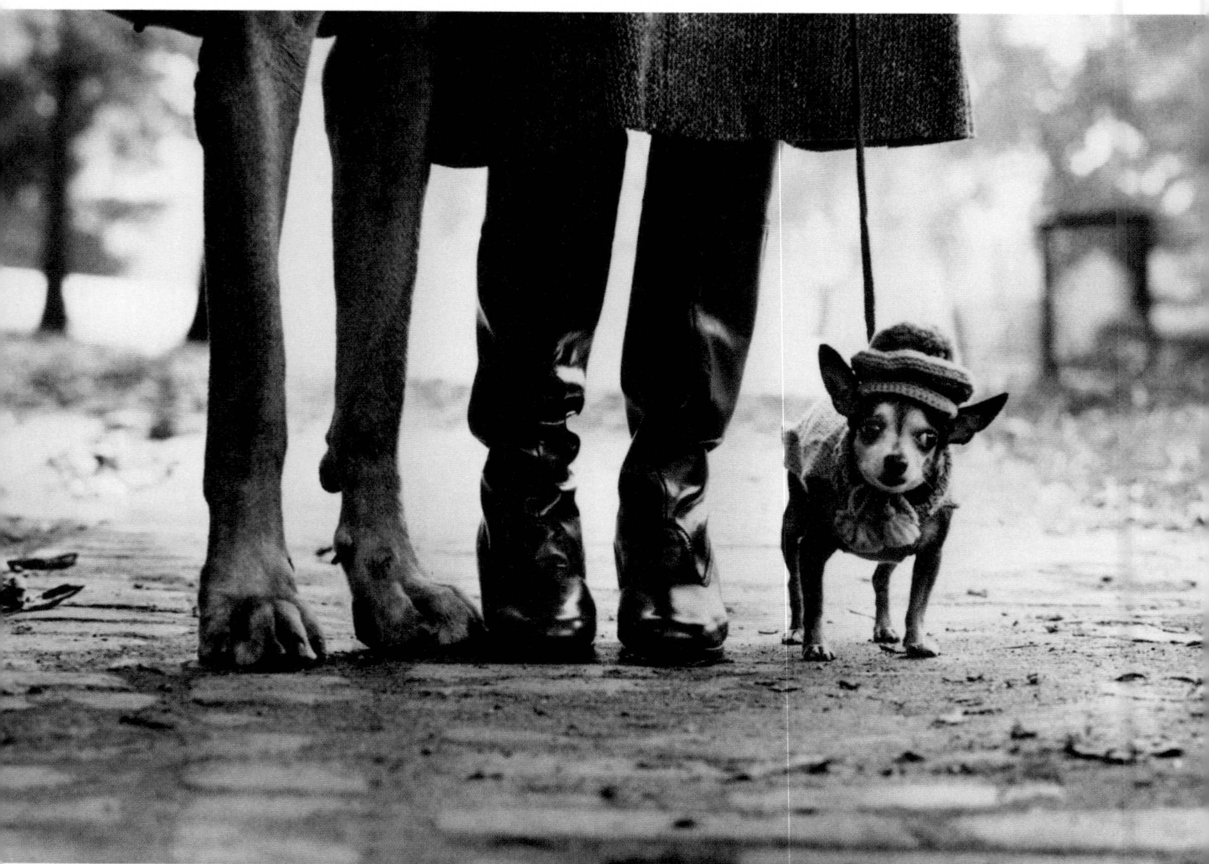

Elliott Erwitt has always had an apparently effortless ability to impeccably navigate the line between visual wit and silliness. His photographs are often described as playful, they celebrate life's inconsequential, serendipitous moments, but never tumble over into the ridiculous. They always remain true to life. 'You just have to care about what's around you and have a concern with humanity and the human comedy,' Erwitt has said, pointing out that there is always humour to be found in the everyday if you care to look for it. After all, photography, he has also said, is 'an art of observation.'

In documentary photography, a serious arm of photography that can sometimes take itself a little too seriously, Elliott's casual, seemingly carefree take is refreshing. His photographs of dogs, for which he is best known, are a good example of how documentary can benefit from a lighter touch. They are fun, entertaining, and yet they also reveal a great deal about us as humans – our propensity to love and our innate need to care for something other than ourselves. In short, there is more to an Erwitt photograph than first appears. His photographs are not just quirky or flippant, as unkind commentators might say; they are deeply considered and thought-provoking.

This photograph, of a woman called Gladys, out for a stroll in New York with what we assume are her two dogs, is among Erwitt's most famous dog pictures. It is witty, like many of his best photographs, and most certainly provokes a double-take response: this is no couple out for a walk with their chihuahua; there is not one, but two dogs here. Only Erwitt could have taken a picture like this, to have had the foresight to crop down and photograph on the smallest dog's level, and in doing so create an image that is both funny and deeply human.

+ PHOTOGRAPHER BIO
French-born American, b. 1928

+ GOOGLE THESE
North Carolina, USA (1950), *New York City. (Mother and baby)* (1953), *Berkeley, California* (1956)

+ READ THIS
'Best in Show', an article about Erwitt's life and work by John O'Mahony on the Guardian website, theguardian.com.

Like This? Try These

- → Henri Cartier-Bresson
- → William Wegman
- → Dan Weiner

Weronika Gęsicka

Untitled #52

2017

+ PHOTOGRAPHER BIO
Polish, b. 1984

+ GOOGLE THIS
Holiday (2019–20)

+ READ THIS
Take a look at 'Ideas on Talent: Weronika Gęsicka' on the Photoworks website at photoworks.org.uk.

In this charming scene a woman looks on as two children, presumably hers, walk smiling to greet a man, presumably their father, who appears to have just returned home from work. All appears to be well in this cheery sunlit tableau, the epitome of the American Dream, until the viewer realizes in horror that the children are heading straight for a gaping chasm.

The adults are completely oblivious to the imminent disaster as are the children, who are unaware of what lies moments ahead. Suddenly, everything in the picture is thrown into doubt. Perhaps you are seeing things. Your eyes must be playing a tricks. Blink. No, the ravine is still there. You look away and back again. There it is. You are left feeling perplexed by an image that appears to be at odds with itself. Yet it looks so real.

The image is from Polish artist Weronika Gęsicka's immensely surreal and unsettling series, *Traces* (2015–17), in which she digitally alters stock family photographs – mostly from American archives of the 1950s and 1960s of holiday snapshots or photographs of everyday family scenes. The subjects in the images look like real families but are in reality models. Gęsicka has long been fascinated by found photographs and has described her project as 'a kind of "family album" composed of stock photos.' Each image is subtly but deliberately modified to undermine what is being depicted. The resulting work cleverly blurs the boundary between what is real and what is not and the images are all the more disconcerting because they look so convincing.

Gęsicka is drawn to adapting typical everyday situations that her audience may have encountered at some point, which she turns upside down and inside out. She not only questions photography's truthfulness but also examines notions of memory. A memory is never a completely accurate account of a situation since it is inevitably warped by time, by what others recall and because people misremember. By introducing a sense that all is not as it seems Gęsicka reminds the viewer that neither memory nor photography – the medium often used to preserve memories – is infallible.

Like This? Try These

→ Julie Cockburn

→ Alma Haser

→ John Stezaker

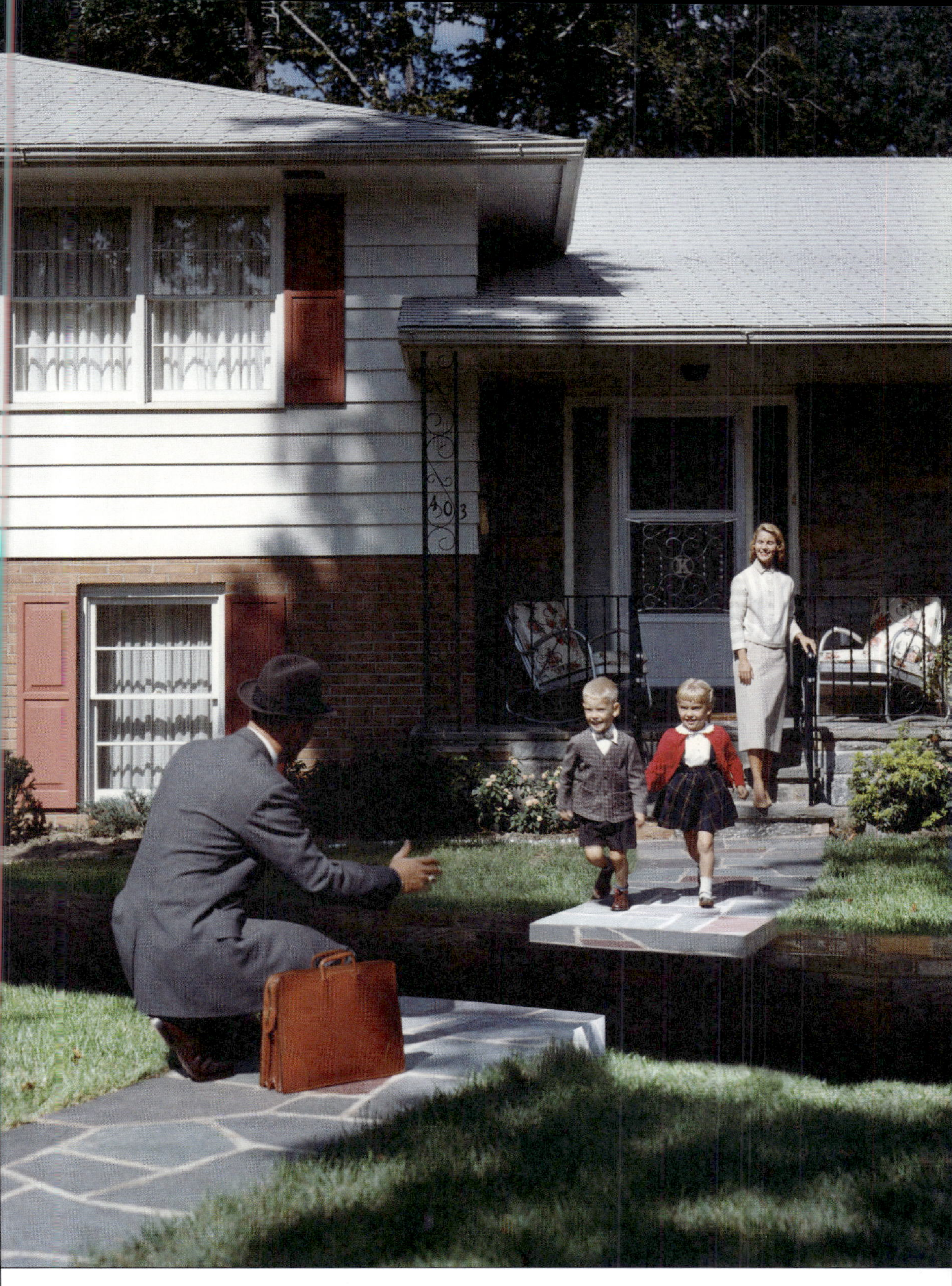

Susan Meiselas

Shortie on the Bally, Barton, Vermont, USA

1974

In Susan Meiselas's bold yet sensitive photograph the viewer cannot rely on the subject's face to make sense of the image. Consequently. every detail, no matter how small, becomes significant, from the position of the hand to the gentle curve of the woman's torso. We may think we know what we are looking at – a young woman, a showgirl perhaps – but to make assumptions is to miss the opportunity to engage on a much deeper level with the photograph and its many nuances.

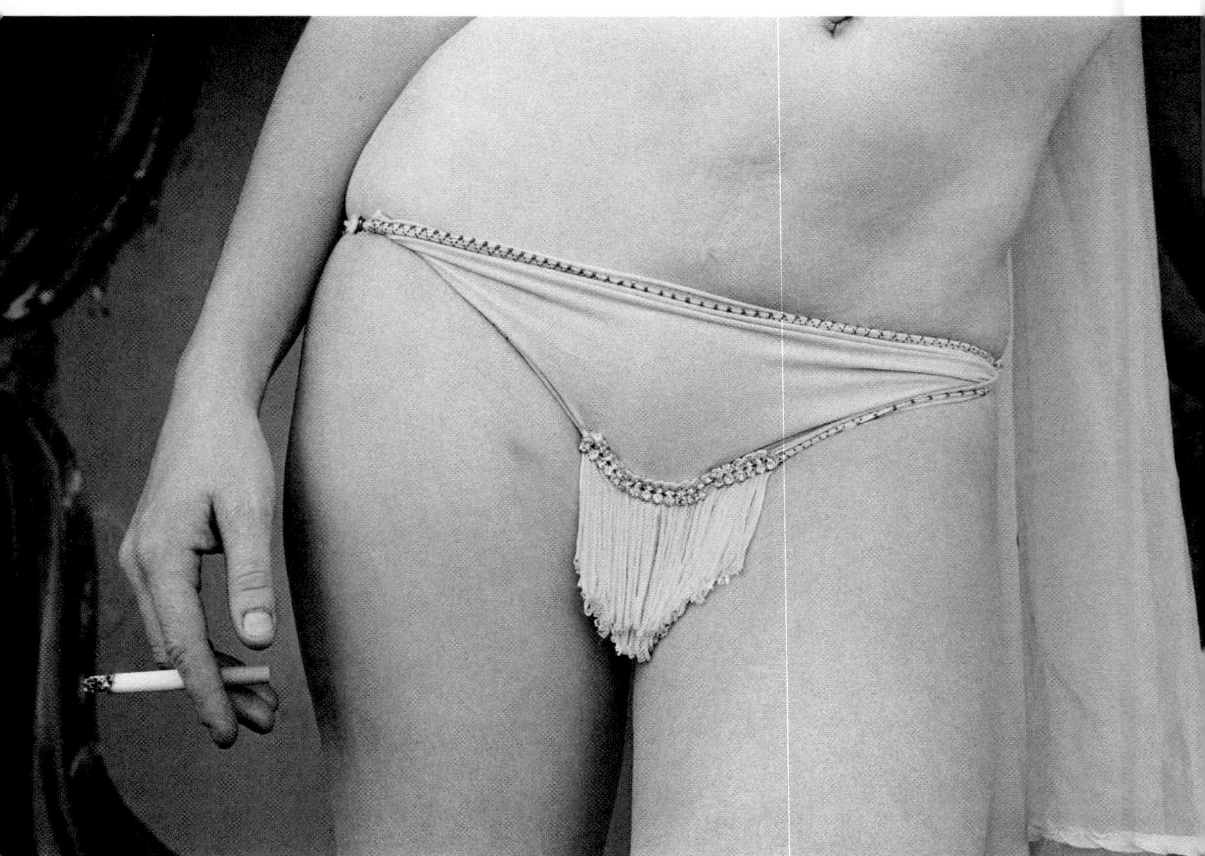

The photograph is from Meiselas's landmark series on carnival strippers shot in the early 1970s. From 1972 to 1975, she followed a troupe of showgirls as they travelled to small-town carnivals in New England, Pennsylvania and South Carolina. Meiselas photographed the women as they performed striptease but also backstage, in private moments. It was the era of the early feminist movement and conversations about how women should project themselves (or not) for male gratification were rife. Through her candid images, Meiselas invites us to engage in discussions around female empowerment and equality for women, issues that are as important today as they were in the 1970s.

Even in an image where only part of her subject's body can be seen, Meiselas draws us into the picture, allowing such dialogues to take place. Formally speaking, the photograph is a masterclass in photographic composition – our eyes are squarely directed to the woman's groin, to tassels that tease and sequins that sparkle. Only one arm is visible and a perfectly sculpted hand, which serves as a counterpoint to a strip of lightweight fabric that hangs softly in the air, emphasizes the other arm's absence. We notice a bruise, a barely-there scar. There is a frankness to the image, but also a tenderness. The realness and directness of the depiction contributes to the photograph's resonance. The woman is anonymous, but Meiselas makes her, and women like her, matter.

+ PHOTOGRAPHER BIO
American, b. 1948

+ GOOGLE THESE
Porch Portraits (1974), *Nicaragua* (1978–79), *Pandora's Box* (1995)

+ WATCH THIS
Watch a short film about the project, called 'Susan Meiselas: Carnival Strippers', on the Magnum Photos Vimeo channel.

Like This? Try These

- → Dorothea Lange
- → Mary Ellen Mark
- → Edward Weston

Anna Fox

Hampshire Village Pram Race

2006

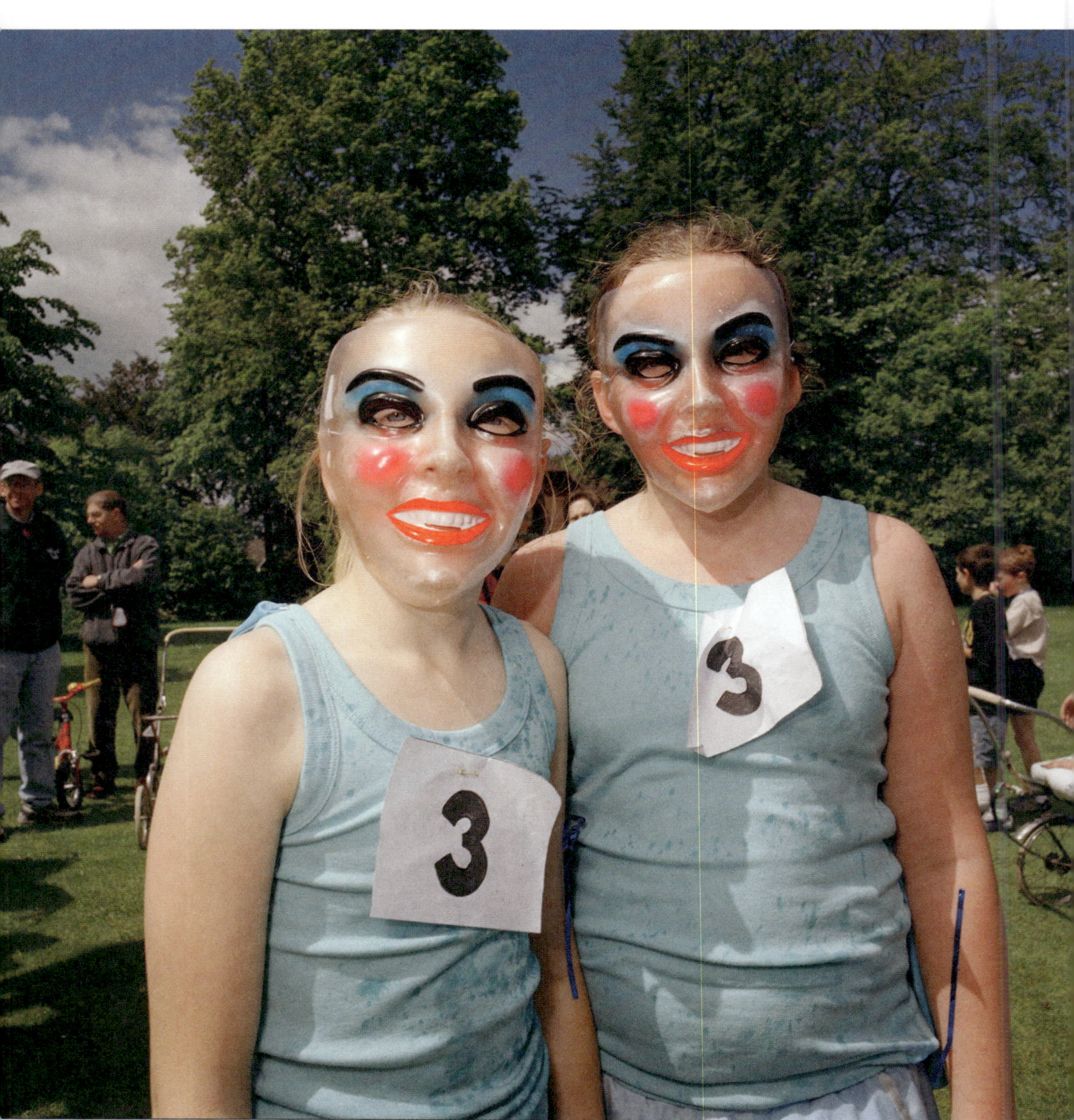

The absurdities of English village life, festivals and rituals have long been of interest to Anna Fox. Influenced by the American New Colourists group of photographers and British documentary photography, Fox photographs the ordinary and the everyday in such a way that pays homage to and seeks to break away from traditional documentary approaches.

The immediacy of colour in photography and its potential to inform and to evoke emotion fascinates Fox, who uses it to create images like this one from the *Back to the Village* (1999–2011) series, which simultaneously imbues a sense of unease and verges on the ridiculous. The two are not mutually exclusive: masked clowns or ones with painted faces have a long history of embodying comedy or silliness as well as something far more sinister or evil.

We may giggle at these masked girls with their exaggerated made-up faces, but a chill runs down our spine. Photographed in bright sunshine and lit by flash, they loom large in the picture, almost unnaturally so. Their smiles become grimaces and there is something even more unsettling about seeing them in daylight – such creatures are the stuff of myths and fairy tales that come out at night on Halloween, we think, not on a sunny summer's day. Placed in the centre of the frame, there is no getting away from them. They are so close to us it feels that they are slowly advancing.

The innocuous activities in the background – indifferent villagers and children at play – jar with Fox's main subject, heightening the tension of the picture. She has been called a satirical observer of rural life and at the heart of the photograph, which was taken in the sleepy village of Selborne in Hampshire, is a sense that all is not as it seems.

Fox has spoken about her interest in the performance side of village life, suggesting everyone is to a greater or lesser degree performing for others or acting out some kind of persona, and the masked figures shown here amplify this. Fox is not recording such customs for posterity; hers is a wry commentary on the way people live and she calls upon us not to take things at face value.

+ PHOTOGRAPHER BIO
British, b. 1961

+ GOOGLE THESE
Country Girls (1996–2001), *My Mother's Cupboards and My Father's Words* (1999)

+ READ THIS
Anna Fox: Photographs 1983–2007, edited by Val Williams (2007).

Like This? Try These

- → Alejandra Carles-Torla
- → David Moore
- → Martin Parr

Simon Norfolk

North Gate of Baghdad (After Corot)

2003

Sometimes the quietest, most unassuming pictures can be the most troubling. At a glance, this picturesque scene bathed in golden light looks innocuous. A charming stream nestled in the landscape beneath an archway of trees that could have been painted by an Impressionist master leads the eye into the frame, while rushing clouds fill the sky overhead.

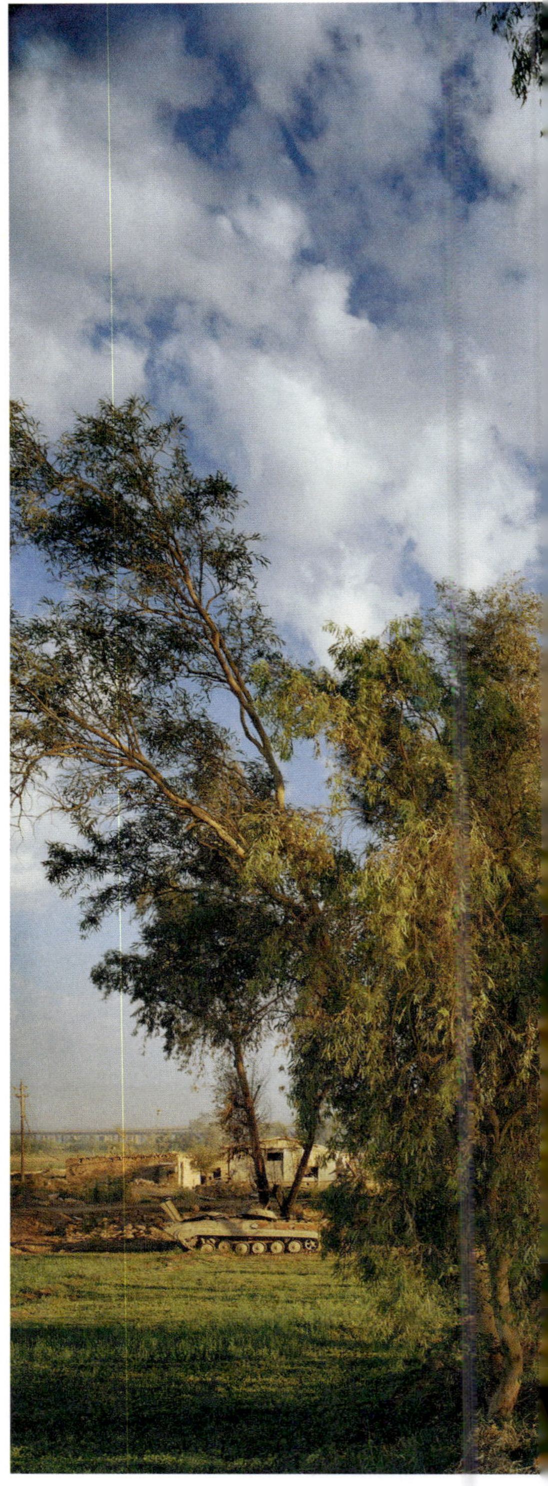

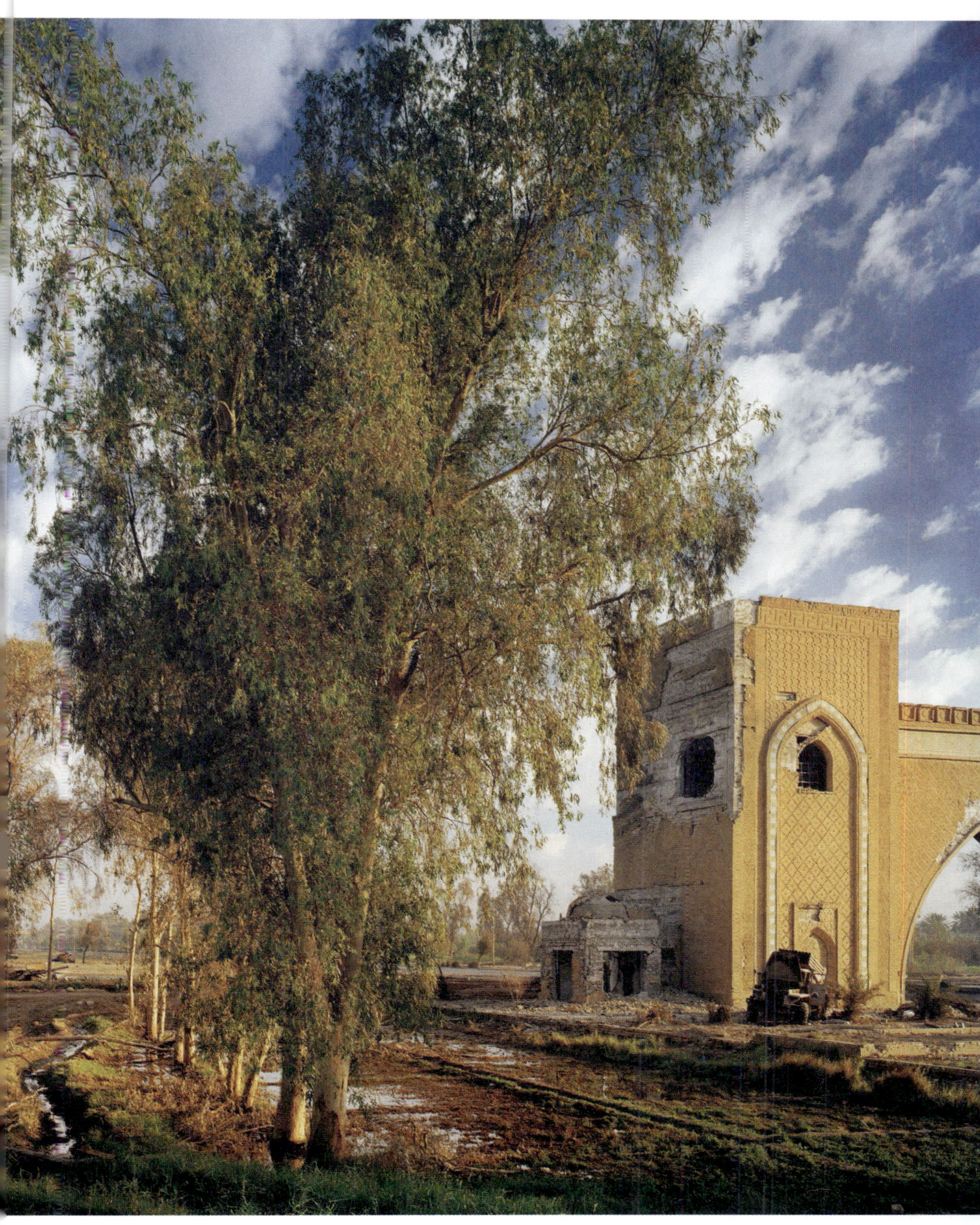

+ PHOTOGRAPHER BIO
British-Nigerian, b. 1963

+ GOOGLE THESE
Former Teahouse in a Park next to the Afghan Exhibition of Economic and Social Achievements in the Shah Shahid district of Kabul (2003), *Abandoned Mortar Shells in a Date Grove in Atifya, Northern Baghdad* (2003), *Flame Line, Lewis Glacier* (2015)

+ LISTEN TO THIS
Simon Norfolk discusses his work in the article 'Forensic Traces of War' on the LensCulture website: lensculture.com.

Like This? Try These

- → Lynsey Addario
- → Alixandra Fazzina
- → Anastasia Taylor-Lind

Simon Norfolk has talked about his photo in the same breath as painters Jean-Baptiste-Camille Corot and Camille Pissarro. We could be forgiven for believing we are looking at rustic slice of village life in France, Italy or the Netherlands at the turn of the nineteenth century – if only that were the case. The reality is far more sinister. Look closely and discarded tanks come into view. Look closer still and the stream is but a muddy furrow leading not to a distant iridescent paradise but to scrubland littered with military paraphernalia – the remnants of war. A majestic Babylonian arch is nothing more than a ruin, a pale imitation of the former at that. As Norfolk says of his photograph: 'It looks like a painting – but this is a place in Iraq where people were slaughtered.' The sunlight does not feel so agreeable now.

What we are looking at is the North Gate of Baghdad built at the behest of Saddam Hussein who, Norfolk says, wanted to associate himself with Babylonian kings. Norfolk, whose work frequently examines war and its effects, took the picture after Saddam's statue had been pulled down in Firdos Square following bloody fighting between Iraqi soldiers and coalition troops during the Battle of Baghdad in April 2003. All appears quiet in this landscape but the recent past weighs heavy on it. Norfolk is fascinated by the portrayal of ruins in art and has talked about the ruins in his own pictures as metaphors for pride and vanity. We could read this ravaged landscape and think that those who died there paid the price for liberation. We might also think the image asks us to remember the terrible atrocities that occurred in a seemingly idyllic landscape.

Joel Meyerowitz

View of the Site from the World Financial Center, Looking East, New York City

2001

There are some world events that need to be photographed no matter how appalling they might be and 9/11 is one of them. In the days and weeks after the terrorist attacks on New York's World Trade Center on 11 September 2001, Joel Meyerowitz was the only photographer granted regular access to Ground Zero.

For the next nine months, Meyerowitz documented the aftermath of the deadliest attack on American soil, creating a photographic record. As a native New Yorker, Meyerowitz had felt compelled to help, and as a photographer he knew the best way he could do so was to take pictures to create an archive in order that future generations would know about the atrocity.

Meyerowitz's dogged efforts meant he was eventually able to gain access to Ground Zero despite New York mayor Rudy Giuliani forbidding photographs of the site. Meyerowitz's visual record comprises almost 9,000 photographs, including this harrowing image that depicts in unflinching detail the devastation that occurred.

The image shows the ruins of the base of the North Tower, looking east towards the Woolworth Building. Shrouded in mist and harshly lit by industrial lighting, the ghostly scene could be a film set. On the face of it, the image shows little more than a tangle of metal but look closer and details begin to reveal themselves. To the right is a barely discernible group of rescue workers dwarfed by the building's remains and in the centre there are glimpses of an unremarkable office interior. From these tiny details Meyerowitz weaves together an image that drives home the scale of the damage. This is no ordinary unsightly pile; it is a mass grave. It is an image that demands the viewer spends time with it, allowing the horror to surface. Meyerowitz's offering may not be easy viewing but it is a vital photographic account that relays a moment in history in a way words never could.

+ PHOTOGRAPHER BIO

American, b. 1938

+ GOOGLE THESE

Land, Provincetown (1976), *Roseville Cottages, Truro, Massachusetts* (1976), *Provincetown, Massachusetts* (1977), *Fort Lauderdale, Florida* (1977)

+ WATCH THIS

Visit the article 'Joel Meyerowitz: Ground Zero, Then and Now' by Neil Harris on time.com to watch 'Ground Zero Rises: Joel Meyerowitz's Photographic Journey' documenting his return to photograph Ground Zero in 2010.

Other Photographers of 9/11 Images

- → Steve McCurry
- → James Nachtwey
- → Gilles Peress

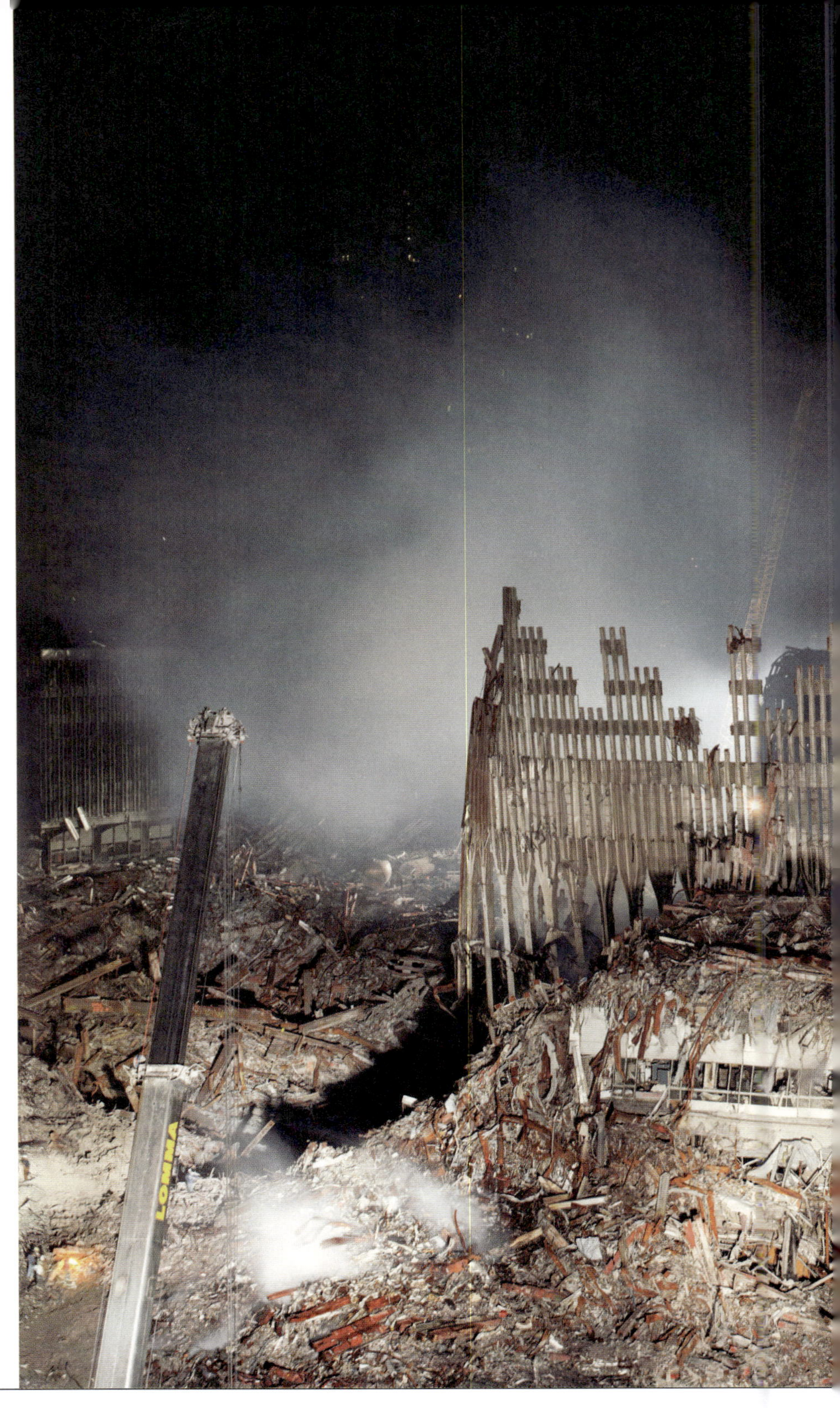

 Joel Meyerowitz—View of the Site from the World Financial Center, Looking East, New York City

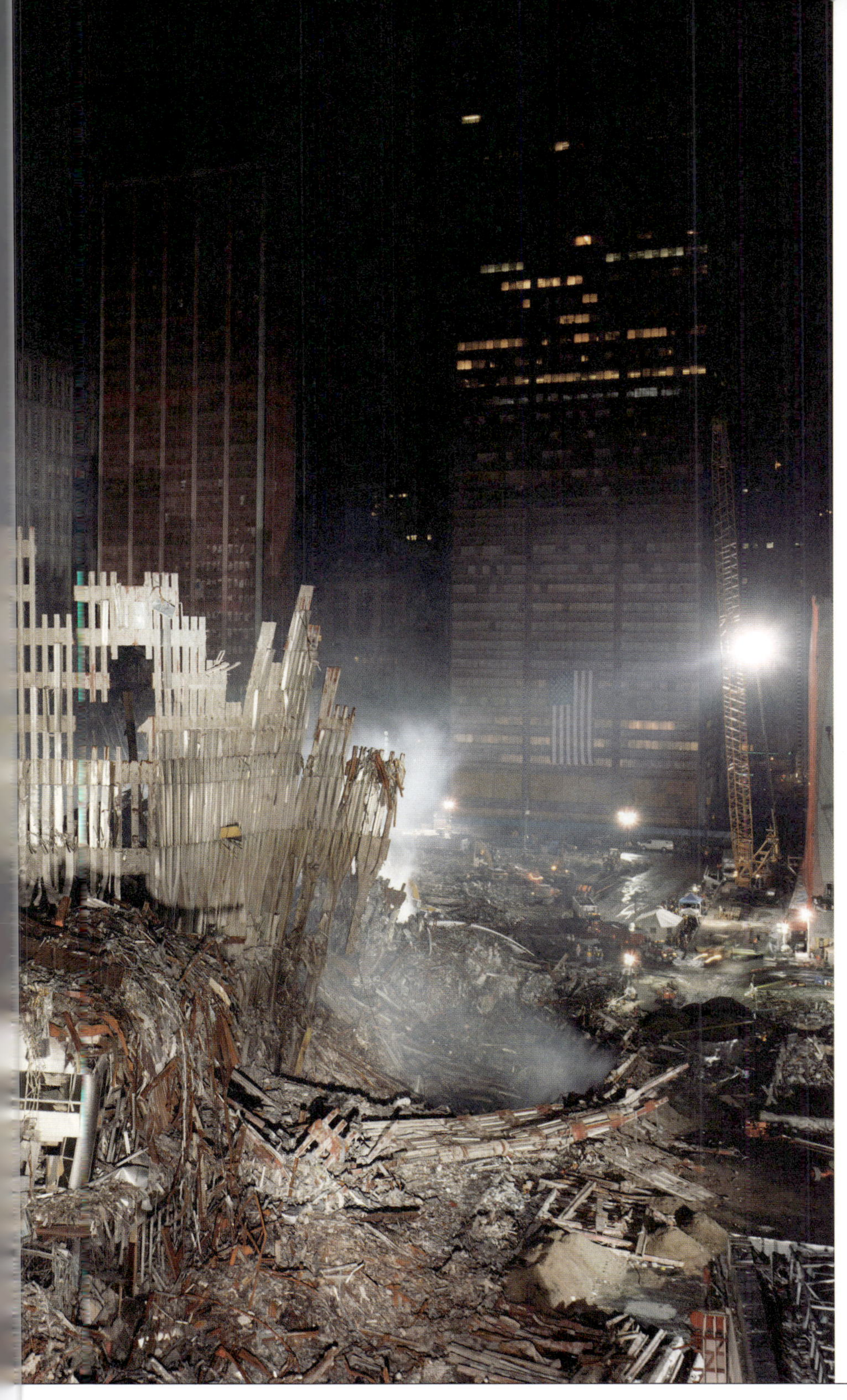

CHAPTER

3

A PUNCH IN THE GUT

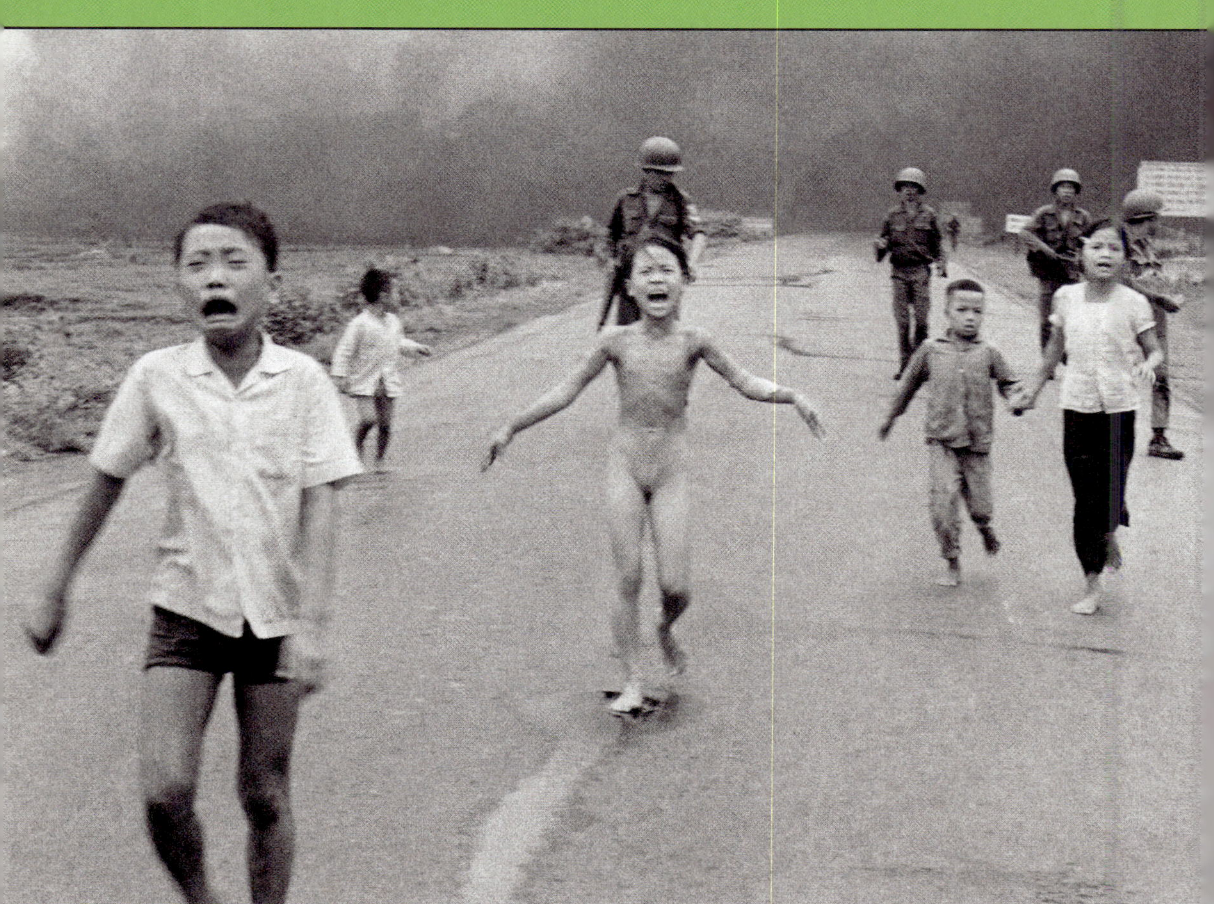

Nick Ut

The Terror of War

1972

History is ridden with mistakes, some more costly than others. When a South Vietnamese plane that was searching for Viet Cong insurgents bombed villagers with napalm during the Vietnam War (1955–75), the consequences were unspeakable yet recordable.

A photographer with Associated Press, Huỳnh Công Út, known professionally as Nick Ut, was close to the town of Trảng Bàng in Tây Ninh Province at the time and made many images in the moments after the disaster, but it is this photograph of nine-year-old Phan Thị Kim Phúc running screaming down Route 1 from the stricken town that has been etched into collective consciousness. Struck by the burning napalm, Kim Phúc had ripped off her clothes as she fled the site. Soldiers from the Vietnam Army 25th Division are visible in the background. The men's apparent nonchalance jars with the pain and terror on the children's faces, adding to the impact of the image.

The debate as to whether conflict photographers should intervene or not is one of the oldest in photojournalism, but on that day – 8 June 1972 – Ut, who was just twenty-one years old, did both. He took a photo that would not only come to epitomize the extent of the devastation of the war at the time but for all time. He also helped Kim Phúc who had suffered horrific third-degree burns across large areas of her body. Together with an ITN correspondent Christopher Wain, Ut assisted in getting her to hospital in the immediate aftermath and later arranged life-saving treatment for her in the United States.

The Pulitzer Prize prize-winning picture is a mainstay on lists of iconic photographs for its utterly compelling, raw depiction of the impact of the war on ordinary people. Yet it is not without controversy. At the time, debates ripped through newsrooms about whether the image should be published on account of its depiction of nudity. Then in 2016, the image made headlines when Facebook removed it after Norwegian newspaper *Aftenposten* shared the image in a post about iconic war photographs.

+ PHOTOGRAPHER BIO
Vietnamese-American, b. 1951

+ GOOGLE THESE
A Refugee Clutches her Baby as a Government Helicopter Carries them Away from Tuy Hòa, 235 Miles North-east of Saigon on March 22, 1975 (1975), *Muhammad Ali Throws a Left Punch at a Sandbag During Workout at a Gym in Tokyo* (1976)

+ WATCH THIS
Search 'Nick Ut' at nbcnews.com to watch Nick Ut talk about what it was like taking this image, in 'How Nick Ut's Photo "Napalm Girl" Changed the Vietnam War'.

Other Compelling Photojournalists

→ Eddie Adams

→ Malcolm Browne

→ Horst Faas

Tom Pilston

A Ranger Strokes a Young Rhino Orphaned by Poachers

2013

Without knowing any context, Tom Pilston's evocative photograph of a rhino and wildlife ranger might be read as an image of utter despair. Initially, it appears that perhaps the animal is dead, especially given the ongoing ferocious poaching of rhinos. Thankfully, the rhino is alive.

Momentary relief quickly gives way to sadness, however, when the captioned image reveals that the young rhino, Hope, was hand-reared after being orphaned by poachers. Pilston took the image in Kenya's Lewa Wildlife Conservancy, a sanctuary that has provided a safe home for rhinos since the early 1980s. So hope, like the animal's name, returns when you learn about the work being done to combat poaching and protect rhinos in Kenya. This is an image where myriad emotions converge, an image that simultaneously exposes the plight of rhinos and celebrates the herculean efforts to prevent their extinction.

At the time of writing, the conservancy cares for approximately 169 rhinos and 14 per cent of the country's rhino population lives on Lewa and the neighbouring Borana Conservancy. The fight continues to protect rhinos by creating secure habitats, involving local people, and ultimately reducing demand for rhino horns, which are used for medicinal purposes, carvings and jewellery in Asia. For as long as there is demand, poaching will continue. Pilston's image, beautifully lit and immaculately composed, resonates deeply. It is a powerful reminder of the incredible work being done not only in Kenya but elsewhere in the world to help these critically endangered creatures, and that there is always hope that they will survive. The presence of a human hand symbolizes universal efforts to help these animals and all threatened species, as the viewer senses a bond between human and animal. Pilston's image serves as reminder to nurture and protect nature not only for the sake of rhinos, but for every living creature, including the human race.

+ PHOTOGRAPHER BIO
British, b. 1963

+ GOOGLE THESE
Pilston's work at the Lewa Wildlife Conservancy in Kenya (begun 2011), *Syria, the World's War* (2011–13)

+ READ THIS
Look up Pilston's profile on Panos Pictures at: panos.co.uk/portfolio/tom-pilston.

Other Compelling Photojournalists

→ Ko Myo

→ Brent Stirton

→ Ami Vitale

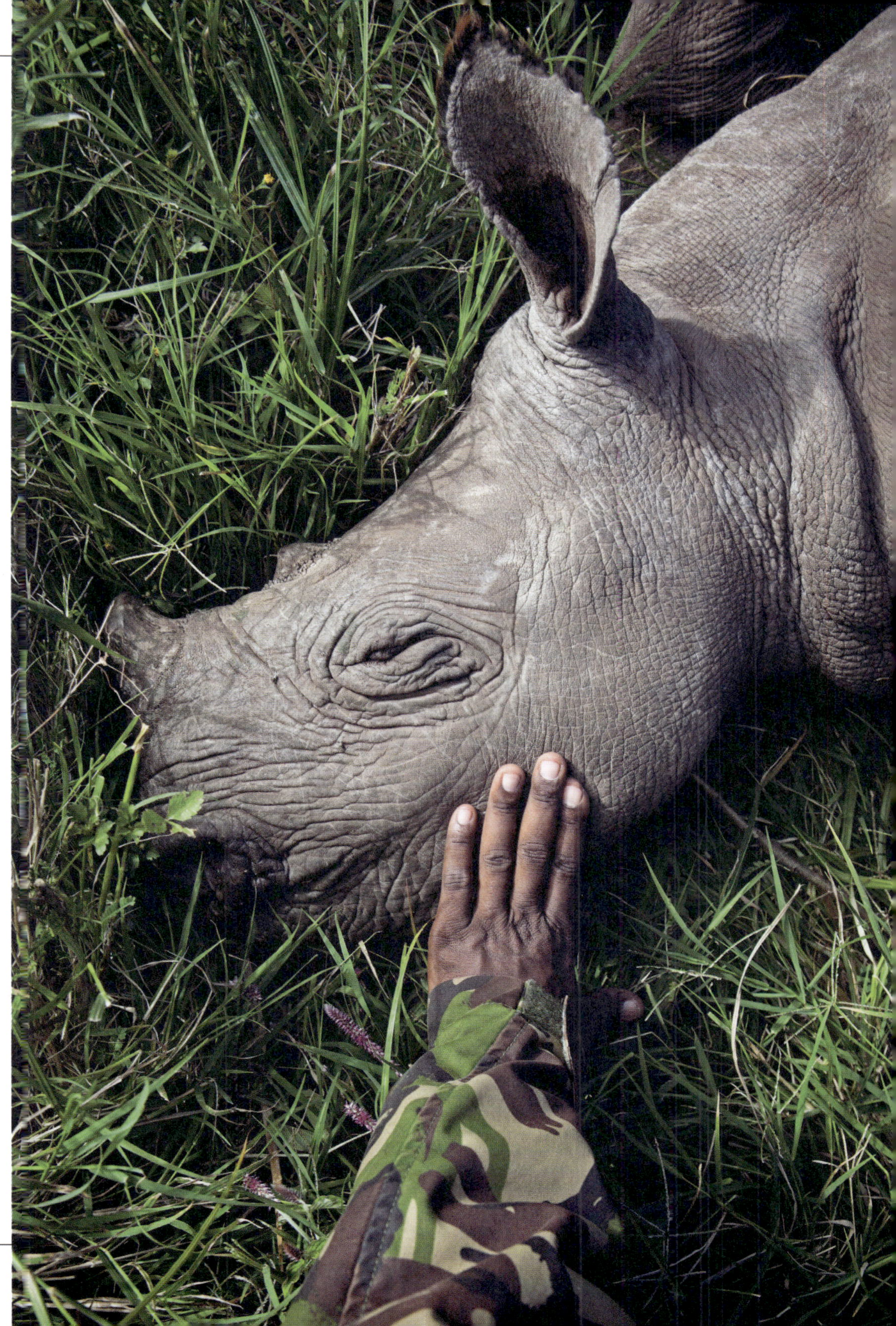

Chris Hondros

Iraqi Girl at Checkpoint

2005

This image shows five-year-old Samar Hassan whose parents were shot and killed moments before the picture was taken on 18 January 2005. Blood-splattered and screaming, her grief and shock could not be more explicit.

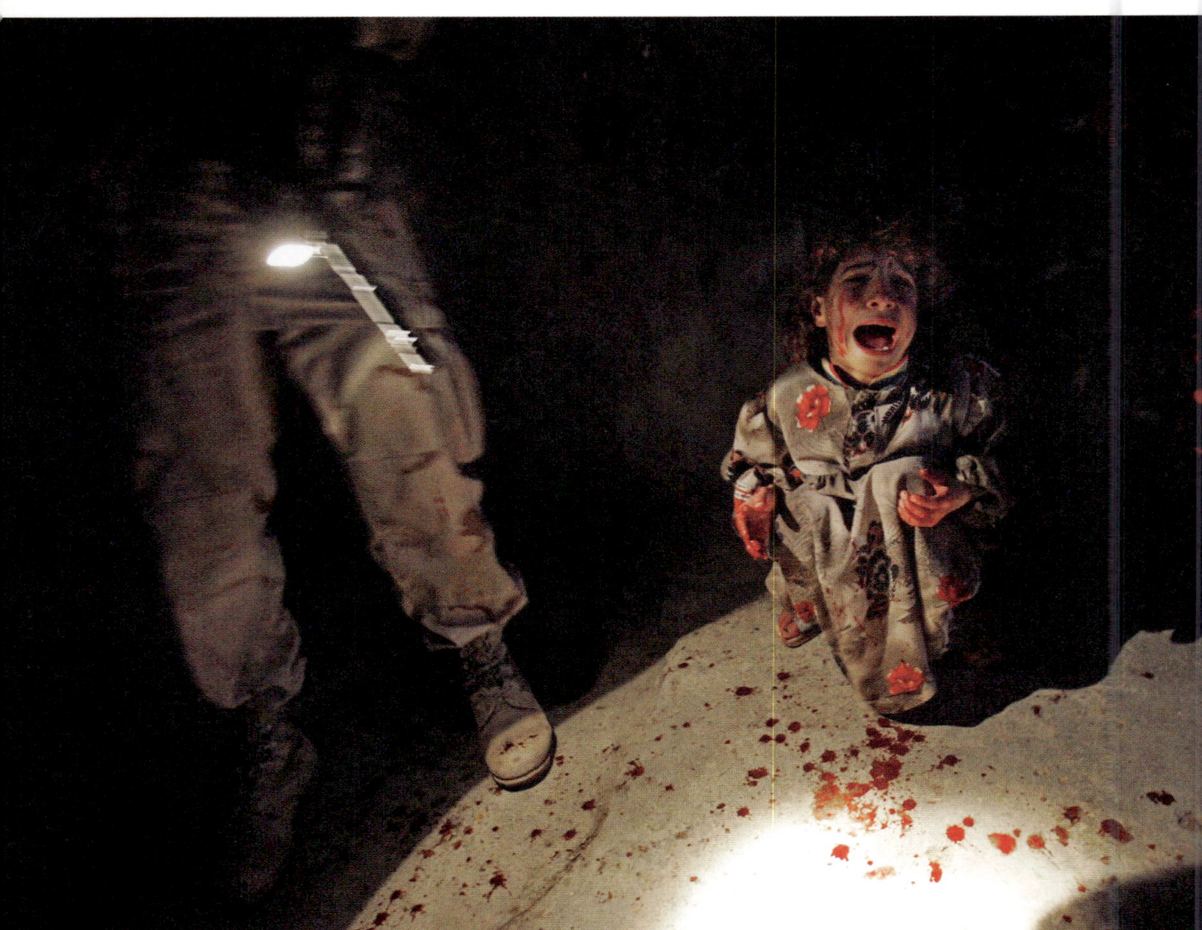

Samar had been travelling home from Tal Afar in Iraq with her family when American troops opened fire on their car mistakenly believing the vehicle contained insurgents or a suicide bomber. Long-time war photographer Chris Hondros was covering the conflict in Iraq, and captured the sequence of events leading up to and after the terrible incident. Hondros was known for his commitment to focusing on the people affected most by the conflicts he was recording and children in particular. Fellow journalist and friend Greg Campbell said that Hondros 'became well-known for being able to find the human thread through everything'.

Hondros's other shots from that night paint a devastating picture of the trauma that unfolded but this image has become the iconic photograph of the Iraq War because of its powerful depiction of the human face and cost of the conflict: Samar's distraught expression and blood-stained face speak volumes. Hondros spoke about the 'stark' light in the photograph and how that led some to comment on the image's apparent links to painting. However, the open and expressive position of the girl's hands, and the way she is crouching and dwarfed by the nearby soldier, give the image its horrific, unforgettable intensity.

If we have become numb to images of human suffering, Hondros's photograph of a young girl who has experienced something no child should ever have to, will surely jolt us out of our stupor. For Samar could be any child; indeed, she is every child who has ever been caught up in conflict anywhere in the world. Hondros was killed during a firefight in Misrata while on assignment covering the civil war in Libya in 2011. His photograph will endure as a symbol and reminder of the appalling and tragic cost of war.

+ PHOTOGRAPHER BIO
American, 1970–2011

+ GOOGLE THESE
A Liberian Militia Commander Loyal to the Government Exults after Firing a Rocket-propelled Grenade at Rebel Forces at a Key Strategic Bridge, July 20, 2003 in Monrovia, Liberia (2003), *U.S. Army Soldiers Shield their Eyes from the Powerful Rotor Wash of a Chinook Cargo Helicopter as They Are Picked up from a Mission October 15, 2009 in Paktika Province, Afghanistan* (2009)

+ WATCH THIS
Find the article 'Testament: Remembering Chris Hondros' Iconic Photograph From Iraq' on Time.com to see a video of Hondros's former editor at Getty Images, Pancho Bernasconi, discuss his work.

+ WATCH THIS
Seek out the documentary *Hondros* (2018), directed by Greg Campbell.

Other Compelling Photojournalists

- Lynsey Addario
- Ron Haviv
- Tim Hetherington

David Hume Kennerly

The Peoples Temple Cult Commits Mass Suicide in Guyana

1978

There is surely no more chilling a sight than this – a view of some of the bodies at the Peoples Temple Agricultural Project in Jonestown, Guyana after the mass murder-suicide of more than 900 men, women and children on 18 November 1978.

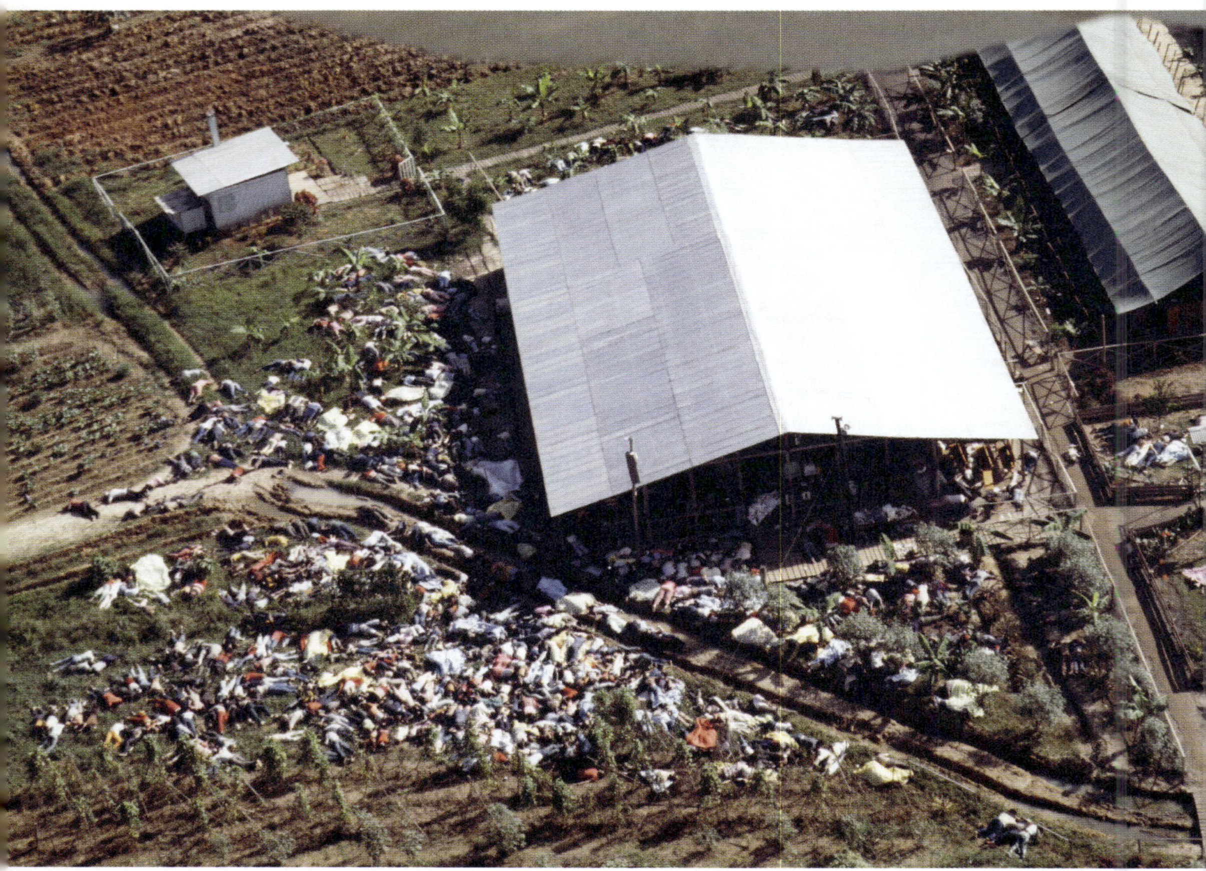

Members of the American cult led by the infamous Reverend Jim Jones poisoned themselves at his behest after Temple members murdered an American Congressman and several journalists. Pulitzer Prize-winning photographer David Hume Kennerly had spent two years in Vietnam covering the war but he has said that nothing prepared him for what he saw in the remote jungle when he arrived three days later. In a fascinating but horrific post on Hume Kennerly's website to mark the 40th anniversary of the tragedy in 2018, he recounts how when he first flew over the scene he thought he was looking at people who were alive. It was only when the aircraft drew closer that he realized the terrible truth. On the ground as he walked around the site, the horrors were amplified: 'I was used to the wounds of war, bodies torn to bits, burned, battered, blown up. This was different. Families with their arms around each other lay face down, in some cases the little feet of their children sticking out between them.'

Hume Kennerly took many pictures that day; his photograph of a large metal vat filled with the purple-coloured poisoned Flavor Aid was used on the cover of *TIME* magazine. The grape drink was laced with Valium, chloral hydrate, cyanide and given to the victims. Nevertheless, nothing is as gut-wrenching as seeing what Hume Kennerly called the 'tableau of death' from above. When the viewer first sees the image it is unclear what it depicts. As is typical with aerial photography, what lies below becomes abstract, a collection of colours and shapes. On closer inspection, the grim reality becomes apparent. When witnessing such a sight from above the true scale of the tragedy is clear. In this image, Hume Kennerly conveys unimaginable horrors leaving the viewer to question how such a massacre could ever have happened.

+ PHOTOGRAPHER BIO
American, b. 1947

+ GOOGLE THESE
Lone soldier walks across a deserted hill in the A Shau Valley (1971), *US Soldier Drinks from his Helmet while on Operation near Da Nang, Vietnam* (1972)

+ READ THIS
'Jonestown, a Personal Recollection' on Hume Kennerly's website at kennerly.com.

+ WATCH THIS
'Telling the Story in 1/60th of a Second: David Hume Kennerly at TEDxBend' on the Tedx Talks YouTube channel.

Other Compelling Photojournalists

- Larry Burrows
- Carolyn Cole
- Ronald L. Haeberle

Idlib Media Center

Children Lie Injured in Khan Sheikhoun Southern Idlib Province, Syria

2017

These children were gassed in Syria early in the morning of 4 April 2017 when warplanes dropped what is believed to have been the deadly nerve agent sarin on the rebel-held town of Khan Sheikhoun in north-western Syria. More than eighty people were killed, and many more were injured.

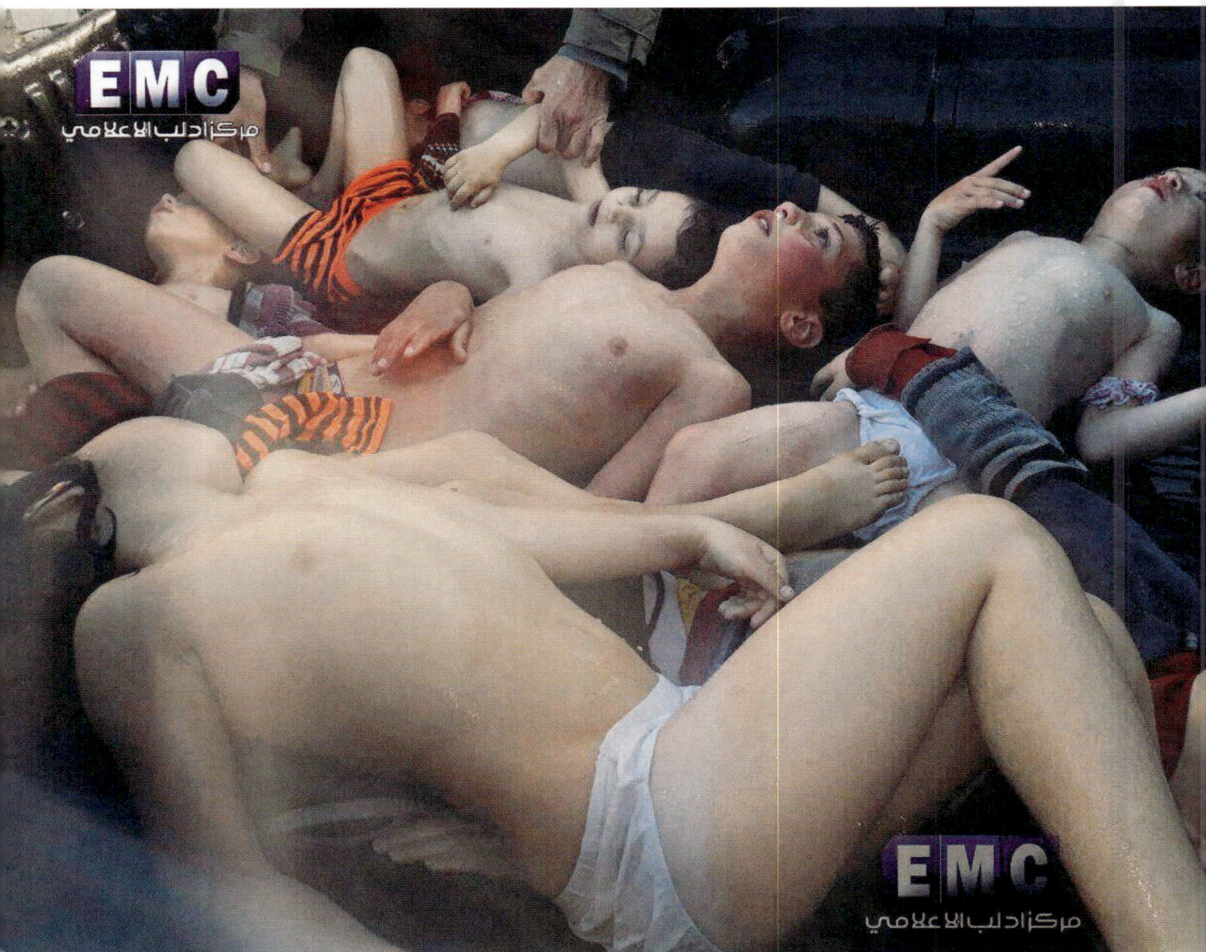

President Bashar al-Assad has denied using chemical weapons and when interviewed about the attack by Agence France-Presse days after the incident, he questioned the reliability of videos that had been released. In June 2017, the Organisation for the Prohibition of Chemical Weapons concluded that the banned nerve agent sarin had been used. It is impossible to fathom an atrocity of this magnitude. Equally, it is a challenge to process such a terrible image, which was used on the front cover of French newspaper *Libération* for its 6 April 2017 edition. Released by Associated Press (AP), the image is a screenshot from a video published by Idlib Media Center, an activist group opposed to the Syrian regime established in 2014. What the viewer sees is chilling: the rigid, contorted bodies of at least seven children with their eyes open and glazed are shown in the back of a pickup truck minutes after the chemical weapon attack. As *TIME* magazine reported, photo editors at the newspaper who had obtained the image from AP were careful to verify that what was being depicted was not a contrived scene and watched videos showing that the children had been placed there by first responders.

This is a difficult image to look at, not only because of the horror it depicts but because the soft colours and light give it an ethereal quality which is at odds with the ghastly subject matter. Some will question *Libération*'s decision to run such a terrible image on their cover, while others will recognize the importance of doing so. Photography, especially in a documentary context, is never straightforward, and even if you cannot agree that there is reason to publish such an image, surely it is right that photography should bear witness and speak truth to power.

+ PHOTOGRAPHER BIO
Syrian

+ GOOGLE THESE
Hope for a new life (2015) by Warren Richardson, *Crying Girl on the Border* (2018) by John Moore, *Palestinian protester Aed Abu Amro in Gaza from Palestinian Right of Return Protests* (2018) by Mustafa Hassona

+ READ THIS
'The Story Behind a Newspaper's Cover Photo of 7 Dead Syrian Children' by Olivier Laurent at time.com.

Other Compelling Photojournalists

- Manu Brabo
- Bassam Khabieh
- Jérôme Sessini

Alex Majoli

Scene #1633 (Controls in the Retirement House, Catania, Sicily)

2020

A heavy mood emanates from this image. What little light is present is stifled by darkness that wraps around everything it touches. Figures emerge from the gloom and we begin to make sense of what we are looking at. The figures seem to have been paralysed, frozen to the spot as though in a dream where movement is slowed to an excruciating pace or halted completely.

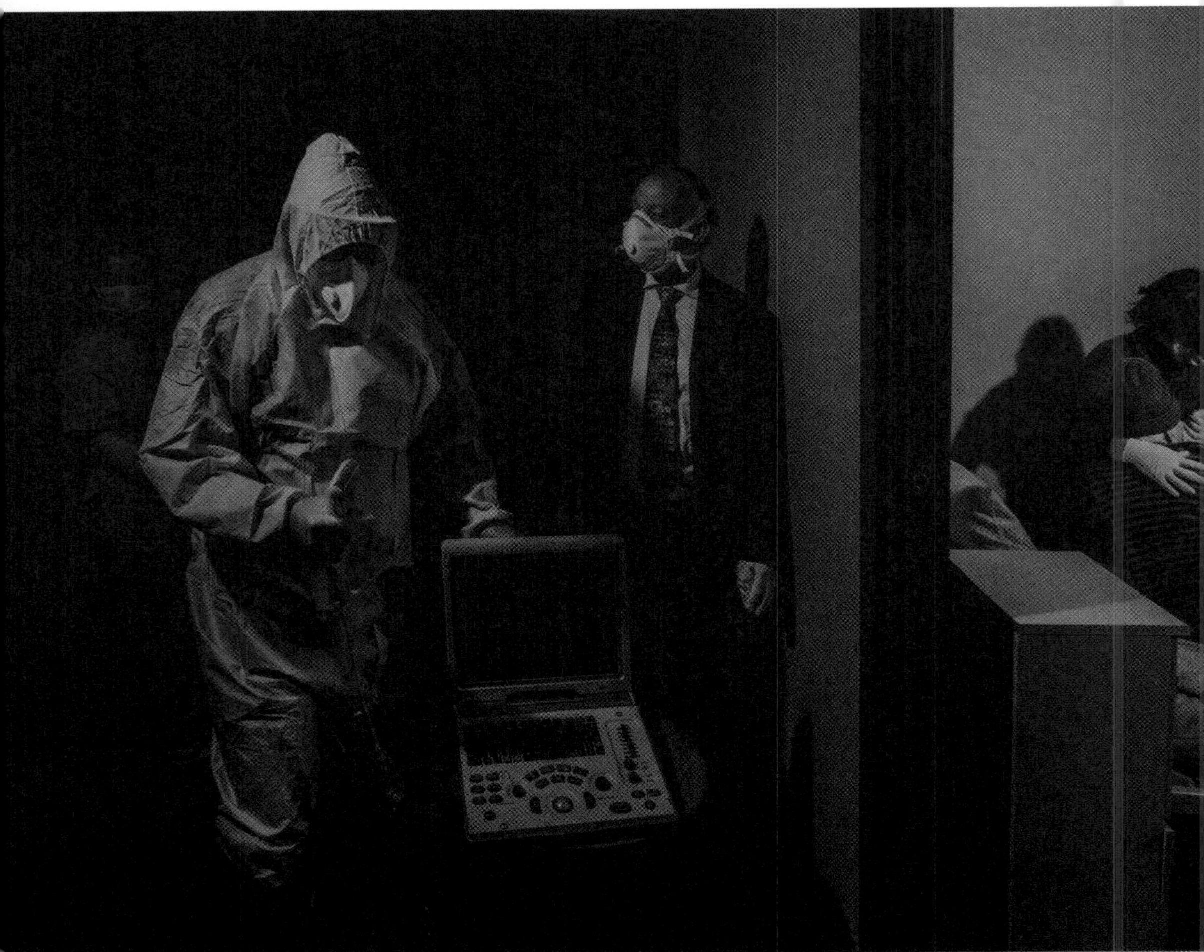

This is the work of COVID-19, an invisible presence in the scene. The PPE-clad figure is a giveaway, his masked companions too. Before 2020, we might have looked at an image like this and thought of Chernobyl or Fukushima; now it could only be the coronavirus pandemic that has swept across the world.

This sombre and eerie photograph is from a series by Italian photographer Alex Majoli who was in Reggio Emilia in northern Italy when COVID-19 took hold in his home country. At the end of February 2020, Majoli began documenting what was unfolding around him before travelling around Italy, from Sicily to Rome, Milan and to the border with Slovenia, recording what he saw. Majoli took this particular image in what the accompanying caption calls an 'Evangelical' nursing home in Catania, Sicily, where residents displayed symptoms of COVID-19.

There is much that is striking. Photographed in a deliberately theatrical way, the photograph reads like a tableau vivant or 'living picture' where actors or models are typically posed and theatrically-lit. Hyperreal, the image looks like a film still or a moment from a play. The doorway that slices through the scene, dividing the image in two, accentuates the film strip feel, while the technique Majoli has used, which involves removing light from the outlines of his subjects, contributes to the image's unnatural almost dreamlike look. As staged as the image looks and feels, however, what Majoli has captured is far from fiction. These are real people with real lives living through a nightmarish reality. By seamlessly blurring the line between reality and fiction, Majoli has created an image that is as troubling as the reality it depicts.

+ PHOTOGRAPHER BIO
Italian, b. 1971

+ GOOGLE THESE
Requiem in Samba (1995–), *Hotel Marinum* (1998–), *Libera Me* (2004)

+ READ THIS
'The COVID-19 Visual Project – A Time of Distance', at covid19visualproject.org.

Other Compelling Photojournalists

- → Gabriele Micalizzi
- → Paolo Pellegrin
- → Ilkka Uimonen

Moises Saman

Displaced Yazidi Man and his Daughters, Fish-Khabur, Iraq, 10 August, 2014

2014

There is no escaping the piercing gaze of the little girl on the right. She looks directly at the viewer, her expression a mix of childish innocence, bemusement, and conversely, an omniscience.

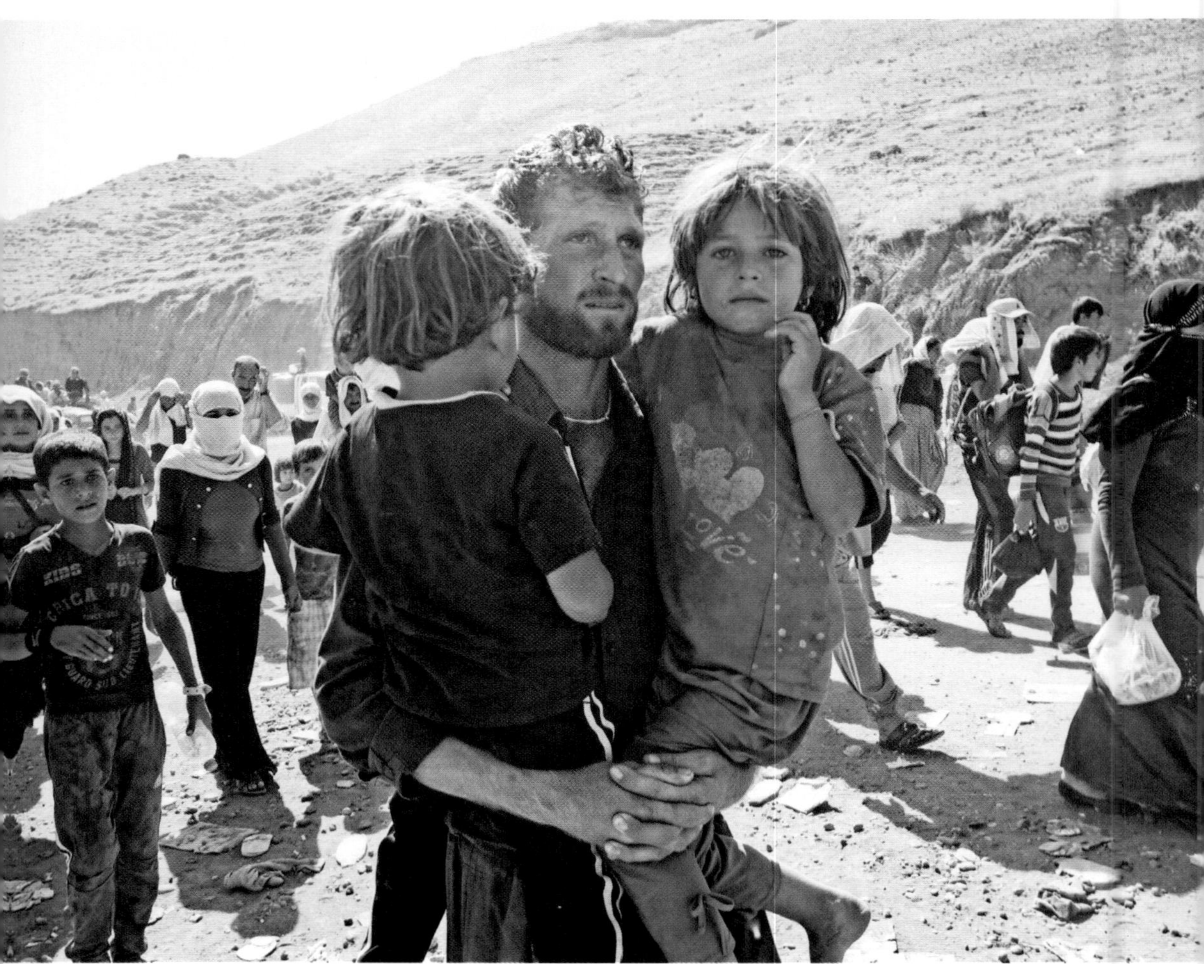

The girl makes the picture, it is she who holds the image together, and gives it weight and substance. Imagine, if her head was turned to the side, her gaze directed towards the commotion around her; would the image make such a strong impression? Possibly not. The viewer needs to see her eyes to fully appreciate the scene photographer Moises Saman has captured. Even the position of her hand, tentatively held up so the tips of her fingers almost touch her face, a tiny gesture here magnified, seems meaningful. Saman, who lives in Jordan, has been recording the humanitarian impact of war in the Middle East since 2001, covering the Arab Spring (2010–12) and the Syrian civil war (2010–). He took this image in Iraq's Sinjar district in 2014 while documenting the plight of Yazidis, a religious minority who have faced persecution.

The photograph shows a Yazidi man with his two young children as they enter Kurdish-controlled northern Iraq near the village of Fish-Khabur. The accompanying caption on the Magnum Photos website, the photographic cooperative to which Saman belongs, explains that thousands of displaced Yazidis from the Sinjar region of northern Iraq – the spiritual heartland of the Yazidis – took refuge in the Kurdish areas of northern Iraq because of the advance of militants Islamic State in Iraq and Syria (ISIS). At a glance, the viewer sees the mass migration of people. But Saman's powerful image offers much more. He has spoken about his desire to capture 'the fleeting moments on the periphery of the more dramatic events,' and he might have been talking about this image, given it fits his remit so well.

Here, Saman has immortalized the briefest of moments when an exhausted father and his children pass by the photographer, so that people might see it and think of the fate of these individuals and the wider context of the suffering that is the backdrop for the image. There is no blood, no screams, yet the image cuts to the quick. Saman's physical proximity to his subjects helps to create impact as he ushers you into their space and permits you to see the nuances of people's expressions clearly. The vacant look on the father's face is haunting – a father trying to do the best for his family, he carries on against the odds, a representation of refugees worldwide.

+ PHOTOGRAPHER BIO
Spanish-American, b. 1974

+ GOOGLE THIS
Discordia: The Arab Spring (2010–14)

+ READ THIS
'In Conversation: Photographer Moises Saman On His Journey Documenting the Arab Spring' published on newsweek.com.

Other Compelling Photojournalists

→ Daniel Etter

→ Alixandra Fazzina

→ Lorenzo Meloni

Photographer Unknown

Terrified African American Girls Flee Police Officers During a Race Riot in the Bedford-Stuyvesant Neighbourhood of Brooklyn

1964

The viewer is immediately drawn to the terrified, screaming girl. As if the girl's fear-stricken face is not sufficiently disturbing, a glance at the police officer behind who appears to be smiling is chilling. Closer inspection shows a group of police officers chasing after the three fleeing figures. The black girls and boy appear to be being hunted.

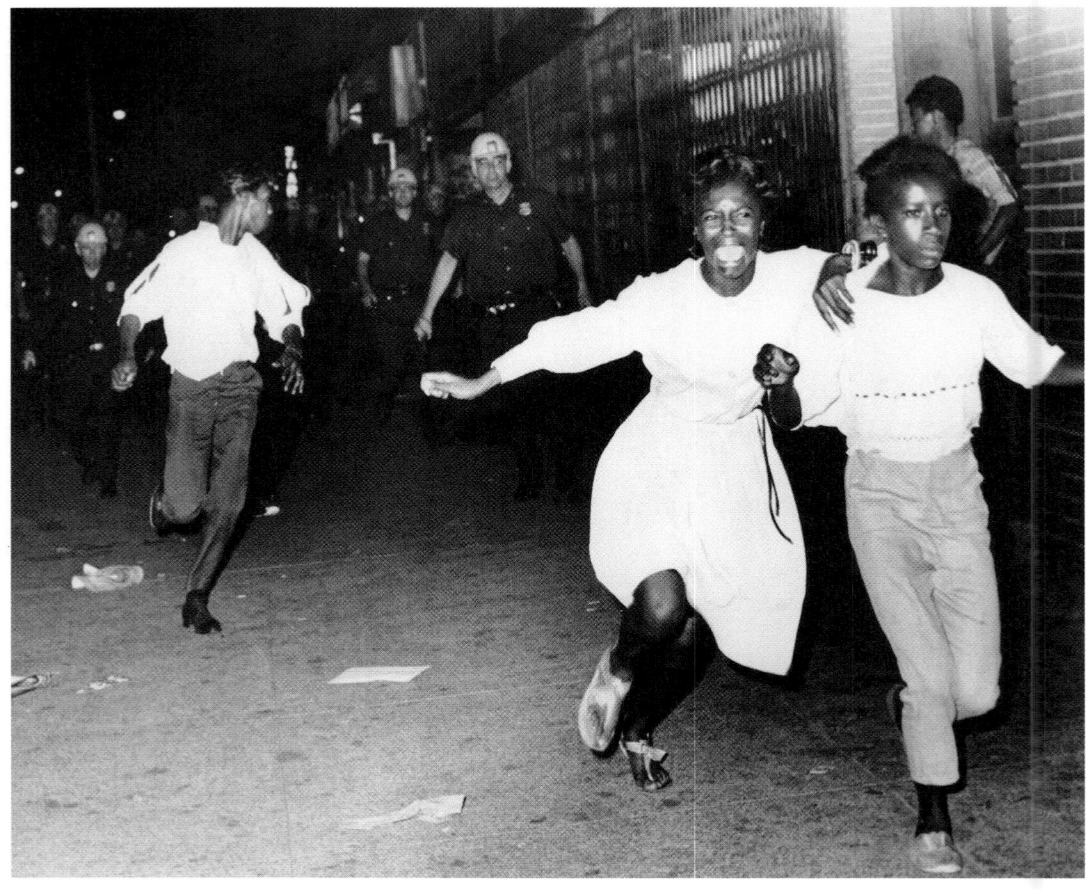

This harrowing photograph was taken during a race riot in Bedford-Stuyvesant or Bed-Stuy, a neighbourhood in Brooklyn, New York that is a major cultural centre for Brooklyn's African Americans. Little is known about the girls or what had just happened, but it is thought they were caught up in riots that began in Harlem and spread to nearby neighbourhoods after the fatal shooting of fifteen-year-old African American James Powell by white police officer Thomas Gilligan in Manhattan on 16 July 1964. Shops were looted and property was vandalized, protestors and police clashed. One person was killed, 118 were injured and 465 arrests were made.

The civil rights movement had started a decade earlier although efforts to end racial discrimination and injustice in the United States got underway much earlier. Harlem itself had experienced two race riots prior to this one, in 1935 and 1943.

In the twenty-first century, African American men, women and children are still being killed because of the colour of their skin, while demands for police reform and racial justice continue to be made. Change has been slow and the fight to eliminate systemic racism is ongoing. The Black Lives Matter movement, which was started in 2013, gained momentum after the killing of George Floyd at the hands of police in Minneapolis on 25 May 2020, and supporters hope that his tragic death brings real, lasting change.

In the 2000s, many people own a smartphone equipped with a camera, so more images of demonstrations are being made and shared than ever before. Nevertheless, the impact of this photograph and its unflinching depiction of the girls' distress endures.

+ PHOTOGRAPHER BIO
American

+ GOOGLE THESE
Innocent bystander, Birmingham, Alabama by Bob Adelman (1963), *Bobby Simmons, Selma to Montgomery March* by Matt Herron (1965), *Taking a Stand in Baton Rouge* by Jonathan Bachman (2016)

+ DISCOVER THIS
This image was used on the cover of the 1999 album *Things Fall Apart* by The Roots.

Other Compelling Photojournalists

- Doris Derby
- Declan Haun
- Ernest Withers

Tim Hetherington

A Soldier from 2nd Platoon Rests at the End of a Day of Heavy Fighting at the 'Restrepo' Outpost, Korengal Valley, Afghanistan

2007

Is this what utter exhaustion looks like? Almost certainly, that is if you are a soldier at the end of a day of intensive fighting in one of the most dangerous areas of Afghanistan during the war against the Taliban.

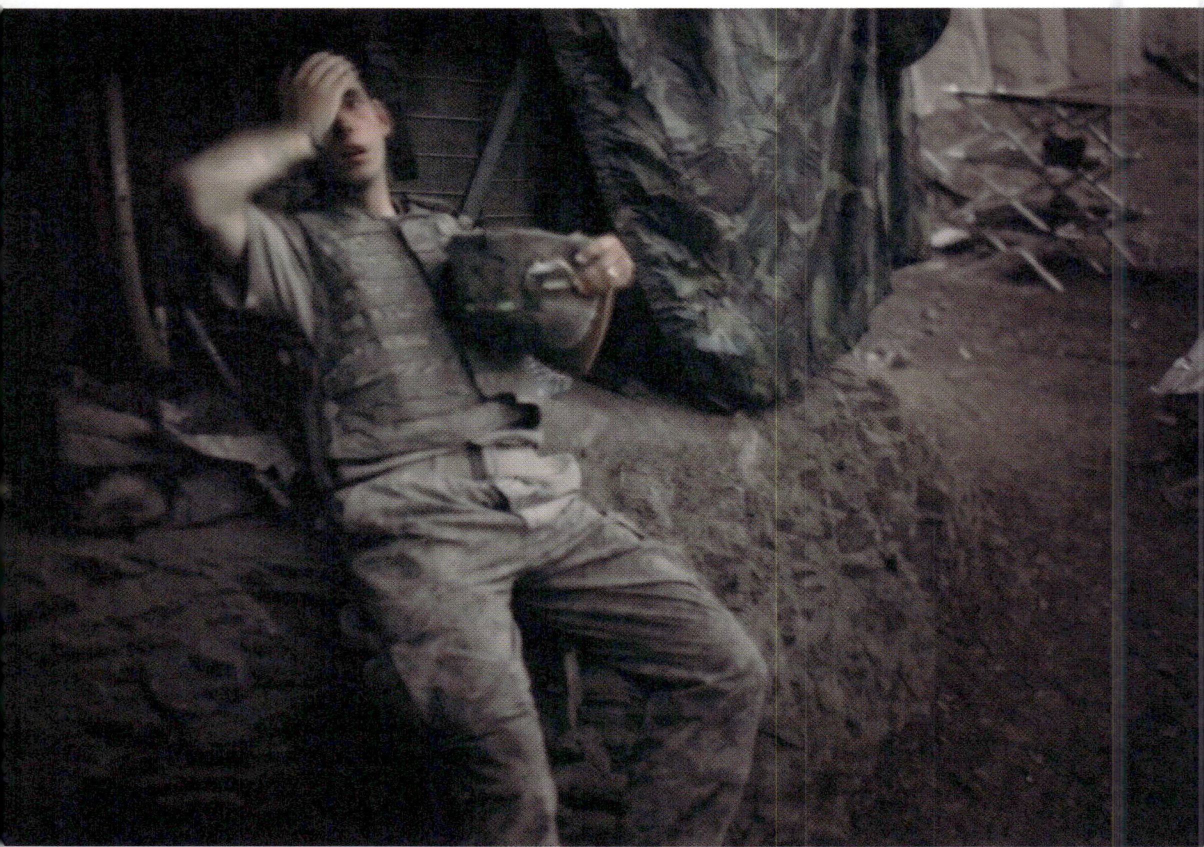

We can only imagine what the man, Brandon Olson, who is often referred to as 'a soldier from 2nd Platoon' or 'exhausted American soldier', may have seen or been through. Rarely do we see soldiers pictured in such an intimate, revealing and vulnerable way. The image by the late Tim Hetherington is from a series he made while embedded for a year between 2007 and 2008 with a US platoon in Afghanistan's Korengal Valley also known as the Valley of Death. Hetherington was on assignment covering the civil war for *Vanity Fair* with American journalist Sebastian Junger. Together, they made the documentary film *Restrepo*. The Oscar-nominated film takes its name from the platoon's remote outpost, which was named after Colombian-born medic Private Juan Sebastián Restrepo who was killed during the fighting in July 2007. Hetherington said the film aimed to provide an honest account of their experiences. His images do so too and this one in particular. Hetherington's career as a war photographer was cut short when he died in Libya in 2011 in the same mortar attack that killed American photographer Chris Hondros.

Hungarian war photographer Robert Capa said: 'If your pictures aren't good enough, you aren't close enough.' No such criticism can be levied here. You can almost feel the photographer's presence although there is no engagement between photographer and subject. The soldier is facing the camera, but he is looking past Hetherington and us, vacant, traumatized, miles away in his thoughts. We do not know what events led up to this moment, or what happened after, but for a brief moment we glimpse a soldier, a man and a son, who is ashen, numb and beaten down: a symbol of the toll of war and its psychological impact on soldiers.

Hetherington won World Press Photo of the Year with this image in 2008. The chairman of the judges, Gary Knight, said the image 'represents the exhaustion of a man – and the exhaustion of a nation.' Hetherington talked about the need to see and understand the soldiers' experiences; in this photograph alone, he does just that.

+ PHOTOGRAPHER BIO
British, 1970–2011

+ GOOGLE THIS
Sleeping Soldiers (2008)

+ WATCH THIS
The documentary *Restrepo* (2010) by Hetherington and journalist Sebastian Junger.

Other Compelling Photojournalists

→ Chris Hondros

→ Ed Kashi

→ Finbarr O'Reilly

Nilüfer Demir

Alan Kurdi

2015

It is one of the most talked about photos of 2015 if not the twenty-first century: an image of a tiny, lifeless child, lying face down in the sand on a Turkish beach. Three-year-old Alan Kurdi was one of twelve Syrians who reportedly died when the boats they were in sank on their way to Greece on 2 September 2015.

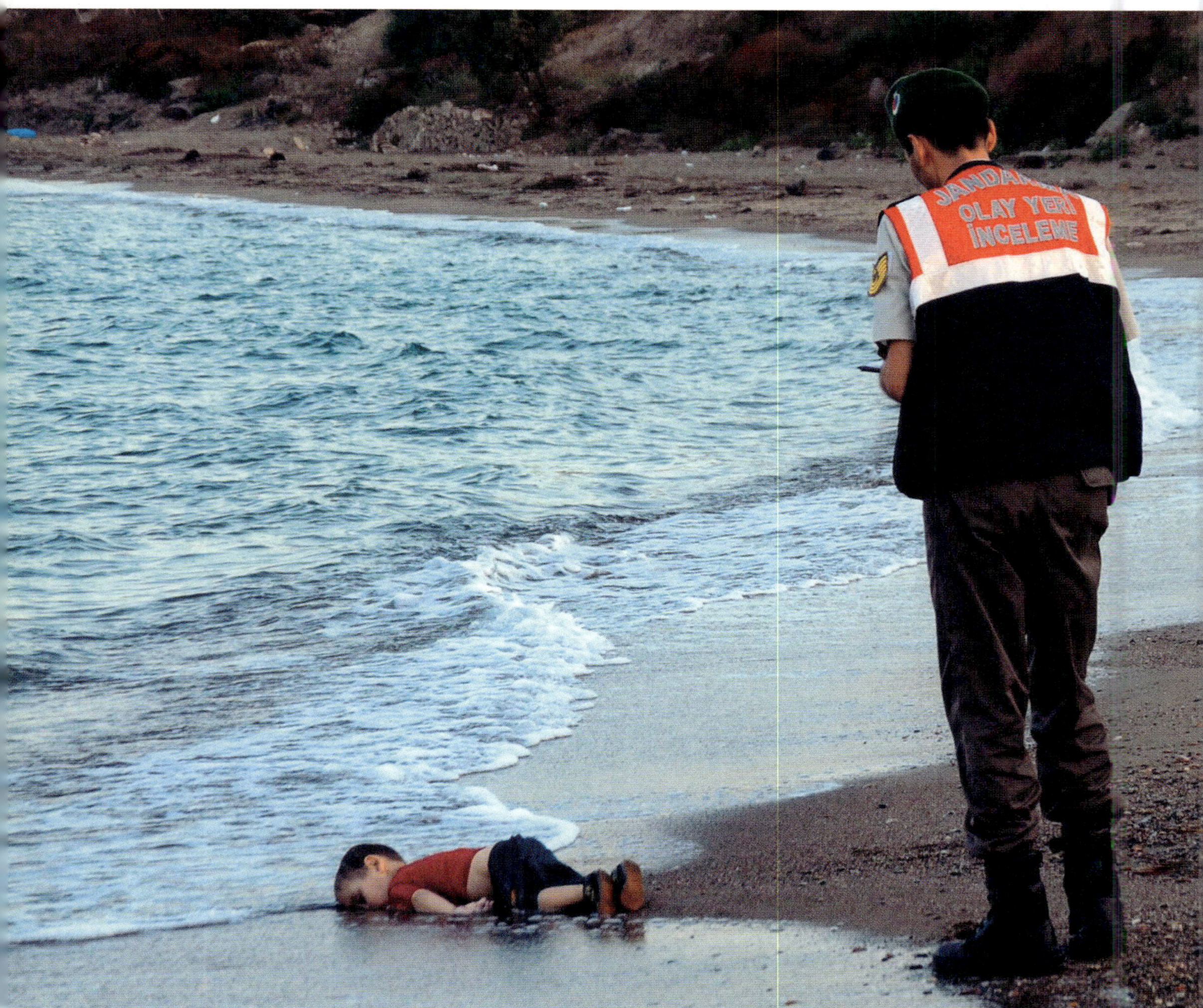

The Syrian toddler had been travelling with his mother Rehana, father Abdullah and older brother Galip towards the Greek island of Kos from the Turkish seaside town of Bodrum. Of the four, only his father survived. Five-year-old Galip's body was found washed up on the shore a short distance from his younger brother. Shortly after the tragedy, Abdullah told reporters how his two young sons had slipped from his hands as the rubber dinghy they were in deflated.

Many of the thousands of refugees who attempt to cross the Mediterranean Sea in a bid to reach Europe do so in vessels that are inadequate for such journeys. Some do not even have lifejackets. The *Washington Post* reported that in 2015 the Turkish coast guard rescued more than 42,000 migrants from the Aegean Sea. Others are less fortunate. Press photographer Nilüfer Demir of the Doğan News Agency was on the beach at the time and captured this photograph of Alan as an official approaches. Demir, who has spent many years documenting refugees at Bodrum's beaches, had been photographing a group of Pakistani refugees as they attempted to take off in a dinghy, but it is this photograph that has become a symbol of the refugee crisis.

At the time the image was published, much discussion occurred as to whether news outlets were right to run the picture. Those that ran it reasoned it was a way to draw attention to Europe's handling of the refugee crisis and it has been argued that Demir's images of the moment have done more than any other photographs to highlight what is going on. World leaders called for action in the wake of the disaster and the images resonated among the public internationally. The publication of the images may or may not have resulted in change yet we can hope that they have in some way moved humanity towards a more compassionate and informed attitude to the crisis.

+ PHOTOGRAPHER BIO
Turkish, b. 1986

+ GOOGLE THESE
A Turkish police officer carries a young boy who drowned in a failed attempt to sail to the Greek island of Kos (2015), *A 5-year-old boy, identified in news reports as Omran Daqneesh, sits in an ambulance Wednesday after reportedly being pulled out of a building hit by an airstrike in Aleppo, Syria* by Mahmoud Raslan (2016)

+ READ THIS
Nilüfer Demir discusses her controversial photograph in 'We Spoke to the Photographer Behind the Picture of the Drowned Syrian Boy', on Vice.com.

Other Compelling Photojournalists

- César Dezfuli
- Mauricio Lima
- John Moore

CHAPTER

4 REFLECTING ON WHO WE ARE

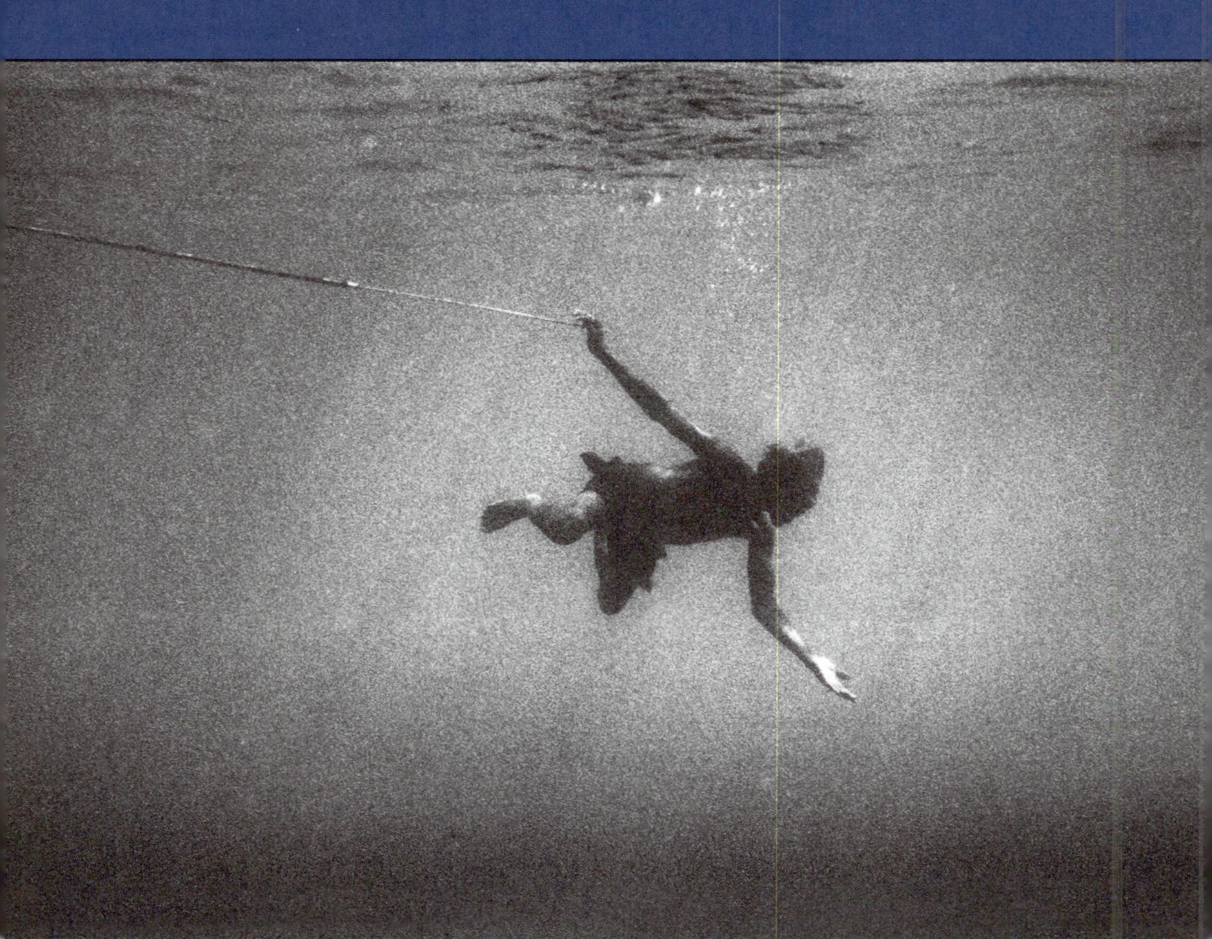

 Andrew Testa—Moken Child Fishing

Andrew Testa

Moken Child Fishing

2004

The Moken are a nomadic tribe of sea gypsies that live on the Surin Islands off the western coast of Thailand. The indigenous people learn to swim before they can walk and are known for their extraordinary ability to see underwater.

The Moken are highly skilled freedivers, who hunt for fish and mussels on the seabed. Years of practice have allowed them to develop their eyesight to an exceptional level. Scientific studies have shown that the underwater eyesight of Moken children is approximately 50 per cent better than that of most other children.

Andrew Testa visited the islands and spent time with the people who live there, photographing them as they fished and went about their lives for his photographic series *Eyes Wide Open* (2004). This ethereal image of a Moken child fishing resonates on many levels. It appeals aesthetically for its exquisite use of light and shadow with the sunlight through the water providing a luminous backdrop for the silhouetted child who appears suspended in space and time. A line appears to link the child to something outside of the frame, prompting a comparison with a foetus in utero as if the line is a metaphorical lifeline.

The scene appears primal and universal because it depicts the most fundamental of animal behaviours, the search for food. The idea of seeking and receiving is heightened by the outstretched hand although ironically the self-sufficient Moken do not have a word for 'want'. It follows that an image whose subject matter is about seeing and searching should place an emphasis on looking. By placing his subject in the centre of the frame Testa focuses attention on the sylph-like child, asking the viewer to reflect on this most intriguing and resilient of peoples whose ancient and simple way of life may be under threat from tourism.

As the viewer looks at Testa's image they might also reflect upon human beings collectively. The image seems to ask who are you and how do you see yourself? What impact is the human race having on the world? How can humanity reconnect with nature? The Moken are intrinsically in tune with nature and swim with their eyes open as they have done for thousands of years, but perhaps it is the rest of the world that should open their eyes.

+ PHOTOGRAPHER BIO
British, b. 1965

+ GOOGLE THESE
Acid Attacks in Bangladesh (2005), *20 Years after Srebrenica* (2015)

+ WATCH THIS
Andrew Testa discusses his experiences as a war photographer in Kosovo in 2011 on Zorye Kolektiv's Vimeo channel.

Like This? Try These

- → Robin Hammond
- → Krisanne Johnson
- → Stephan Vanfleteren

Cristina de Middel

Hamba

2011

Cristina de Middel had been working as a photojournalist for some years before she made her name with the series *The Afronauts* (2012) to which this image belongs. Her star rose rapidly after a copy of her book dummy fell into the hands of British photographer Martin Parr.

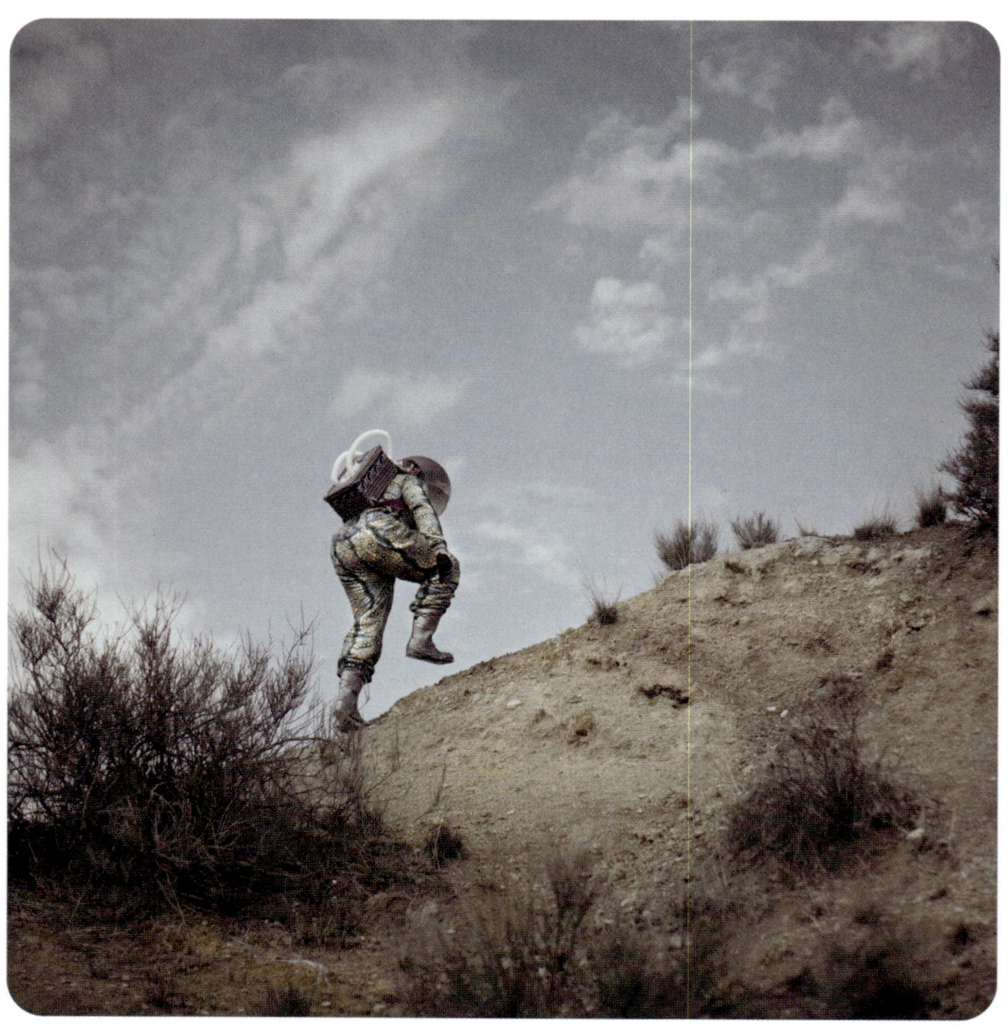

Early copies of De Middel's highly sought-after book have gone on to fetch hundreds of pounds and she has since joined the prestigious Magnum Photos agency.

Part of her project's enormous success can be attributed to the uniqueness of the story De Middel told. The work weaves a fictitious narrative around Zambia's attempt to join the United States and the Soviet Union in the so-called 'Space Race' following the country's independence in 1964. Science teacher Edward Makuka Nkoloso led the programme, which was heartfelt if misjudged. He made it his mission to recruit and train a group of Zambians, and selected a young woman, a missionary and two cats to fly to the moon and then on to Mars. Nkoloso even designed a rocket and a catapult system to launch it into space. It was a serious but naive undertaking says De Middel, who came across the story while doing research into unusual experiments. She uses reconstructions and fake archival materials to create her narrative.

Although Nkoloso's plan never came to fruition, it was not so much its failure that De Middel wanted to focus on but rather the belief that such a thing was possible. It is this sense of unfaltering human endeavour and of striving to push beyond what is humanly possible that this image encapsulates so well in the stoop of the figure steadily climbing, head down, undeterred and with one foot raised in a wry reference to American astronaut Neil Armstrong's phrase when he first stepped on the moon: 'One small step…'

De Middel has spoken about her desire to question photography and the ways it is used to represent the world. In this photograph as in the project as a whole, she asks us to reflect upon our blind faith in the truthfulness of photography. Yet she also celebrates photography's capacity to tell a powerful and inspiring story of undaunted human spirit.

+ PHOTOGRAPHER BIO
Spanish, b. 1975

+ GOOGLE THESE
Iko Iko (2011), *Jambo* (2011), *This is What Hatred Did* (2015)

+ WATCH THIS
Parr interviews De Middel for his series *Sofa Sessions*, in the Archive at martinparrfoundation.org.

+ READ THIS
De Middel discusses her practice in 'Music, Pleasure and Photography' at magnumphotos.com.

Like This? Try These

- Sanne De Wilde
- Joan Fontcuberta
- Ouka Leele

Herbert List

Goldfish Bowl, Santorini, Greece

1937

+ PHOTOGRAPHER BIO
German, 1903–75

+ GOOGLE THESE
Picnic by the Baltic, Germany (1930), *Lake Lucerne (Lac des Quatre-Cantons), Switzerland* (1936), *Ashtray, London, England* (1936)

+ READ THIS
Herbert List: The Monograph (2000) by Max Ferdinand Scheler *et al.*

Thinking about a photo's possible meanings is one of the great pleasures of looking at an image. German-born photographer Herbert List was among the most skilled at constructing photographs, and still lifes in particular, which invite us to reflect upon their meaning.

We can enjoy both the visual qualities of a List photograph and what it might say about us as individuals and collectively with regard to the human condition. His images are incredibly poetic and he had a knack for cleverly suggesting things to the viewer – always showing, hinting, but never dictating. In 1929, he met the American photographer Andreas Feininger, whose own eye was drawn to the everyday surreal. Feininger gave him a Rolleiflex camera and List went on to be known for artfully juxtaposing elements in his compositions and using tonal contrast to evoke a sense of the fantastical. He spoke of his attempt to capture in his photographs 'the magical essence' that inhabited and animated the world of appearances, and drew inspiration from surrealism's preoccupation with dreams and the *Pittura Metafisica* (Metaphysical Art) Italian art movement with its own surreal overtones.

How an image appears differs from person to person depending on our experiences, which also affect the feelings and memories it triggers. Perhaps the fish in this photograph reminds you of a pet you had as a child or of trips to see a relative who lovingly kept a goldfish in a bowl on their windowsill. List fled Nazi Germany in 1936, so we could read the image as a metaphorical meditation on exile or the futility of existence. The photographer helpfully hinted at one possible reading of his image, when he said: 'The captive fish in its bowl and the open sea symbolize man who, being tied to earth, can never quite break free from matter, and who, while having intimations of a sublime world, is yet unable to immerse himself in it because he is trapped in his body'.

Ultimately, it does not matter what we see or think we see, whether the fish in the goldfish bowl symbolizes man's unfulfilled potential or the endless possibilities that stretch out before us if only we are bold enough to seize them. What matters is we are moved to think and feel at all.

Like This? Try These

- → Werner Bischof
- → Henri Cartier-Bresson
- → Andreas Feininger

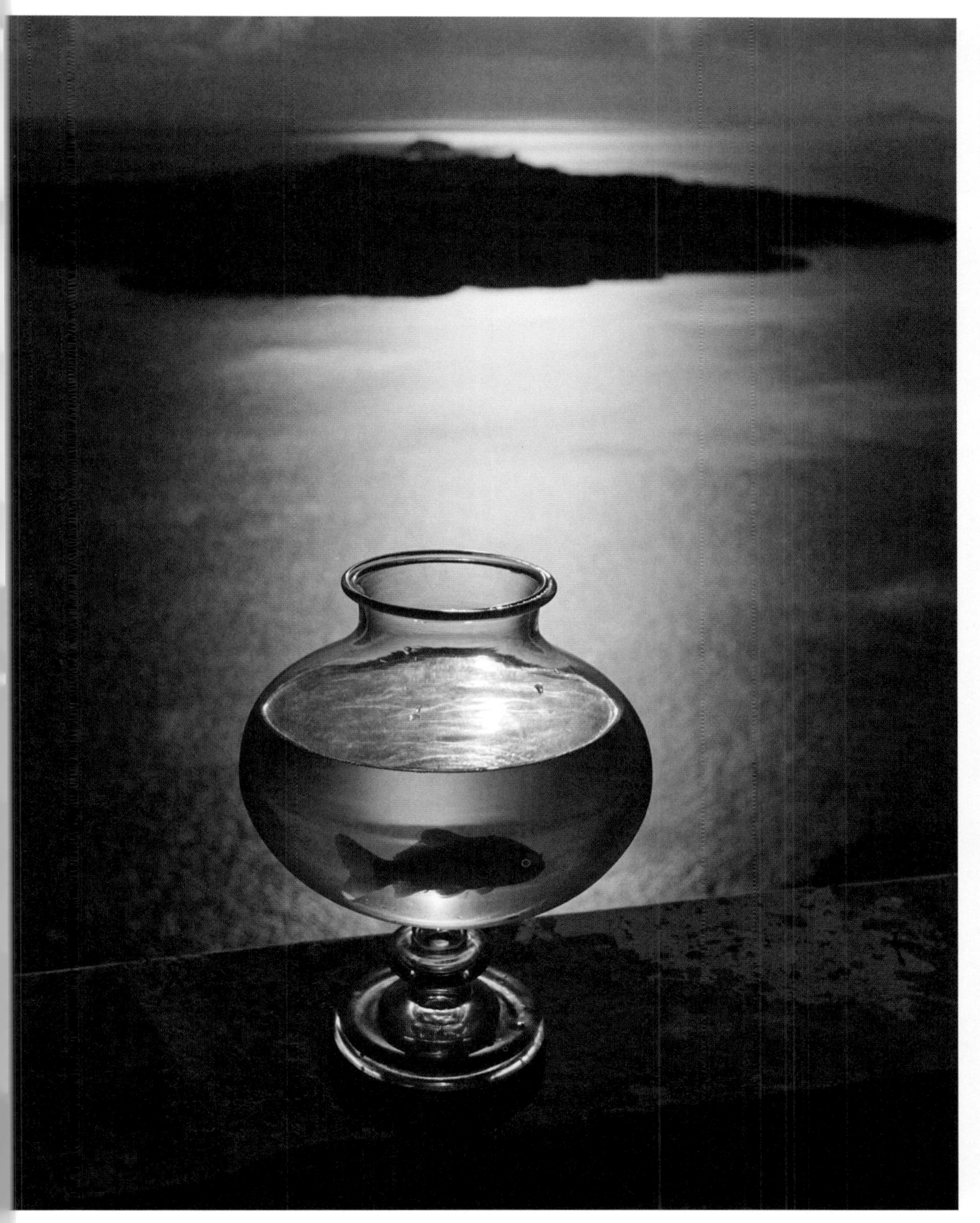

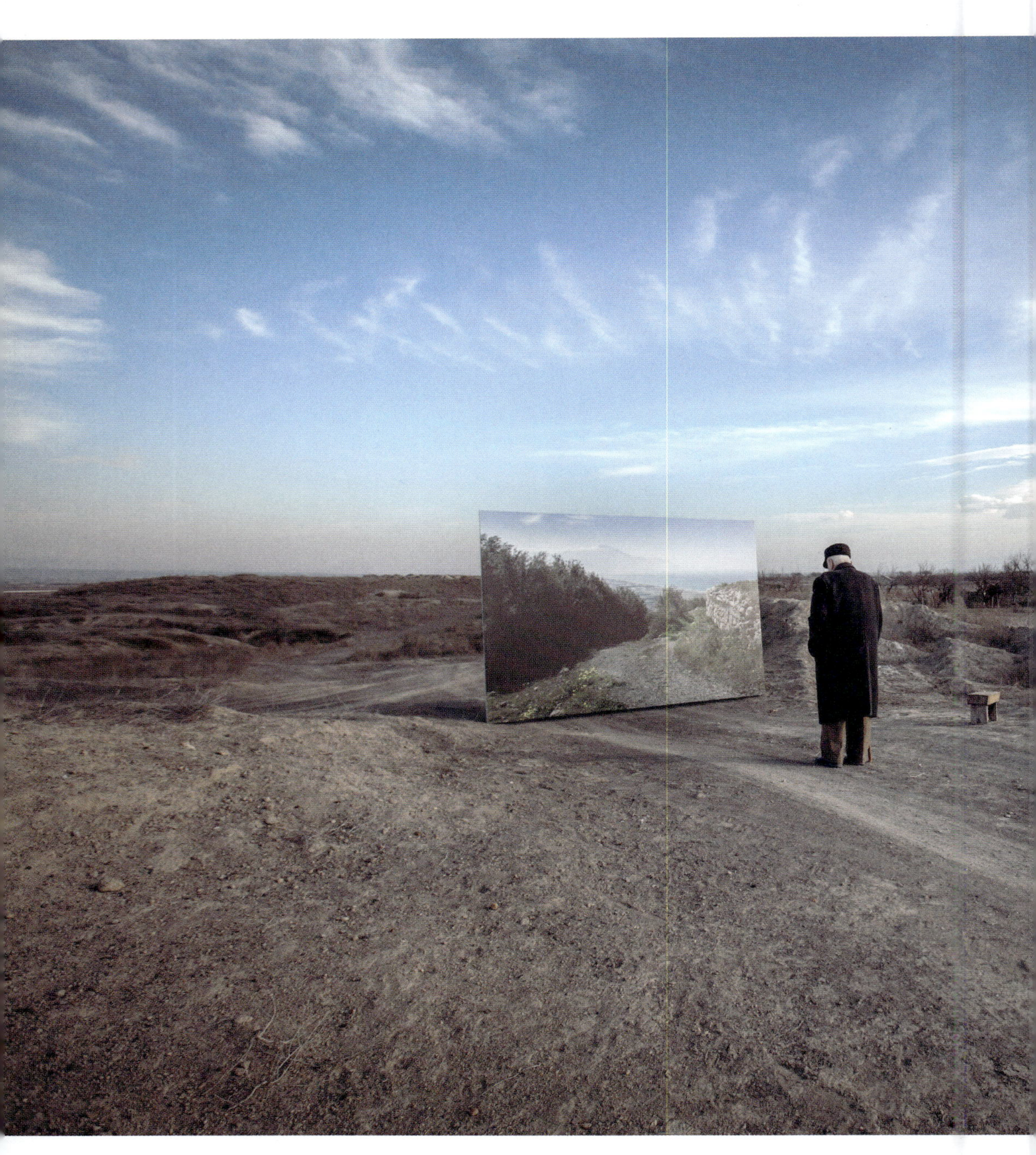

 Diana Markosian—Holding a Cane in his Right Hand, Movses Haneshyan

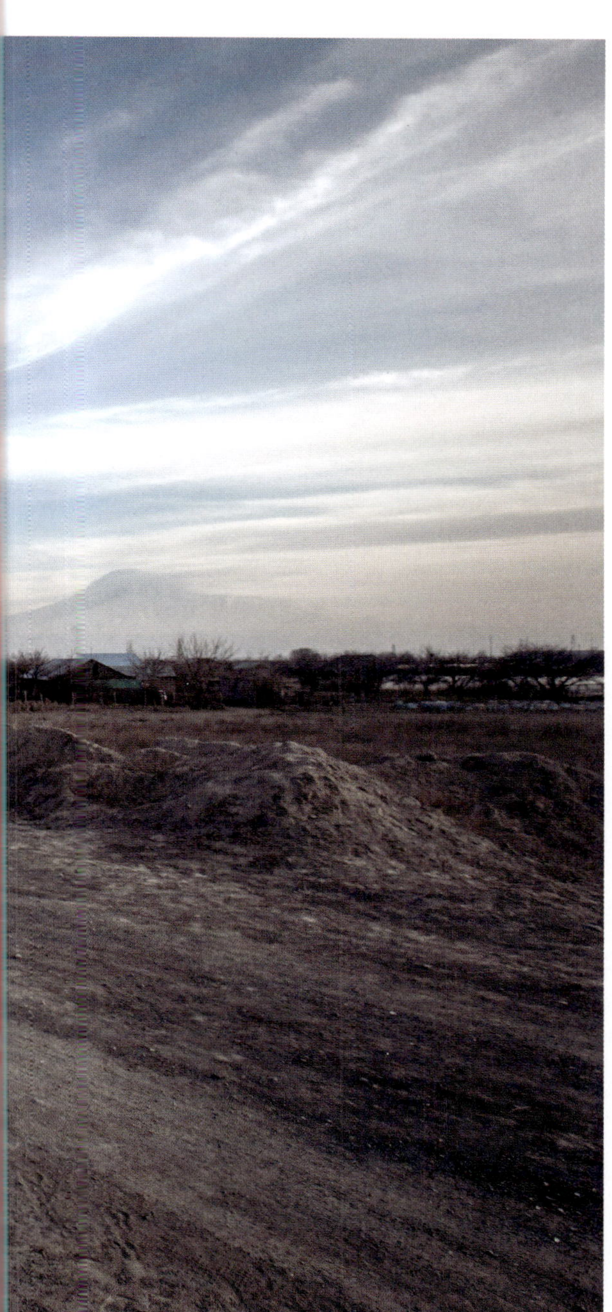

Diana Markosian

Holding a Cane in his Right Hand, Movses Haneshyan, 105, Slowly Approaches a Life-size Landscape

2015

The open expanse of endless blue sky with its hypnotic, rushing clouds beckons, as do the teasing mountains just visible through the distant haze and the humble, unassuming dirt track that is but a step away.

+ PHOTOGRAPHER BIO
Russian. b. 1989

+ GOOGLE THESE
Inventing My Father (2014), *My Family Arrived to America in 1996. My Mother Described it as the Arrival to Nowhere, with the Hope of Going Somewhere, USA* (2018)

+ READ THIS
Diana Markosian discusses how walking inspires her practice in 'I don't know where I'm going when I walk' at magnumphotos.com.

Diana Markosian's photograph, like a window onto the world, is wide open. A conflation of past and present, it invites us to step over the threshold into the beatific landscape contained within. But to do so is to confront untold horrors hidden from sight but not so easily forgotten. This is 105-year-old Movses Haneshyan, standing before a photograph of his former home in modern Turkey. Movses was one of 1.5 million ethnic Armenians who were murdered or driven from their homes during the Armenian Genocide between 1914 and 1923.

Markosian was born in Moscow of Armenian descent and moved to the United States when she was seven years old. In 2015, she travelled to Armenia to meet survivors and ask them about their memories of home. She also travelled to Turkey to retrace their steps. The result is her series *1915* (2015). In this image from the series, she uses photography to bring a piece of Movses's former home to him. It is the first time he has seen his home since he fled ninety-eight years ago in 1915. Markosian presents Movses with his head slightly bowed reverently, transported back in time and reliving memories we can barely begin to imagine.

Just as we are drawn into Markosian's photograph, Movses too is drawn into the photograph within the photograph. Markosian seems to suggest that everything is one continuum: time moves on but the past is always present. At a glance, the photograph depicted could be mistaken for a mirror, suggesting ideas about looking and reflecting. In 1859, American writer Oliver Wendell Holmes called the daguerreotype 'the mirror with a memory' and photography has long been associated with remembrance. Australian historian Geoffrey Batchen writes on this topic in *Forget Me Not: Photography and Remembrance* (2004), noting that English photographer Julia Margaret Cameron's portrait *Mnemosyne*, or *Memory* (1868), seems to suggest that 'photography itself is an art of memory'. By intervening in the landscape in this image in such a bold yet sensitive way Markosian reminds us of photography's unique power to traverse time.

Like This? Try These

→ Dario Mitidieri

→ Tomás Munita

→ Daniella Zalcman

+ PHOTOGRAPHER BIO
American, b. 1946

+ GOOGLE THESE
Harlem Story (1987), *Benaco Refugee Camp, Tanzania* (1995), *Million Man March, Washington, D.C.* (1995)

+ READ THIS
Eli Reed: A Long Walk Home (2015) by Eli Reed.

+ READ THIS
'The World as Seen by Magnum's First Black Photographer' on Slate.com.

Like This? Try These

→ Dana Lixenberg

→ Gordon Parks

→ Jamel Shabazz

Eli Reed

Homeless Mother with Children, St Louis, Missouri

1987

At a glance this image could show the aftermath of a car crash. The woman and child are lying amid what appears to be tangled metal and the girl's dead-eyed expression seem to herald a scene of death and tragedy. However, they are sleeping and resting, having made the car into a temporary place of refuge.

We are relieved to know they are not the victims of some terrible road accident, but what kind of a life is this for a young family in one of the richest countries in the world?

Eli Reed has visited many places, including Lebanon, Liberia, Beirut, Guatemala, Panama and Haiti, in his search to understand the human condition, yet he photographed the homeless woman and her children in St Louis, Missouri in 1987. A year later, he documented the effects of poverty on the youth in the United States for the documentary film *Poorest in the Land of Plenty* (1988). In truth, his eye has never wandered far from what is happening on his doorstep. He has a strong interest in social justice and has made some of his most arresting work in his homeland, turning his lens on life in small towns and putting those who are often overlooked into the spotlight as he has done here.

Reed grew up in a housing project in Perth Amboy, New Jersey. Interested in history and literature, and curious about the world around him, he embarked on what has become his life's mission to uncover and photograph 'beauty inside the visual framework of life.' San Francisco's so-called 'Pink Palace' housing project became his subject in 1981 and his work there earned him a place as a finalist for a Pulitzer Prize. Since then, he has never stopped paying 'attention to people and what's going on with them'. We do not know what the people in this photograph have been through, but Reed's picture is empathetic towards their situation and critical of the establishment that has let them down. The mother and young girl may not meet our gaze but the child in the centre does not shy away. The child's eyes are in shadow, but the steely stare, only just discernible, makes us all culpable.

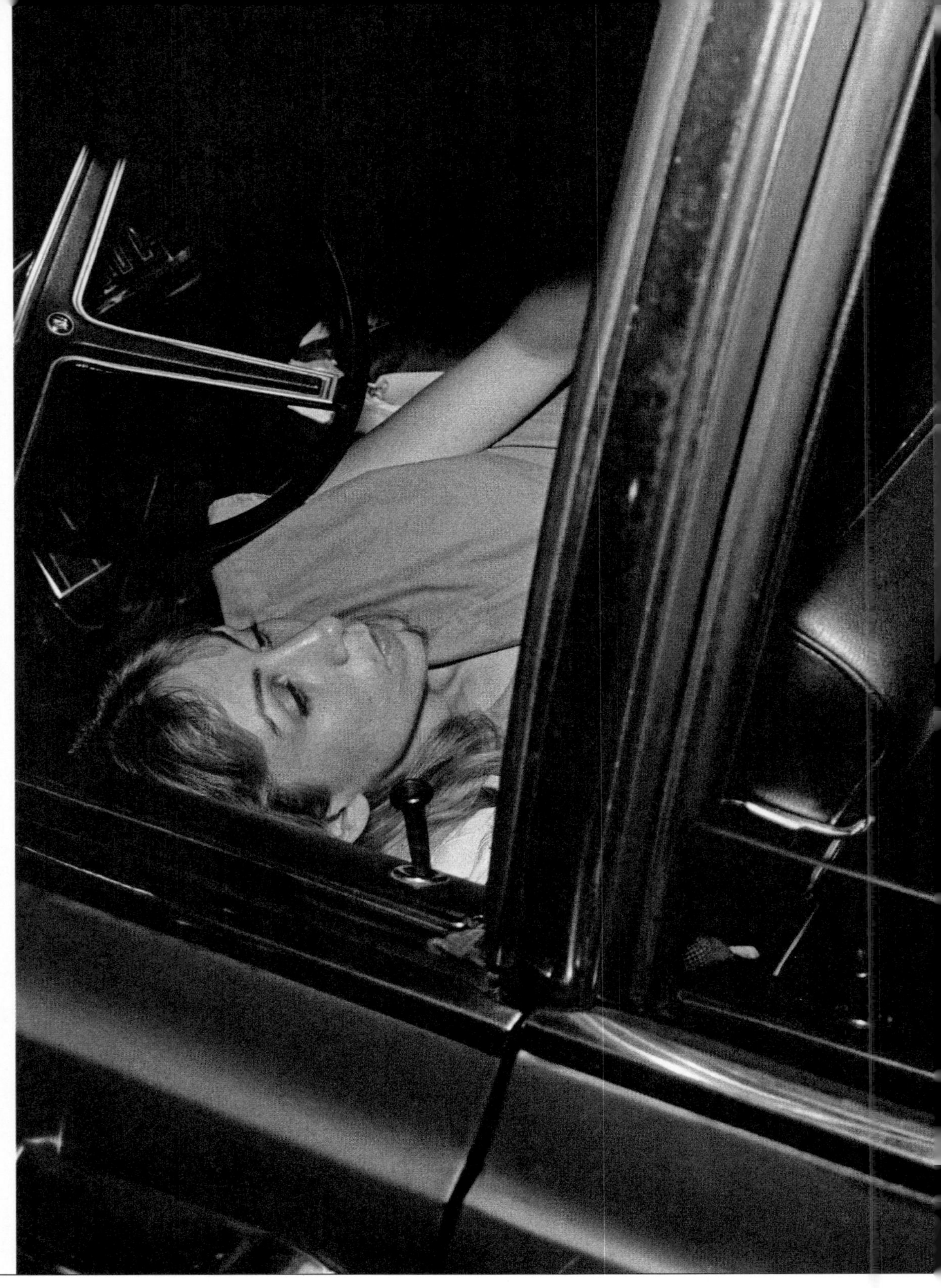

 Eli Reed—Homeless Mother with Children, St Louis, Missouri

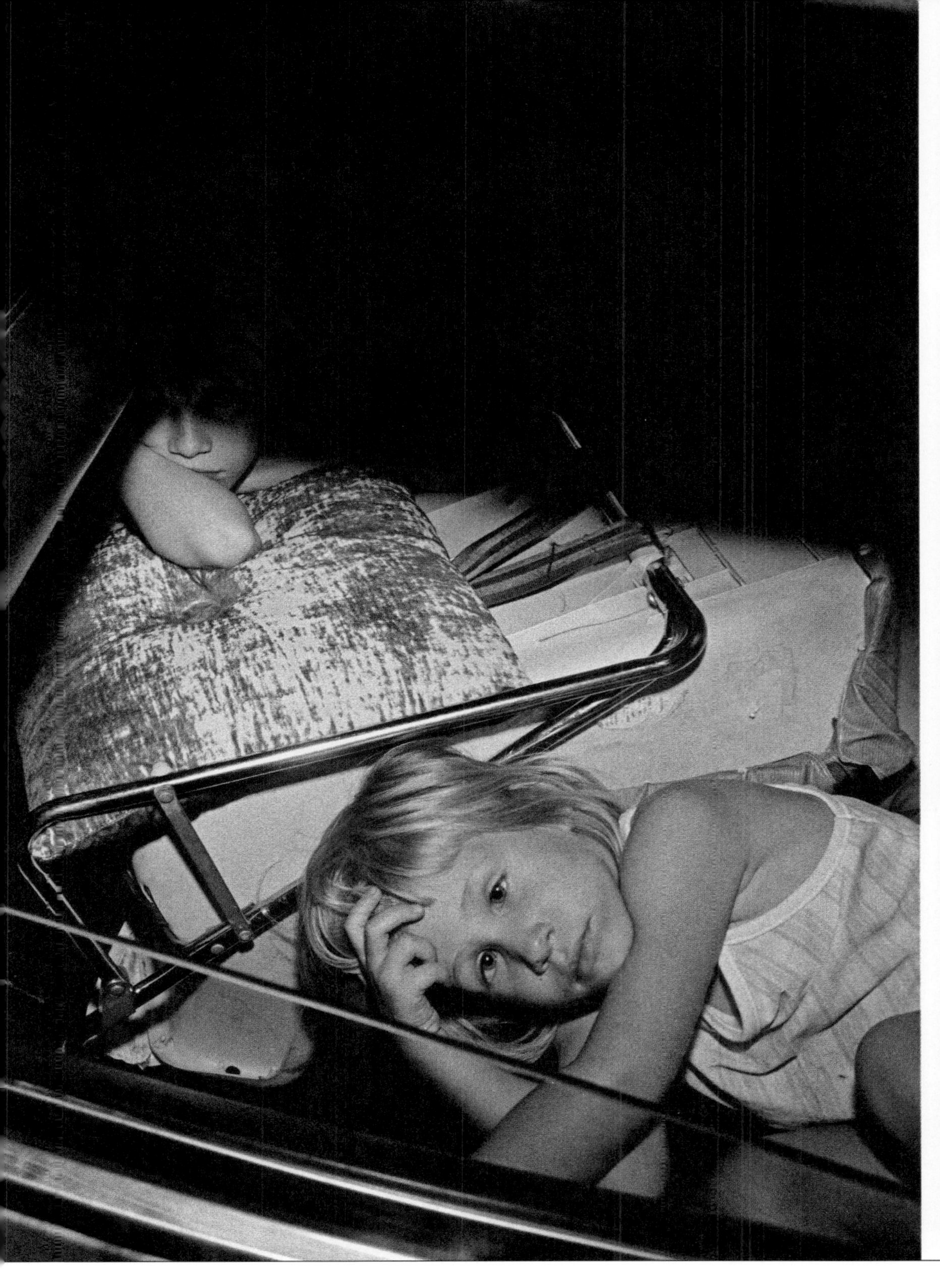

Mads Nissen

Jon and Alex

2014

It has been said that this intimate, atmospheric photograph of a gay couple, *Jon and Alex*, by Danish photographer Mads Nissen has the potential to become iconic. It is certainly a powerful and affecting image.

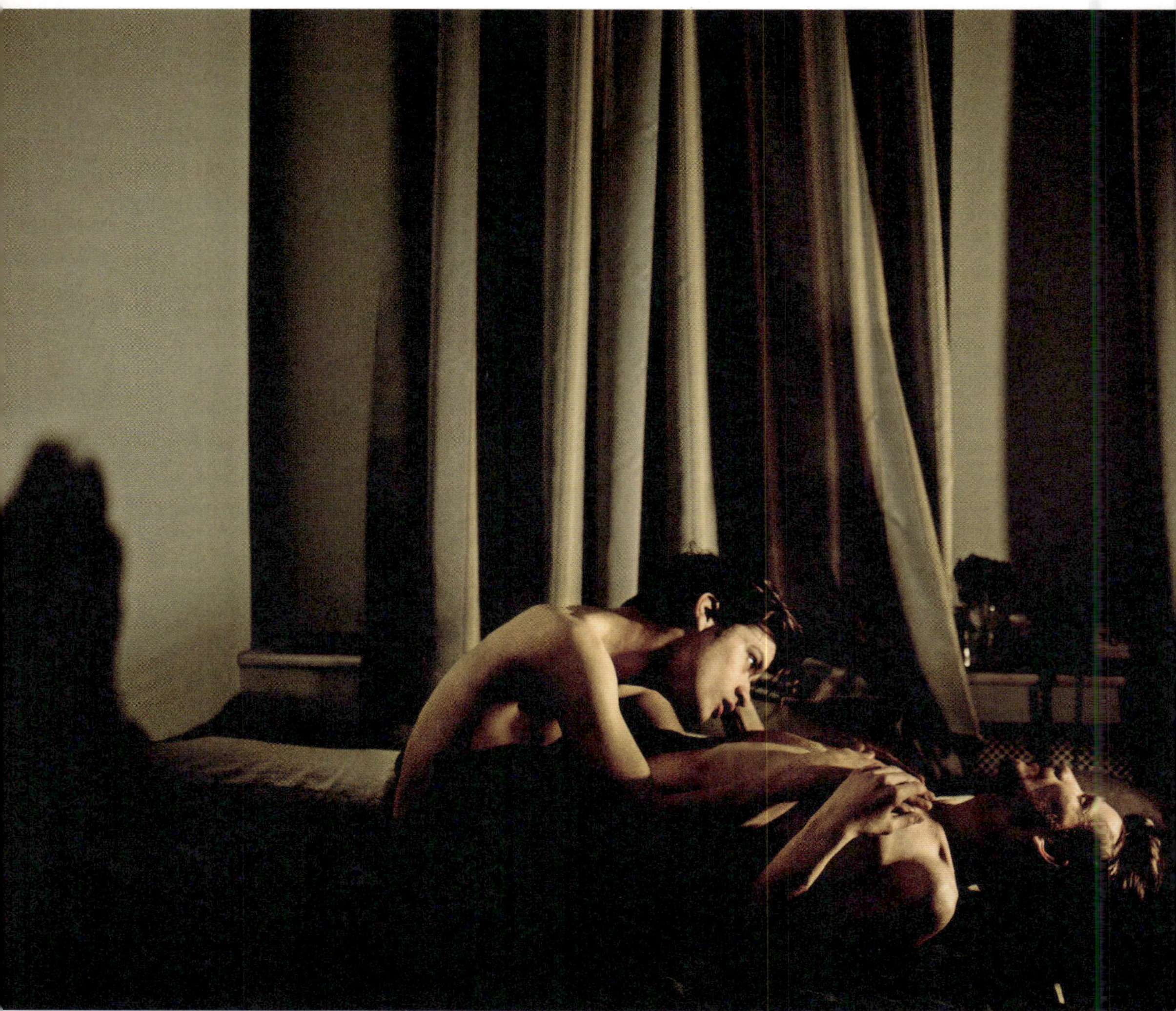

Nissen took the photo in St Petersburg, Russia when he was working as a photographer for Danish newspaper *Politiken*. Life for LGBTQI+ people across the state is incredibly difficult in light of laws that curtail civil liberties and effectively legalize discrimination, leaving them vulnerable to hate speech and harassment in an increasingly hostile environment, including from religious and neo-Nazi groups. The image won World Press Photo of the Year in 2015 and is part of a series Nissen made called *Homophobia in Russia* (2014). With guidance from LGBTQI+ organisation, Coming Out, he joined gay-rights activists at rallies and witnessed their treatment firsthand; on one occasion the friend he was with was assaulted after kissing his boyfriend goodbye.

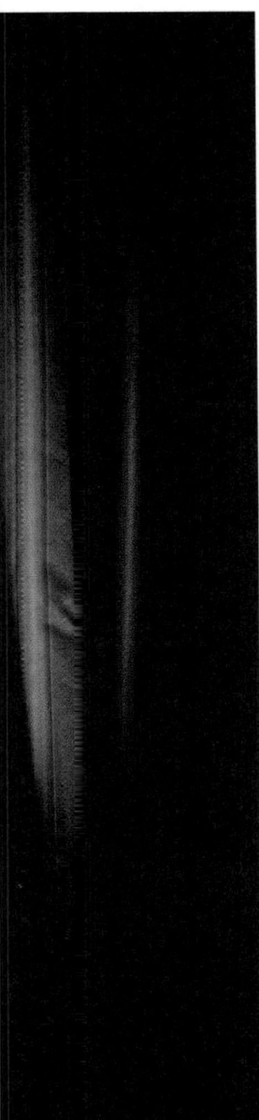

Nissen belongs to a school of Danish photojournalists that have been known to get in close to create their images and tell their stories through photos that are emotive and descriptive. Here, he has created an image that succeeds aesthetically and emotionally. His evocative use of light is reminiscent of great painters such as Michelangelo Merisi da Caravaggio. Moreover, he directs our gaze to the men who are the embodiment of love and tenderness, they are a shining light in a dark, ugly world, who symbolize all those who face discrimination.

One World Press Photo judge said that the image is the result of 'commitment and compassion and thoughtfulness' on Nissen's part, an image that speaks to the many thousands of people across the world for whom loving someone means risking persecution. It is not a typical press shot, as the World Press Photo jury pointed out when it awarded the image the top prize, rather its strength lies in its ability to transcend politics and geographical borders and to highlight a pressing global issue.

+ PHOTOGRAPHER BIO
Danish, b. 1979

+ GOOGLE THESE
Amazonas (2006–13), Nissen's images of Colombia's civil war (2010–)

+ WATCH THIS
Search for Mads Nissen on the Mashable website and click on Brian Ries' article to watch a video of two photography experts discussing Nissen's *Jon and Alex*.

Like This? Try These

→ Robin Hammond

→ Tatiana Vinogradova

→ Mario Wezel

Newsha Tavakolian

Portrait of Somayyeh

2014

Perhaps the tangled branches are drawing the woman in, engulfing her, or maybe she is emerging from their spindly embrace, silently defiant. This is a quiet, contemplative photograph, but one that speaks volumes about life for young people, especially women, in Iran.

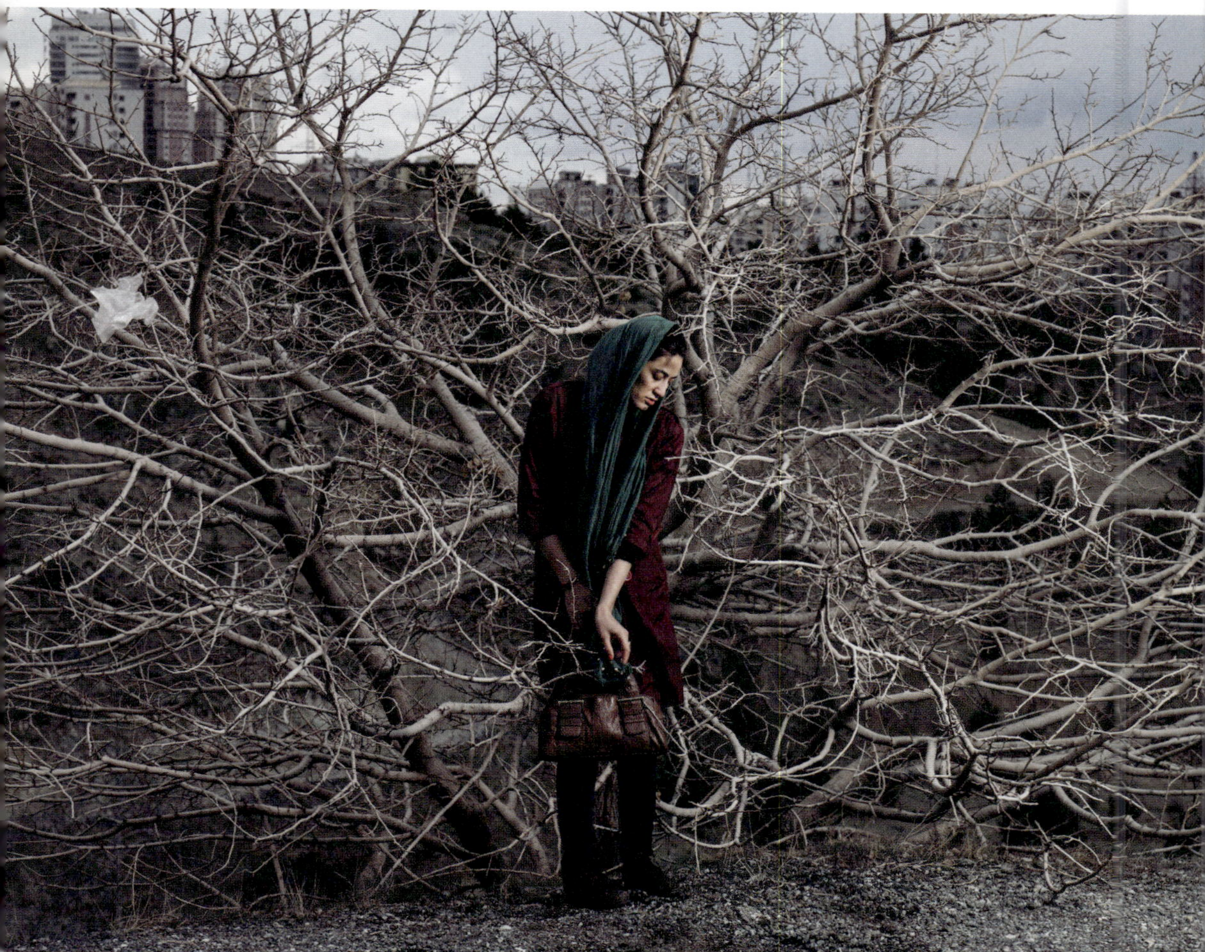

It is impossible to ignore the symbolism of the thorny branches that provide the backdrop for Newsha Tavakolian's powerful portrait taken on a mountainside outside Tehran. Their dominant presence in the frame suggests an oppressive culture from which it is impossible to break free, a feeling which is heightened in the picture by an ominous, inky sky that bears down on everything beneath it. Conversely, as the woman in the picture, Somayyeh, is shown deep in thought as she carefully untangles her headscarf from the branch upon which it appears to have been caught, could this simple act symbolize a new beginning in the shape of an autonomous existence for women?

The photograph belongs to Tavakolian's series, *Blank Pages of an Iranian Photo Album* (2006–2015), which tells the stories of Tavakolian's generation, who grew up after the Iranian Revolution (1978–1979). Somayyeh was one of several people Tavakolian invited to be photographed who she believed represented her generation. The uprising led to huge changes in the way women were able to live, notably the way they dressed and wore their hair; it also became compulsory for women to wear the hijab. In this context, the untangling of the headscarf is especially telling.

Tavakolian's choice of a desolate mountain setting is significant too. Photo albums from thirty years ago commonly had a picture of a beautiful, hopeful mountainside on the front. She has said she wanted to pay homage to them by presenting the opposite: an 'almost hopeless' landscape. There is a bleakness to her photograph, but also a sense of hope and possibility. As Tavakolian has said of her subject: 'Surrounded by the web of branches around her, she's vulnerable but fighting her way out.'

+ PHOTOGRAPHER BIO
Iranian, b. 1981

+ GOOGLE THIS
Blank Pages of an Iranian Photo Album (2006–2015)

+ WATCH THIS
Visit Newshatavakolian.com to see a couple of videos of Tavakolian's work.

Like This? Try These

- → Gohar Dashti
- → Diana Markosian
- → Stephanie Sinclair

Tony Ray-Jones

Glyndebourne

1967

If this couple is to be believed it is the most natural thing in the world to picnic in the company of cows. The English are known for their eccentric ways, but this unconventional scene takes idiosyncratic behaviour to the extreme.

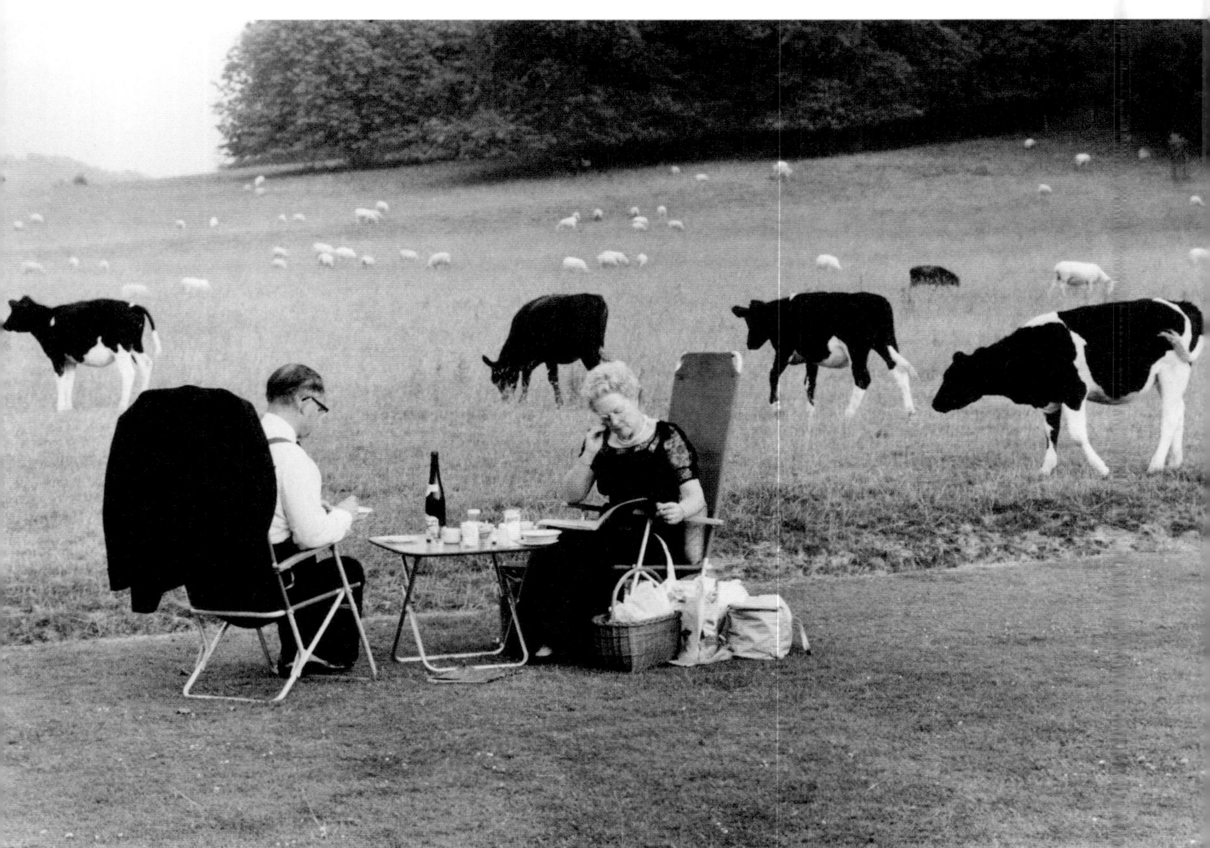

Yet the couple could be oblivious to the cows' presence: engrossed in eating and reading they do not appear to be bothered by their inquisitive neighbours. Whether or not the couple are aware of their bovine compadres, the skill with which Tony Ray-Jones brought them together in the frame to make us believe they are part of the same scene shows his immense skill and wit as a documentarian. Among the principles he set for himself was one that said: 'See if everything in the background relates to the subject matter.' This photograph, taken at Glyndebourne, the famous opera house in the Sussex countryside, is an example of his guiding principle in action. As the couple dines out in style, the cows take lunch too. But if Ray-Jones is poking fun at English eccentricities, he is doing it fondly and reverently.

A master of capturing Englishness in all its quirky forms, Ray-Jones's career saw him embark on a project that took him throughout the UK where he set himself the task of capturing the essence of the English way of life, which resulted in the book *A Day Off: An English Journal* (1974). Between 1966 and 1969 he made hundreds of photographs of the British at work and leisure. People from all walks of life were his subjects, whether holidaying at Brighton Pier or Butlin's Holiday Camp in Clacton-on-Sea, taking the air in Blackpool or Newquay, or dressing up for a festival in Broadstairs. Ray-Jones died suddenly in 1972 aged just thirty years old, however, he had already made his mark on British documentary photography through his unique way of seeing and talent for picturing the English.

+ PHOTOGRAPHER BIO
British, 1941–72

+ GOOGLE THIS
Beachy Head Tripper Boat (1967)

+ WATCH THIS
Martin Parr talks about Ray-Jones' work in 'Only in England: Photographs by Tony Ray-Jones and Martin Parr' on the National Science and Media Museum YouTube channel.

Like This? Try These

- Shirley Baker
- Tish Murtha
- Martin Parr

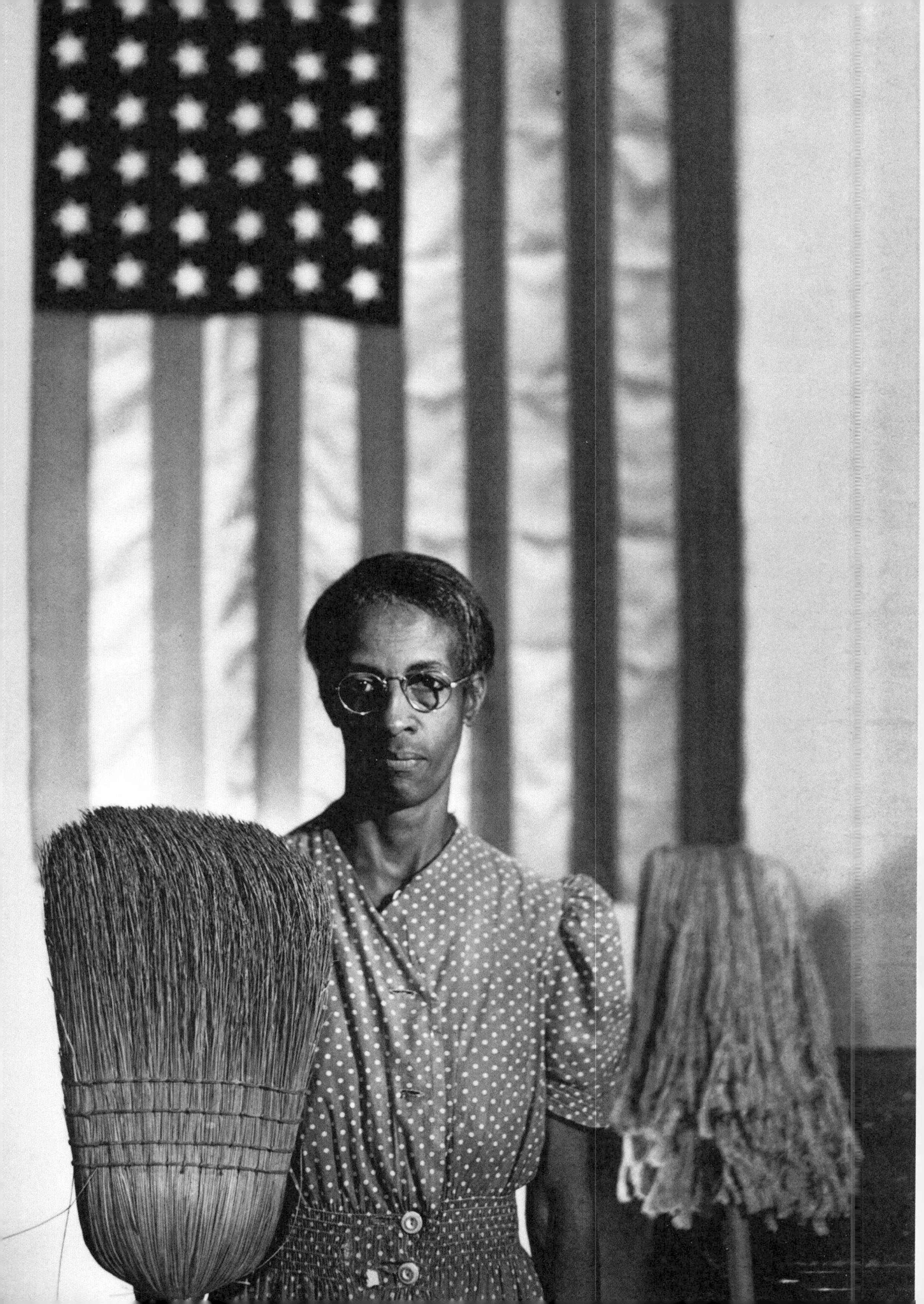

Gordon Parks

American Gothic, Washington, D.C.

1942

– PHOTOGRAPHER BIO
American, 1912–2006

– GOOGLE THESE
Emerging Man, Harlem, New York (1952), *Airline Terminal, Atlanta, Georgia* (1956), *Untitled, Shady Grove, Alabama* (1956)

– WATCH THIS
'Half Past Autumn: The Life and Work of Gordon Parks' on the FunkStudios YouTube channel.

Hers is a stare you cannot ignore. She meets your gaze with a look of defiance, a silent inner rage bubbling just beneath the surface. This is Ella Watson, a cleaner at the Farm Security Administration (FSA) where Gordon Parks was working as a photographer in 1942 when he took the shot.

Flanked by a broom and a mop, Watson stands tall in front of the lens, dignified, proud. In the hands of a lesser photographer the photograph might have been an ordinary portrait, but Parks transforms the scene into something truly remarkable. It is an image that embodies strength, resilience and resistance in the United States prior to the civil rights era. The viewer imagines the difficult life this woman has led but Parks presents her as a figure who refuses to be beaten down. In that sense the image can be read as a symbol of those who endure and rise up against racism, injustice and inequality, past and present.

Parks also takes the opportunity to cleverly parody American artist Grant Wood's iconic painting of the same name created in 1930 in which the painter, through his steadfast characters, sought to offer hope in the face of adversity in Depression-era America. In Parks's photograph, he exposes the American Dream as being hollow, discriminatory and ultimately deeply flawed. In the 'land of the free', not everyone benefits from what is promised. The inclusion of the American flag as backdrop underlines this. In the BBC TV series *Age of the Image* (2020) art historian James Fox said of the image 'by placing his brutalized subject in front of the Stars and Stripes [Parks] reveals America itself to be brutal…It is impossible not to be moved by this haunting commentary on injustice and inequality.'

Parks, who was also a prolific writer, poet, filmmaker and musician, spent his life not just recording the African American experience with his camera but advocating for racial equality. His extensive archive contains many photos that capture with brutal honesty what life was like for African Americans from the 1940s to the 1960s and beyond. He depicted the injustice, poverty, racism and oppression they experienced, and this image is among his most celebrated photos.

Like This? Try These

- Doris Derby
- Ming Smith
- Ernest Withers

Zanele Muholi

Ntozkhe II Parktown

2016

+ PHOTOGRAPHER BIO
South African, b. 1972

+ GOOGLE THESE
Only Half the Picture (2003–06), *Faces and Phases* (2006–), *Somnyama Ngonyama* (2012–)

+ WATCH THIS
Visit the International Center of Photography website to see an interview with Muholi: icp.org/infinity-awards/zanele-muholi.

In the age of the selfie vision has turned inwards, towards the self, even as people use photography to project carefully curated idealized visions of themselves to the world for virtual approval. But self portraiture has a long history and it has not always been a way of masking the self to seek approbation. South African visual activist Zanele Muholi falls within that tradition.

Muholi's self-portraits challenge racist, stereotypical and oppressive ideas regarding Eurocentrism, gender and black identity. The artist, who does not use gender-specific pronouns, says: 'By exaggerating the darkness of my skin tone, I'm reclaiming my blackness.' This image belongs to their series *Somnyama Ngonyama* (2012–), which translates as 'hail the dark lioness'. They have featured in their previous bodies of work but their face, body and persona takes on greater prominance here. Muholi appears regal, statuesque and heroic, and is often pictured wearing elaborate headdresses made from repurposed everyday objects, including clothes pegs or pieces of fabric. The highly stylized portraits prompt the viewer to rethink racist and colonial depictions and notions of beauty. By drawing on traditions of portrait photography, Muholi pays homage to black women in history. They also reclaim photographic histories where black South African women and/or those who identify as LGBTQI+ have typically been overlooked.

In this self-portrait, Muholi's fierce, defiant presence and strength dominate the picture. It is disarming, even though they gaze upwards out of the frame rather directly at the viewer. The portrait is all the more powerful for its apparent simplicity evident in the use of a plain backdrop and traditional composition. The photographer told the *New York Times*: 'I wanted to use my face so that people will always remember just how important our black faces are when confronted by them. For this black face to be recognized as belonging to a sensible, thinking being in their own right.' This is a performance of the self far removed from selfie culture, rather it is a call to action to the viewer whoever they are, irrespective of race, gender or sexual orientation.

Like This? Try These

- → Rotimi Fani-Kayode
- → Deana Lawson
- → Lina Iris Viktor

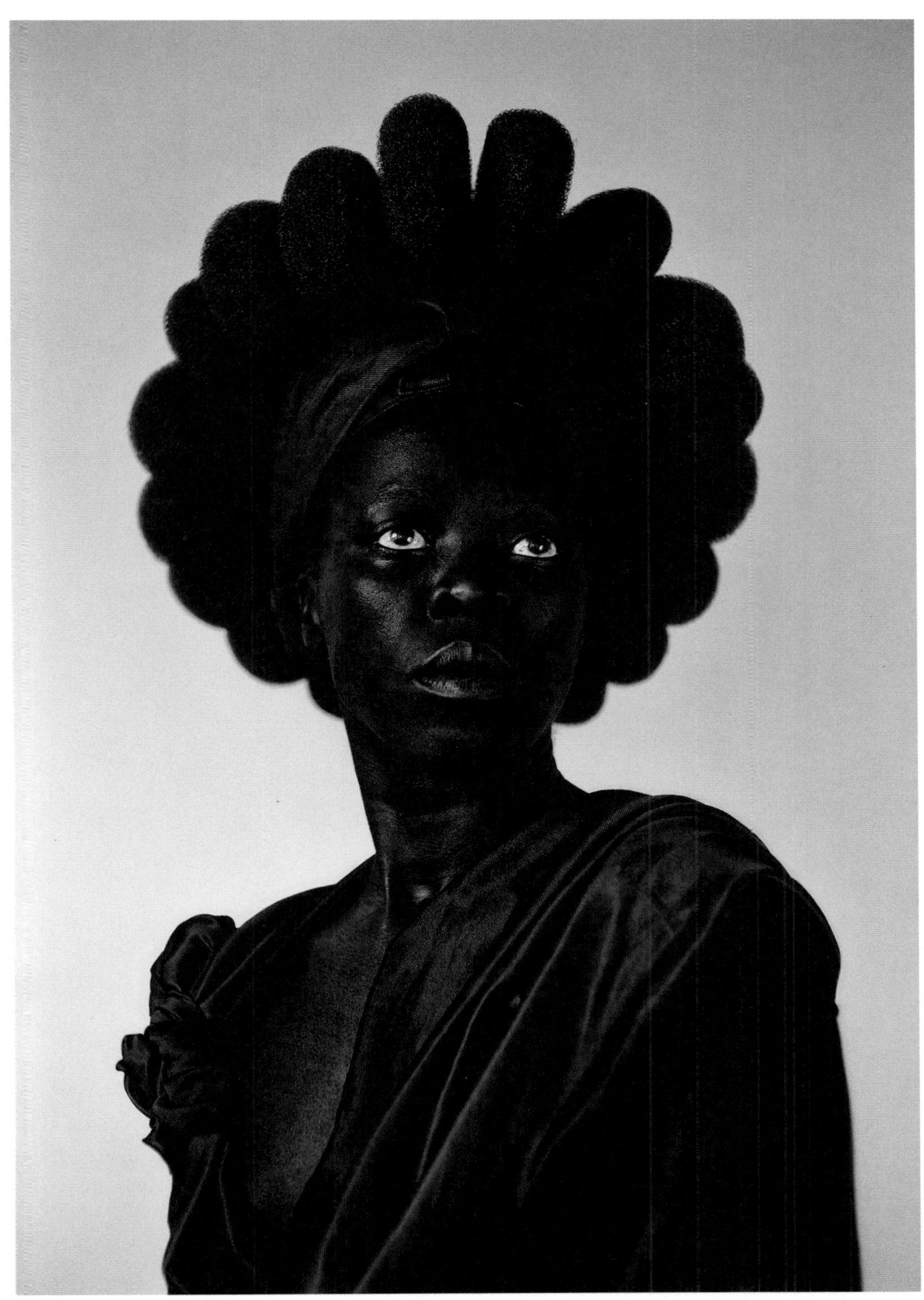

CHAPTER

5

FLIRTING WITH OTHER ART FORMS

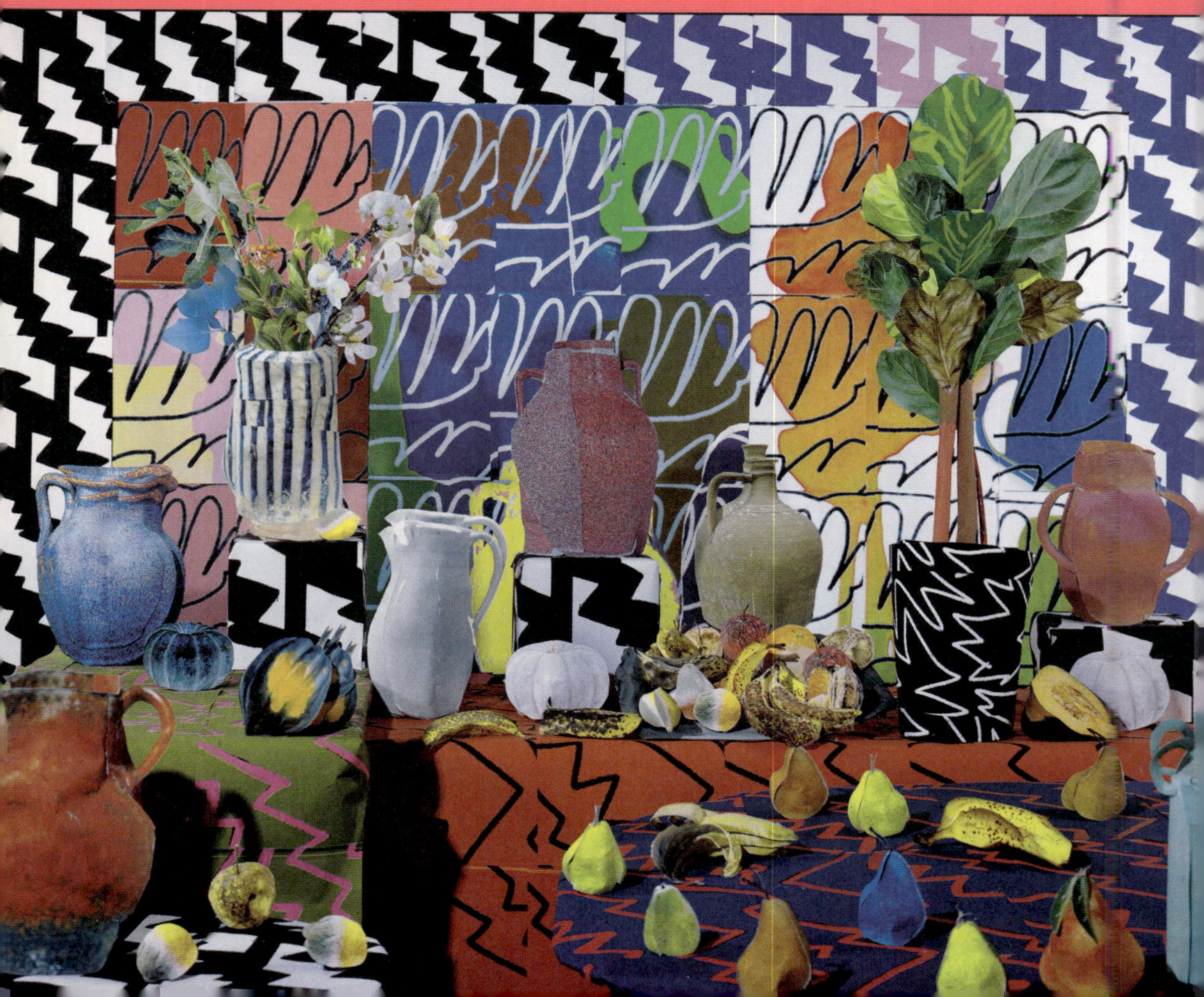

Daniel Gordon

Still Life with Fruit and Ficus

2016

If the lurid colours do not draw you in, the crazy patterns and shapes surely will. In Daniel Gordon's genre-bending work, 3D meets 2D with electrifying consequences.

In this playful image, it is difficult to know where sculpture and collage end and the photograph begins. Yet it is this quality that makes Gordon's artworks so much fun. You do not just look at one of them; you drink and breathe it in. It washes over you as it is a sensory experience not limited to sight. Walking a precarious line between photography, collage, painting and sculpture, each Gordon piece begins life in 3D. Gordon carefully builds set pieces using found imagery sourced from the internet, and objects ranging from cutouts and paper constructions to real-life entities. He then photographs the results using an 8x10 view camera to render the scenes in 2D. The final photograph with its flattened perspective is the artwork. Each scene only exists in this form because the sets are dismantled and reused.

Every photograph is a construction of reality to some extent, a bringing together of real elements in photographic space, but Gordon's artworks take this to another level by combining the real and fabricated in a literal fashion. The joins and overlaps are just visible enough to tease the eye, causing us to question what it is we're looking at.

One of the best, pithiest descriptions of Gordon's work describes it as 'Dutch still life on acid ….' The connections to seventeenth-century Dutch still-life painting are obvious – the fruit, plants and jugs are giveaways. Yet this image is no remake. Less interested in subverting or critiquing still life Gordon turns the genre on its head, and he uses zingy colours and zany patterns to do it.

+ PHOTOGRAPHER BIO
American, b. 1980

+ GOOGLE THESE
Portrait with Blue Hair (2013), *Still Life with Bowl of Lemons* (2018)

+ WATCH THIS
Search 'Daniel Gordon Nowness' on Vimeo to watch a video about Gordon's practice.

Like This? Try These

→ Nico Krijno

→ Sandy Skoglund

→ Kate Steciw

Lorenzo Vitturi

Green Stripes #1

2013

+ PHOTOGRAPHER BIO
Italian, b. 1980

+ GOOGLE THIS
Yellow Chalk #1&2 (2013), *White Tarpaulin, Chinese Cloth and Ewe Agoin* (2017), *Praying Mat Fragments, Egg and Blue* (2017), *Yam, Calabashes, Aso-oke, Egg and Pink Sponge* (2017)

+ WATCH THIS
'Lorenzo Vitturi on Dalston Anatomy' on the Photographers' Gallery channel on Vimeo.

+ WATCH THIS
Alessia Glaviano's video interview with Vitturi for *Vogue Italia* at vogue.it.

Precariously balanced fruit and vegetables, the head of some kind of shrivelled creature and a smattering of dried beans topped off with what looks to be powder or pigment: Lorenzo Vitturi's curious creation is a sight to behold.

The spectacle, which sits somewhere between a vanitas painting and an exploded or deconstructed still life, belongs to the artist's landmark series, *Dalston Anatomy* (2013), a visual celebration of Ridley Road Market in Dalston, east London. The market has long been a multicultural melting pot where traders from diverse backgrounds congregate to sell their wares, but the possibility of gentrification looms large over its future. Vitturi moved to London in 2006. He was intrigued by the area he lived in and in 2011, began working on his *Dalston Anatomy* project, which combines sculptural installations with photography. Using items from the market, such as fabrics and fresh produce, he created sculptures in his nearby studio, which he then photographed. His work is a dialogue between street and studio, two arms of photography that Vitturi draws on to create a new hybrid genre. Irish writer Sean O'Hagan has described his pictures as being 'as far away from traditional street photography as it is possible to go, while still evoking the cacophonous energy of the street'.

Vitturi's background is in set painting for films and experience in this area is evident in this image where built elements meet photographic space in the most inventive way. He has talked about his interest in building set pieces in order to film or photograph them, creating tableaux designed to be viewed in a certain way. Here, every element has been carefully placed in physical space with a mind to what the scene will look like as a photograph. What Vitturi presents seems to defy logic and gravity and can be described as a photographic sculpture as much as a sculptural photograph. Vitturi had a clear purpose in creating his series of images that he hoped would capture the energy of a location before it transformed beyond recognition: 'The ephemerality of these sculptures mirrors the impermanent nature of a rapidly changing neighbourhood, while their reintroduction in the exhibition space as photographic images allows reflections on constant cycles of production, destruction, and recreation.'

Like This? Try These

→ Lucas Blalock
→ Sara Cwynar
→ Daniel Gordon

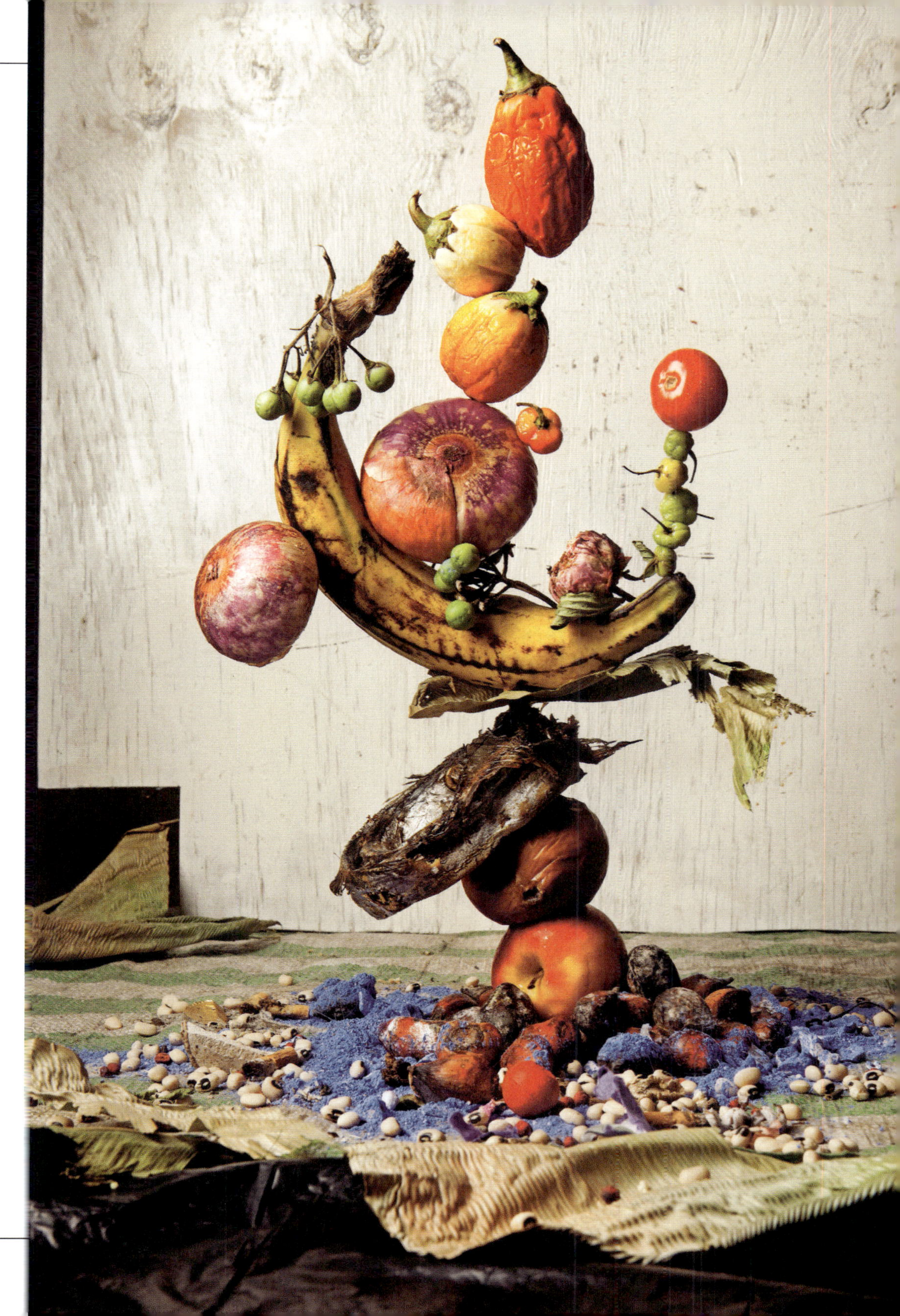

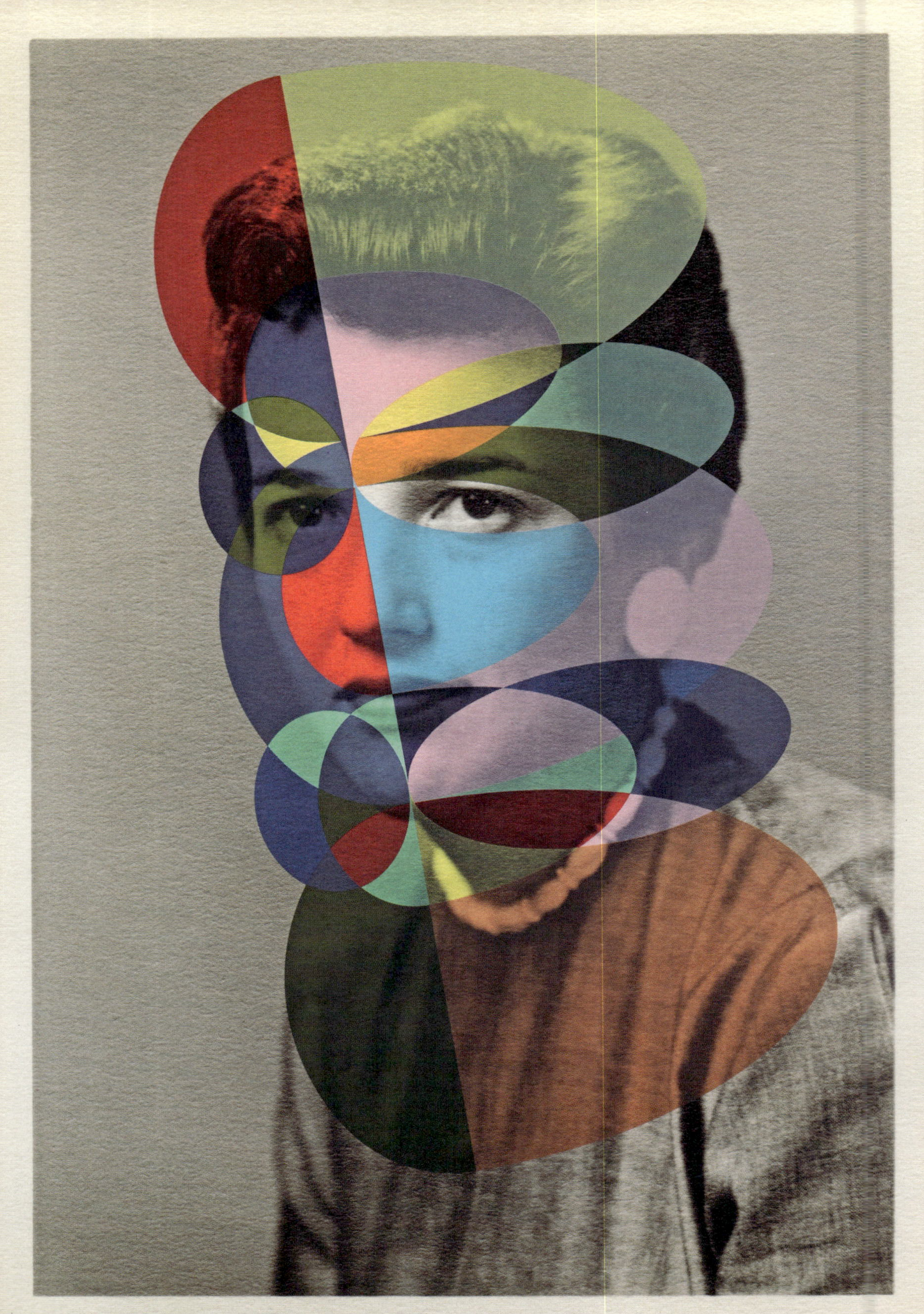

Julie Cockburn

It's Complicated 2

2017

+ **PHOTOGRAPHER BIO**
British, b. 1966

+ **GOOGLE THESE**
The Parachutist (2017), *Five Senses* (2019), *Moonscape* (2019), *Feed the Birds (Women)* (2019)

+ **READ THIS**
Stickybeak (2019) by Julie Cockburn.

Julie Cockburn works with found photographs and paintings, postcards, printed matter or other objects that catch her eye to transform them into works of art.

Guided by intuition and feeling as much as design, Cockburn breathes life into forgotten objects sourced from car-boot sales, junk shops, charity shops and online sales to elevate them to a place where they can be appreciated anew.

Cockburn has a background in sculpture, and works at the fringes of photography where it meets needlework, screen printing, collage and painting. The found photos are her canvases, which she embellishes as the mood takes her, although she adopts a methodical process to work through an idea meticulously. Her subjects include generic landscape photos and studio portraits of a formal nature. She has spoken about how she finds the 'character-less' nature of studio portraits appealing because of their 'stillness' and the space around the subject. She has said that she works with and responds to what is already present in the photograph, since every image has its own history that serves as a starting point from which a new image emerges.

For *It's Complicated 2*, she swapped embroidery for screen printing and collaborated with printing specialist Suki Hayes-Watkins at The Print Block studio in Whitstable, Kent. The image is part of Cockburn's series of screen prints *It's Complicated* (2017). The working process was complex and intricate. She enlarged an old found photograph of a young woman and mapped out a design detailing the position of each colour and shape. Colours were screen printed on top of the enlarged photo. Cockburn brings the portrait back to life with her use of colour, creating an image that sparkles with mischief and magic. The colours hang like a semitranslucent veil over the woman's face paradoxically calling the viewer to look even closer even as they obscure the sitter's features. Cockburn's colourful subject, whoever she may be, invites discussion regarding photography and memory, photography and identity, and photography and truth. However, just as importantly the image reminds the viewer how exciting, interesting and beautiful photography can be in the hands of an artist whose vision knows no bounds and who is unafraid to combine photography with other art forms and see where the results might lead.

Like This? Try These

- → Joana Choumali
- → Jessa Fairbrother
- → Alma Haser

John MacLean

Hometown of John Baldessari, National City, California

2013

+ PHOTOGRAPHER BIO
British, b. 1969

+ GOOGLE THESE
Hometown of Takashi Homma, Ottowa, Tokyo (2014), *Hometown of John Gossage, Staten Island, New York* (2014), *Hometown of Robert Cumming, Mattapan, Massachusetts* (2014)

+ READ THIS
John MacLean discusses *Hometowns* on the Photoworks website: photoworks.org.uk/interview-john-maclean.

This is such a fun image. Bright, cheerful splashes of colour instantly turn a drab, nondescript industrial-looking setting into something more appealing.

What is interesting on a first look is how photographer John MacLean flirts with notions of sculpture, installation and even performance art by appearing to have intervened in the scene; we are led to believe that the colourful discs have been placed there, surreptitiously slipped into gaps in the fence prior to the photograph being made. That would be novel enough, but there is more to this image than first appears. It belongs to his series *Hometowns* (2011–16) for which MacLean visited and photographed the places where artists he admires spent their formative years. The project sprung from a simple idea jotted down in a notebook – 'photograph the hometowns of your heroes' – and it evolved into what MacLean calls 'a layered investigation into the places which influenced those artists whose work has coloured my own.' He visited twenty-five towns and cities across the world, places where artists such as William Eggleston, Ed Ruscha, Robert Frank and Gabriel Orozco lived, making images that MacLean says pay 'tribute to the spirit in which each artist worked'. But, as American artist, writer, editor and curator Aaron Schuman points out in the introductory text for the book of the work, MacLean's images go beyond echoing or referencing and are 'strikingly original, visually arresting and deeply personal in their own right.'

In this image MacLean features American conceptual artist John Baldessari. He channels the conceptual provocateur who turned the art world upside down with his quirky pieces. Baldessari was interested in language, text, games, structures and rules, and his work spanned painting, photography, film, video, sculpture and Installation. MacLean deftly yet reverently nods to the artist and his way of making art by constructing his image in a similarly playful way. At the same time, he ruminates on the nature of influence and how people learn from those that precede them.

Like This? Try These

→ John Baldessari

→ Gabriel Orozco

→ David Spero

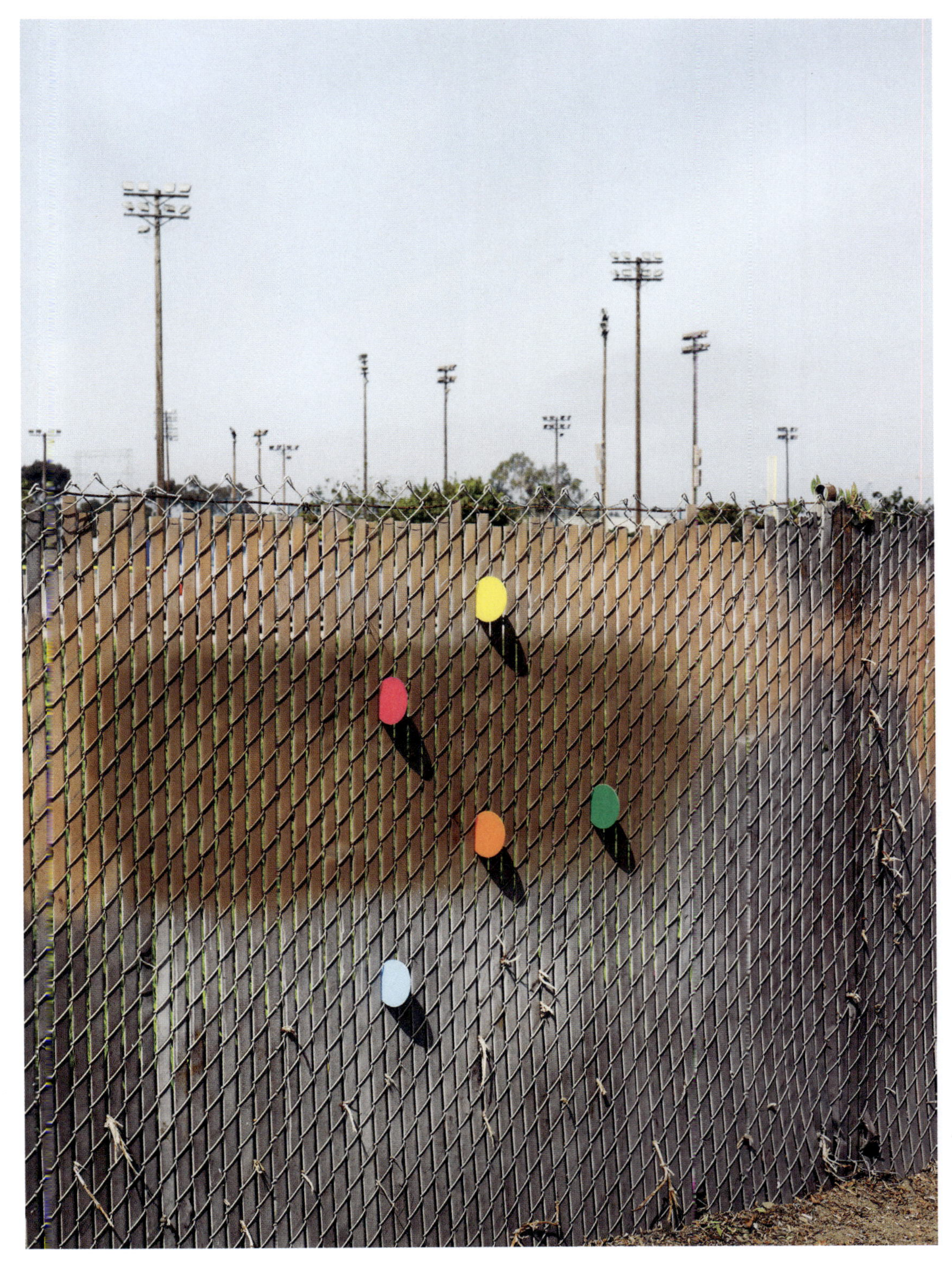

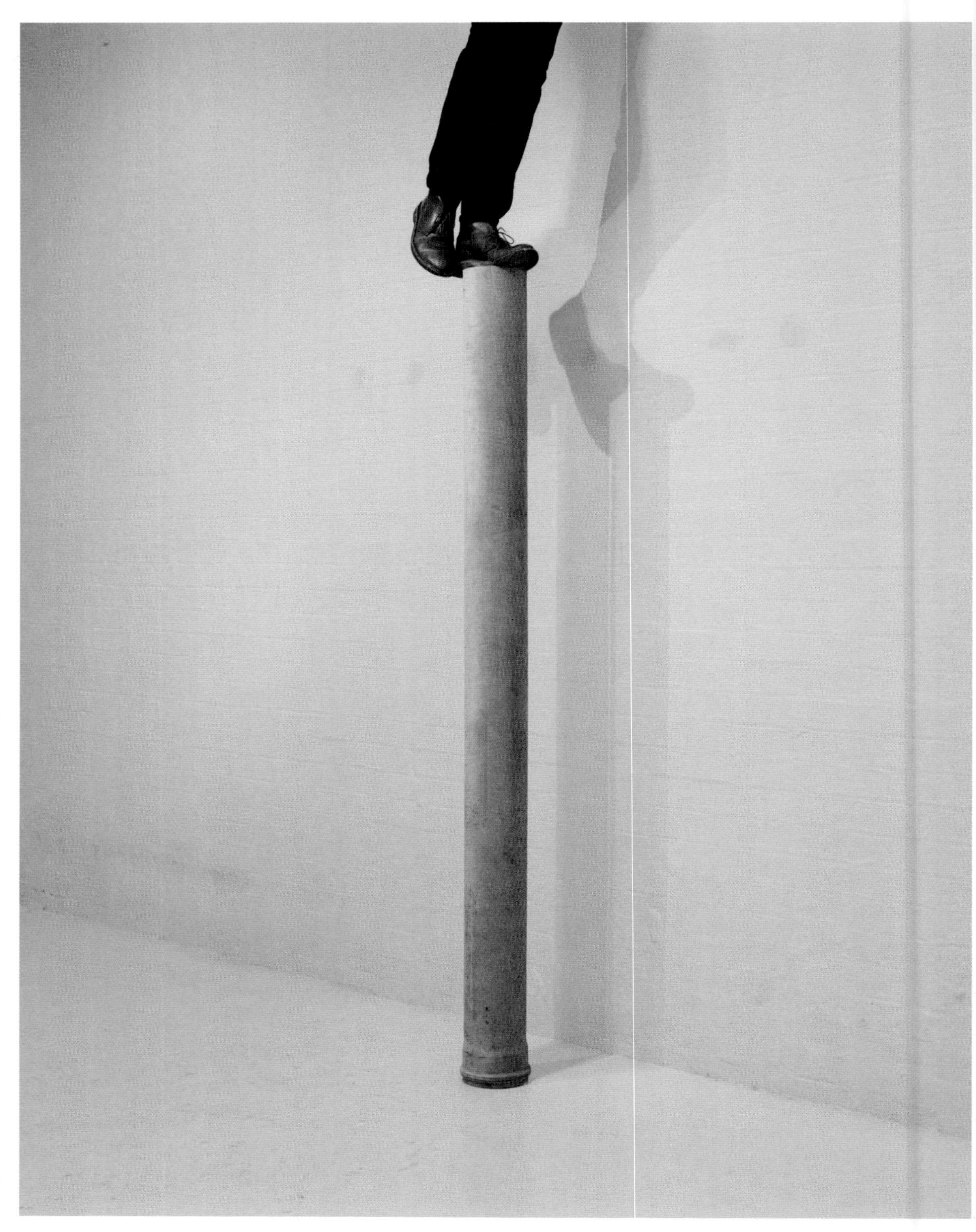

Tom Lovelace

In Preparation No. 09

2012

Two feet teeter on a column that appears inadequately secured to the ground. Questions abound as the viewer wonders who the person is, what they are doing, how and why they got on top of the column, and how they will get down.

Lovelace's photograph first succeeds by ensnaring the viewer's attention, then the relationship with the artwork becomes even more interesting. Lovelace wants to question the nature of photography, particularly where and how photography intersects with sculpture and performance. The image is part of an on-going series of works called *In Preparation* (2010–) for which Lovelace created temporary site-specific compositions from industrial materials. In these complex works 'the event and image take place in a gallery where the resulting image is then displayed,' Lovelace has said. 'The picture is hung in close proximity to where the image was made so [visitors to the gallery] have to literally stand in the space where the image was made – they become caught within the image.'

Everything in the image is carefully positioned to draw attention to the properties of the objects and play with notions of balance, weight and tension. Each element is dependent on the other, and the objects or individuals featured in the image are precisely balanced. Together, this creates a sense of weight, whether it be heaviness, weightlessness or lightness, which pervades the scene. Elements in the images appear to fluctuate from one state to the other as the viewer wonders whether, as in this case, the column is heavy or light.

Lovelace also uses the series to explore the relationship between functional, workaday objects that were never intended to be pieces of art and the viewer's expectations regarding what to see in an art gallery, thus subverting or destabilizing accepted ideas of what constitutes art. With *In Preparation No.09* he emphasizes this goal by the inclusion of the column that could be interpreted as a plinth upon which artworks such as busts are typically displayed. In a clever twist, the viewer wonders if it is the artist himself who is on display. Lovelace investigates the limits of the photograph and how it might collaborate with other media, while simultaneously creating artworks that are often whimsical and prompt the viewer to reflect on their understanding of what photography is.

+ PHOTOGRAPHER BIO
British, b. 1981

+ GOOGLE THESE
Platform at Pontresina (2015), *Stargazing* (2015), *Coastal Blocks* (2016)

+ VISIT THIS
Lovelace's website, tomlovelace.co.uk, is full of information and showcases a range of his work.

Like This? Try These

→ Thom Bridge

→ Joanna Piotrowska

→ Eva Stenram

Darren Harvey-Regan

The Halt

2011

+ **PHOTOGRAPHER BIO**
British, b. 1974

+ **GOOGLE THESE**
More or Less Obvious Forms (2012), *The Erratics (Part 1)* (2015)

+ **READ THIS**
An interview with Darren Harvey-Regan by Brad Feuerhelm on American Suburb X, at americansuburbx.com.

You are not looking at a reflection, although you would be forgiven for thinking that what you are seeing is a mirror image. There really is an axe pinning this photographic print of an axe to the wall.

To complicate things further, since a physical object could not be printed in the pages of a book, the photograph published here is of the axe that is pinning a print of an image of the same axe to the wall. This never-ending loop alludes to the reciprocal and certainly fraught relationship between an object and a photograph that lies at the centre of this work by Darren Harvey-Regan. Here he brings image and object together in the same space so that the work exists at the point where flat representation and 3D object meet. Consequently, we experience the photograph of the object and the object itself in the same moment. As Harvey-Regan says: 'The aspect of this piece I like to draw attention to is that of grounding the image in the present moment. Rather than the photograph being an image of the past, the literal joining with its subject embeds it in a continual present'.

If there is a tug between past and present at work in *The Halt*, there is also a tension between the photograph as object and the photographic subject. Harvey-Regan reminds us in the most brutal fashion that both are inextricably entwined. Ultimately, at the heart of this piece, and much of his work, is a questioning of photographic representation and an interest in how photography butts up against sculpture. He has admitted to having a 'love-hate relationship with photography' and talked about his keenness to be hands-on and to engage physically with materials. In addition to investigating photography's relationship to itself his interest lies in its relationship to the world at large. As he says: 'For me, photographs of/with/as objects create an intriguing context offering the most overlap with the world as it is and the world as photography makes it.'

Like This? Try These

→ Marianne Bjørnmyr

→ Tom Lovelace

→ Peter Watkins

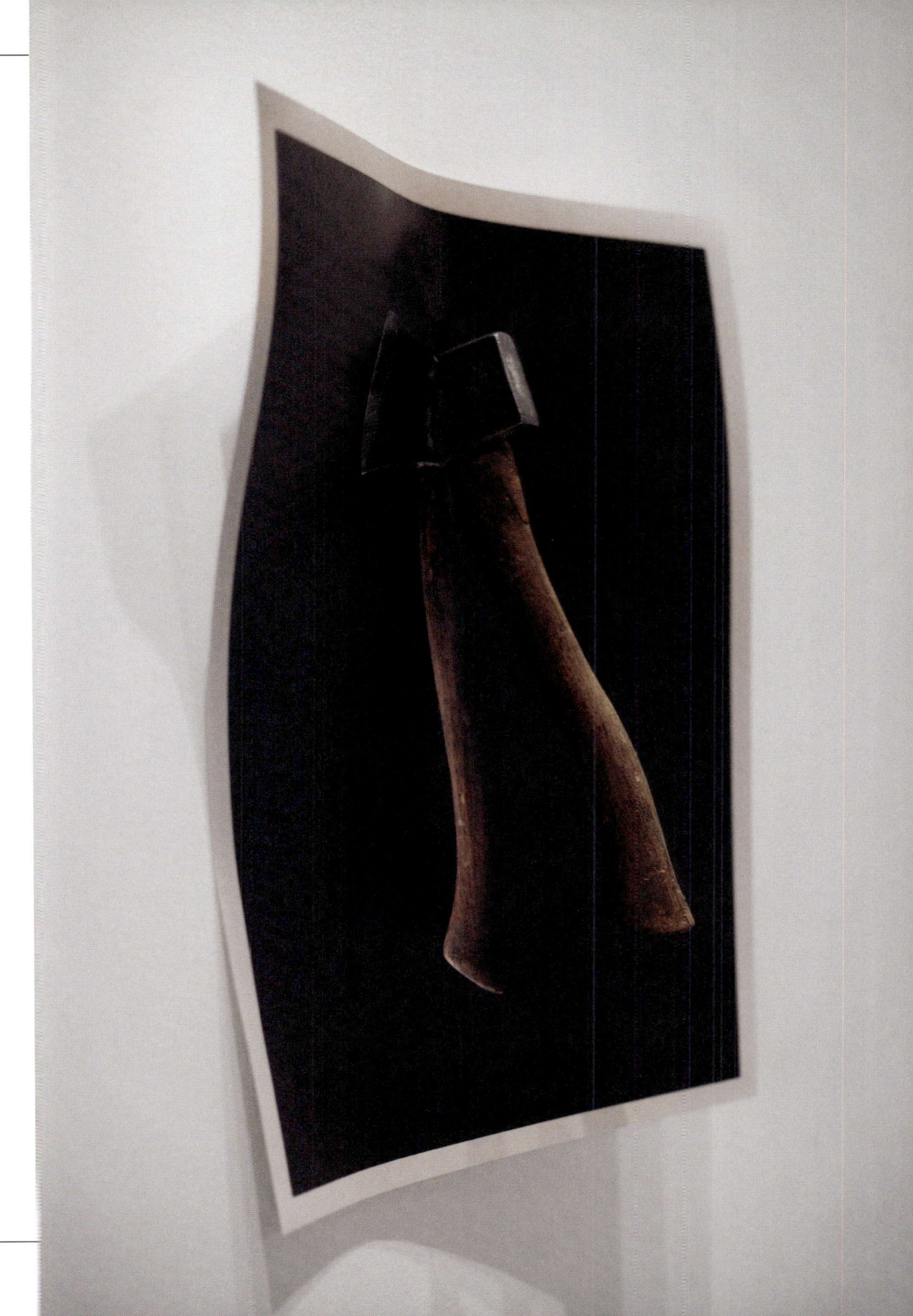

Hannah Hughes

Mirror Image #33

2019

Photography has always had a complex and fraught relationship with three-dimensional space. A photograph is the depiction of something with physical form that has been rendered two dimensional.

The flat photograph can point to the physicality of its subject, but it will always remain two-dimensional in that it will always be a reproduction of a three-dimensional object and give an impression of physical space.

Hannah Hughes's work plays with such tensions: the ideas of physical and photographic space, what is there and what has been removed, the flat and the sculptural. In the *Flatland* series, the precursor to the series to which this artwork belongs, she combines fragments selected from her archive of vintage fashion magazines, auction catalogues and other published material to create photo collages that are at once flat and yet strikingly three- dimensional.

In this earlier work, Hughes is drawn to what she has called the 'unimportant sections of a photograph', meaning the parts that surround the main subject that are carefully removed from their original contexts and reconfigured to form her sculptural-looking collages. In contrast, in the *Mirror Image* collages, of which this is one, the opposite happens: image fragments are used to project shadows in new photographs, which are then cut out and reassembled to create collages.

If there is a tension between two- and three-dimensional space in the work and between sculpture and photography, there is also a dialogue between presence and absence, the essence of a photograph and its lack of substance. While the viewer can readily enjoy the image for its playful take on collage and sculpture as well as its visually challenging aesthetic, Hughes's intentions run deeper. She has said: 'I'm interested in the idea of creating new languages from pre-existing forms as a completely alternative way of seeing what's around you.' This artwork's beguiling sculptural presence questions the way we experience things in space and how space is presented in images.

+ PHOTOGRAPHER BIO
British, b. 1975

+ GOOGLE THESE
Flatland Series (2014–),
Room With Its Own Sun (2019),
Outer Movements (2020)

+ READ THIS
'Playful Collages Inverting the Value of Negative Spaces' interview with Hannah Hughes by Maisie Skidmore at AnOthermag.com.

Like This? Try These

→ Ruth van Beek

→ Nico Krijno

→ Dafna Talmor

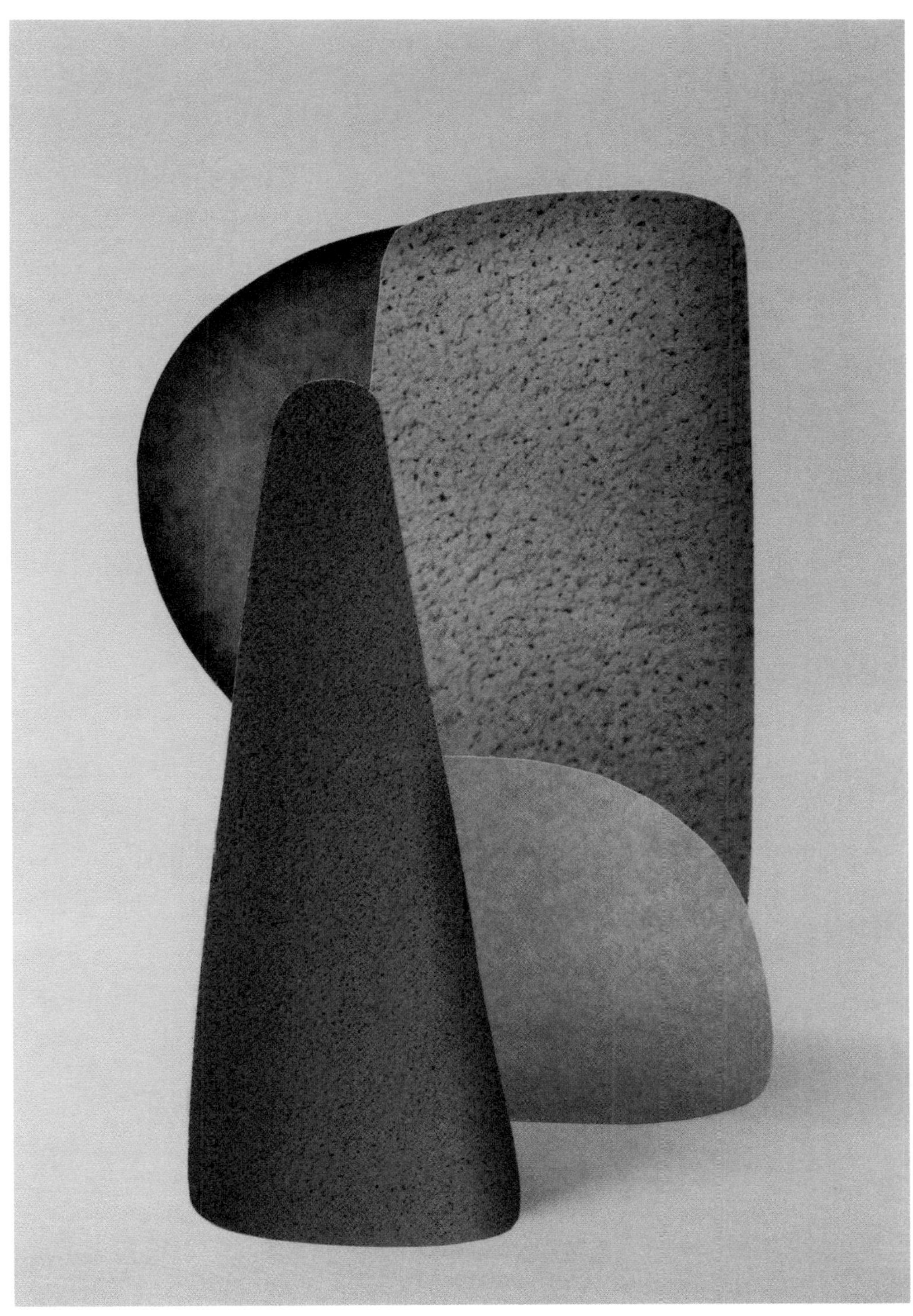

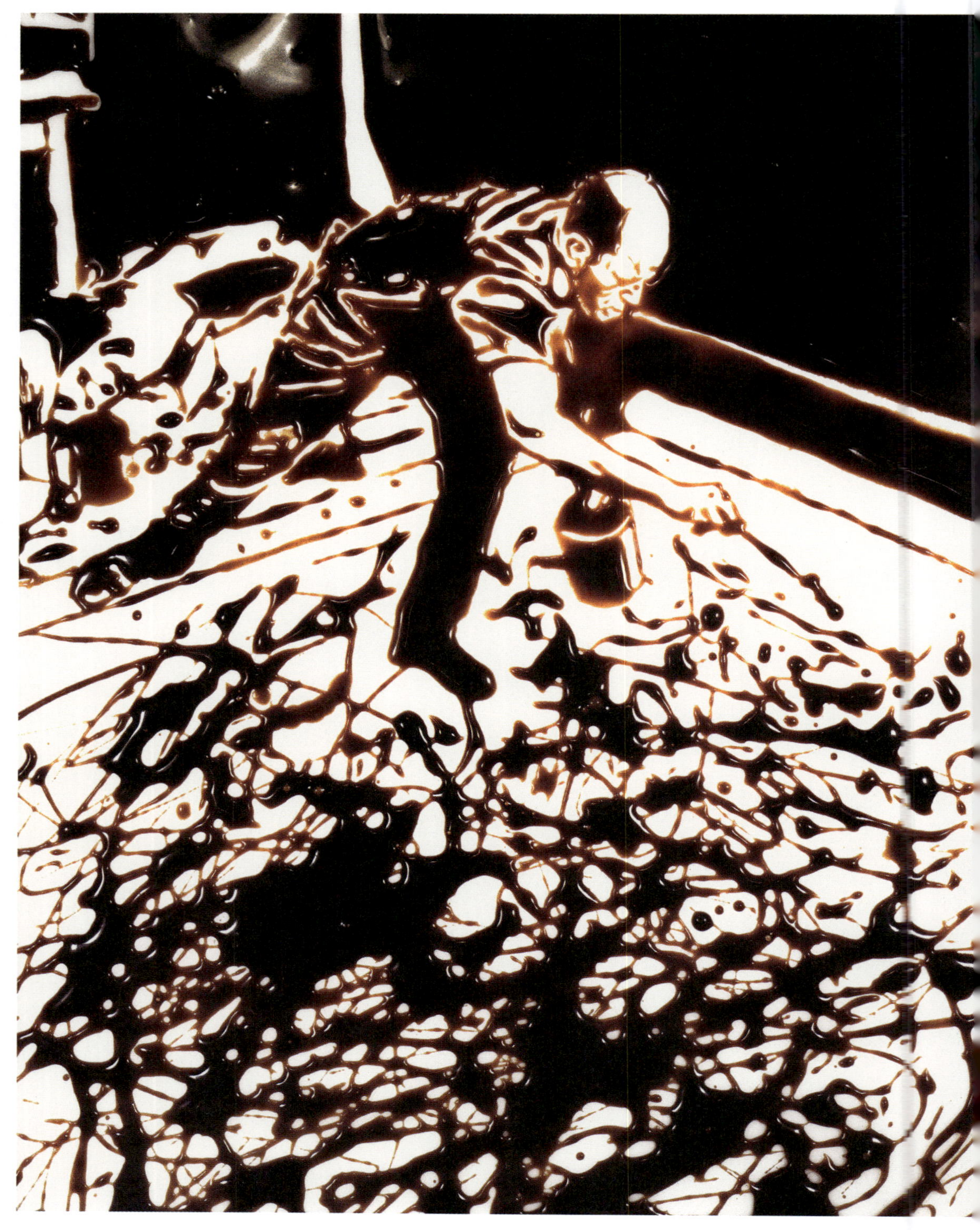

 Vik Muniz—Action Photo, after Hans Namuth

Vik Muniz

Action Photo, after Hans Namuth

1997

When German photographer Hans Namuth took a photograph for *LIFE* magazine of the great American abstract expressionist artist Jackson Pollock as he was making one of his action paintings in 1950, he could never have imagined that it would be recreated in chocolate syrup and re-photographed decades later.

New York-based Muniz has made it his life's work to play with the notion of visual representation, to question what we think when we look at art. He is renowned for his innovative use of eclectic everyday materials, which he uses to recreate images ingrained in popular consciousness, often from pop culture or art history. Sugar, ink, string and wire as well as chocolate syrup and peanut butter have all featured in his artist's tool bag, his subjects ranging from the *Mona Lisa* to Marilyn Monroe and Van Gogh's *Starry Night*. After he has created his interpretation of the original image, Muniz photographs the results to create a permanent photographic record. He uses a photographic process called Ilfochrome whereby several layers of emulsion are perceived as one to make his vibrant 'dye destruction' prints.

This work is from a series called *Pictures of Chocolate* (1997) and is one of several images by Namuth that Muniz remade in chocolate syrup. What is fascinating about Muniz's image and the way he went about making it, is how it cleverly draws attention to the interplay, or rather the relationship, between painting or drawing and photography. It is an image that operates on many levels, which can be peeled back in an attempt to get to the heart of the picture. But what we see depends on how we look and think as individuals: there is Pollock, the painter, immortalized in Namuth's photograph. At the same time, Muniz's syrupy impermanent rendition involves an act of creation akin to painting, indeed, with deliberate parallels to Pollock's process of dripping household paint on canvas. Finally, the photograph of Muniz's work is realized as a photographic print. It is a strange experience to look at such an image, which slips between painting and photography. Muniz opens up a raft of questions about what photography is and what it can do, how it can help us to see or indeed understand the world around us.

+ PHOTOGRAPHER BIO
Brazilian, b. 1961

+ GOOGLE THESE:
The Sugar Children Series (1996), *Nadia Comaneci*, (from *Pictures of Ink*) (2000), *The Steerage, after Stieglitz* (2000), *Starry Night, after Van Gogh* (2012)

+ WATCH THIS
'Art with Wire, Sugar, Chocolate and String', a talk by Vik Muniz on Ted.com.

Like This? Try These

→ Jan Dibbets

→ Gabriel Orozco

→ Martha Rosler

Edward Steichen

The Pond – Moonrise

1904

If you thought the manipulation of photographs was a recent phenomenon, one look at Edward Steichen's Pictorialist masterpiece *The Pond – Moonrise* will convince you otherwise. Its painterly look is no accident.

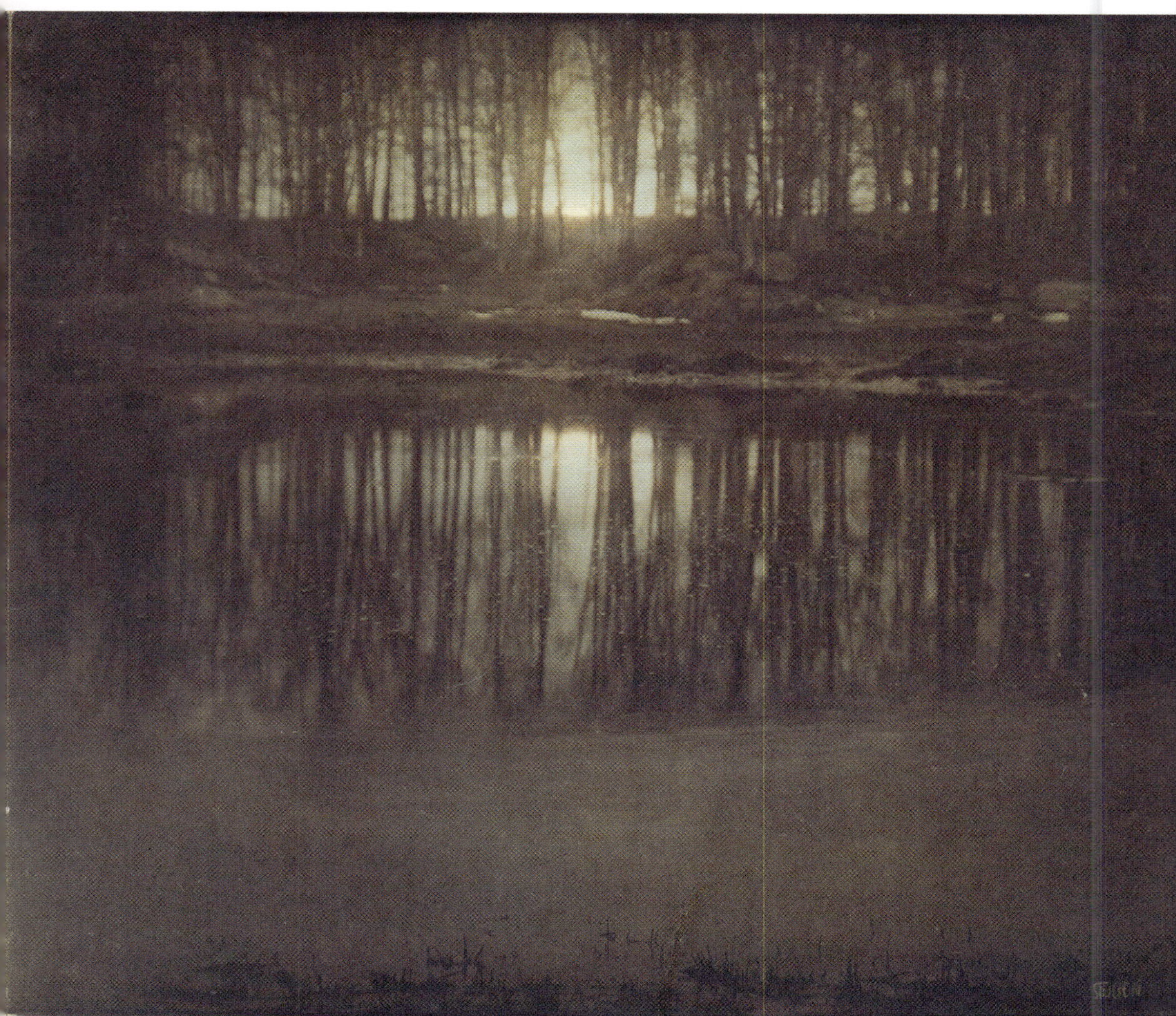

Steichen, whose artistic roots were in painting, applied multiple emulsions – layers of gum bichromate added by hand with a brush – to a platinum print, giving the photograph its luminous, ethereal quality and blue-green hue. Steichen would have worked to bring out different parts of the image, accentuating darker areas and balancing those with lighter patches. Some commentators believe that he may even have added in the moon. New York's Metropolitan Museum of Art, which sold one of the copies in its collection for a record-breaking $2.9 million in 2006, describes it as 'a tone poem of twilight, indistinction and suggestiveness'.

Steichen took the photograph in woods near Mamaroneck, Westchester County in New York, on the tidal estuary of Long Island Sound. At this point in his photographic career, he was an advocate of Pictorialism and the Photo-Secession, a movement led by Alfred Stieglitz that sought to promote photography as art by rejecting the point-and-shoot approach of snapshot photography that had become popular among amateur photographers. It involved manipulating photographs to make them look more akin to paintings and less rigidly true to life. The uniqueness and character of each print, lovingly made by hand, was paramount.

Steichen eventually moved away from Pictorialism, embracing straight photography after the First World War (1914–18), and in doing so he contributed to the global art movement of modernism. But Steichen's early works including this, his atmospheric, soft-focused images of landscapes, cityscapes and portraits remain a fundamental part of photography's rich history. Photographs such as *The Pond – Moonrise* reveal the medium's propensity for expression, which has since been explored successfully by successive generations of photographers and artists working with photography.

+ PHOTOGRAPHER BIO

Luxembourgish-American, 1879–1973

+ GOOGLE THESE

The Pool (1899), *The Flatiron* (1904), *Balzac, The Silhouette – 4 a.m.* (1908)

+ READ THIS

Edward Steichen: Lives in Photography (2007) by Todd Brandow and William A. Ewing.

Like This? Try These

→ Imogen Cunningham

→ Frank Eugene

→ Gertrude Käsebier

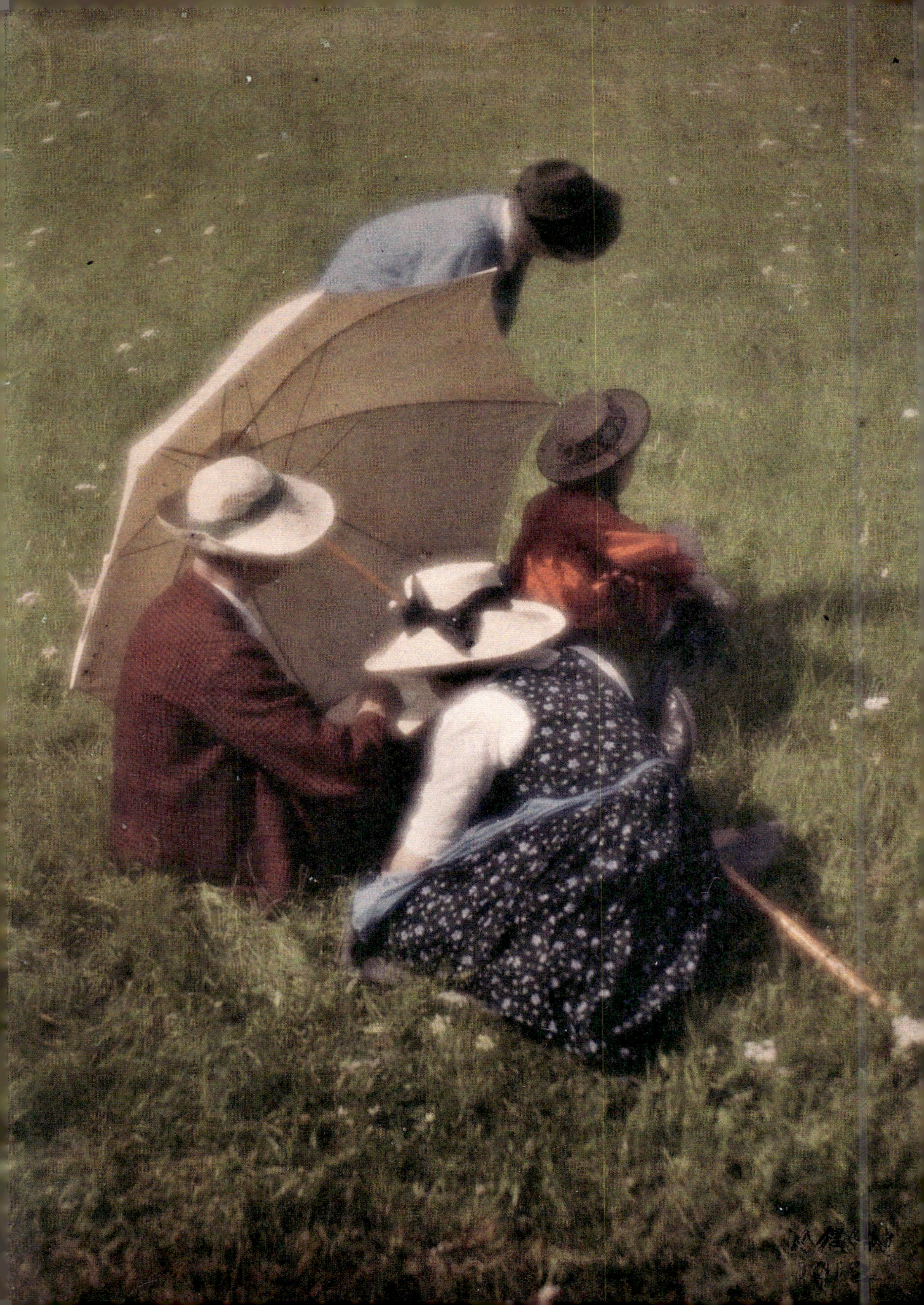

Heinrich Kühn

The Kühn Siblings in the Meadow

1912

Looking at this autochrome photograph it is almost impossible not to think of the work of Impressionists such as Claude Monet, Berthe Morisot or Pierre-Auguste Renoir.

The countryside setting, rich colours and soft haze invite comparisons with Impressionism, as does the dotted texture, which is an intrinsic quality of the autochrome colour photography process.

Autochrome was the first commercially successful colour photography process. The Lumière brothers, Auguste and Louis, patented the process in France in 1903 and began the commercial manufacture of autochrome plates in 1907. By 1913, 6,000 Autochrome plates were being produced every day in the Lumière brothers' factory in Lyon. Autochromes are glass plates coated with tiny grains of potato starch that were dyed green, orange-red and blue-violet and then covered with emulsion. They had a painterly look, which was especially gratifying for early photographers such as Heinrich Kühn who were passionate about exploring photography's artistic possibilities. Kühn had taken his first art photograph several years earlier in 1894 and had thrown himself into the Pictorialist way of making pictures, which privileged beauty in tone and composition over true to life depictions of subject matter. His images were even used by American photographer Alfred Stieglitz, who advocated photography as fine art, to show that photographs could be considered artworks.

Kühn's early landscapes from the 1900s were already exquisite examples of how the boundaries between photography and painting could be blurred brilliantly.

However, it was Kühn's photographs of his family that really startle in this respect. Kühn often photographed his children and their nanny in the landscapes of the Austrian Tyrol where they lived. Here they are in a meadow, looking out into an unseen distance. The subjects' hats, colourful patterned clothes and the parasol suggest the universal, timeless and romantic idyll of a family at leisure on a balmy summer's day. That such an intricate combination of light, colour and texture could be achieved in the early twentieth century is remarkable, and the beauty of the scene has proved to be eternally moving.

+ PHOTOGRAPHER BIO
German-Austrian, 1866–1944

+ GOOGLE THESE
Playmates (1907), *Children on the Hill* (c. 1908), *Miss Mary and Edeltrude Lying on Grass* (c. 1910)

+ WATCH THIS
'Heinrich Kuehn and the Development of Color Autochromes' on Neue Galerie New York's YouTube channel.

Like This? Try These

→ Etheldreda Laing

→ Mervyn O'Gorman

→ John Cimon Warburg

CHAPTER

6

PHOTOS THAT COULD BE DREAMS

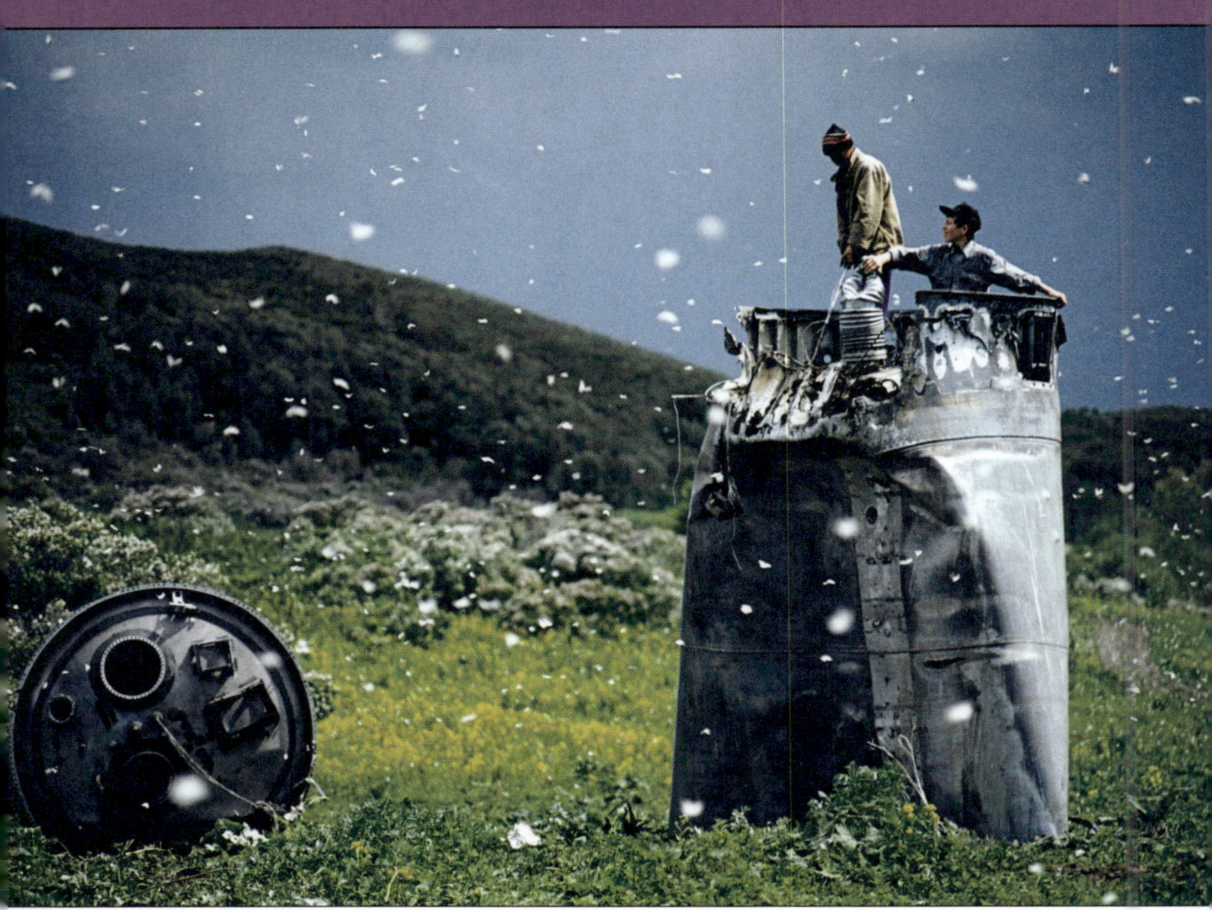

 Jonas Bendiksen—Russia, Altai Territory

Jonas Bendiksen

Russia, Altai Territory

2000

From the odd sense of perspective and confusing scale to the white flecks that could be ash or snow and ethereal light that bathes the scene, Jonas Bendiksen's photograph could not be more otherworldly.

The reality is less magical although still rather unusual. What you are looking at is the remnants of a crashed spacecraft in Altai, Russia, where two men are scavenging for scrap. The white flecks are thousands of butterflies. The Altai region is a remote and mountainous stretch of land, which is often referred to as 'spaceship junkyard' or 'space graveyard'. It lies below the main flight path of the world's largest and oldest spaceport, Baikonur Cosmodrome, and debris from rockets crashes down onto the land below. Wrecks are left to rust or are stripped by local scrap-metal merchants for any valuable metals in what is an area where there is little economic stability, so the activity provides a modest but vital income for those who do so.

Bendiksen has spoken about how all the elements of his picture came together saying it was 'a truly magical situation'. The dark, brooding sky with the bright light cutting through adds to the picture's fantastical and surreal mood. If you spend time looking through the other images from his *Satellites* (2006) series to which this photograph belongs, you will find that Bendiksen has an uncanny way of using light, colour and movement to whisk viewers off into worlds that could belong to the realm of dreams. What he depicts is always real but Bendiksen – in this image especially – has a way of using the otherworldliness of humble human events to create images that are almost transcendent.

+ PHOTOGRAPHER BIO
Norwegian, b. 1977

+ GOOGLE THESE
Sukhumi Beach, Abkhazia Georgia (2005), *Klo, Vesteraalen, Norway* (2012)

+ READ THIS
The Last Testament (2017) by Jonas Bendiksen.

+ WATCH THIS
Visit the Magnum Photos YouTube channel and search for 'Behind the Picture – Jonas Bendiksen, Satellites' to see him talk about his photograph.

Like This? Try These

→ Evgenia Arbugaeva

→ Bieke Depoorter

→ Rafal Milach

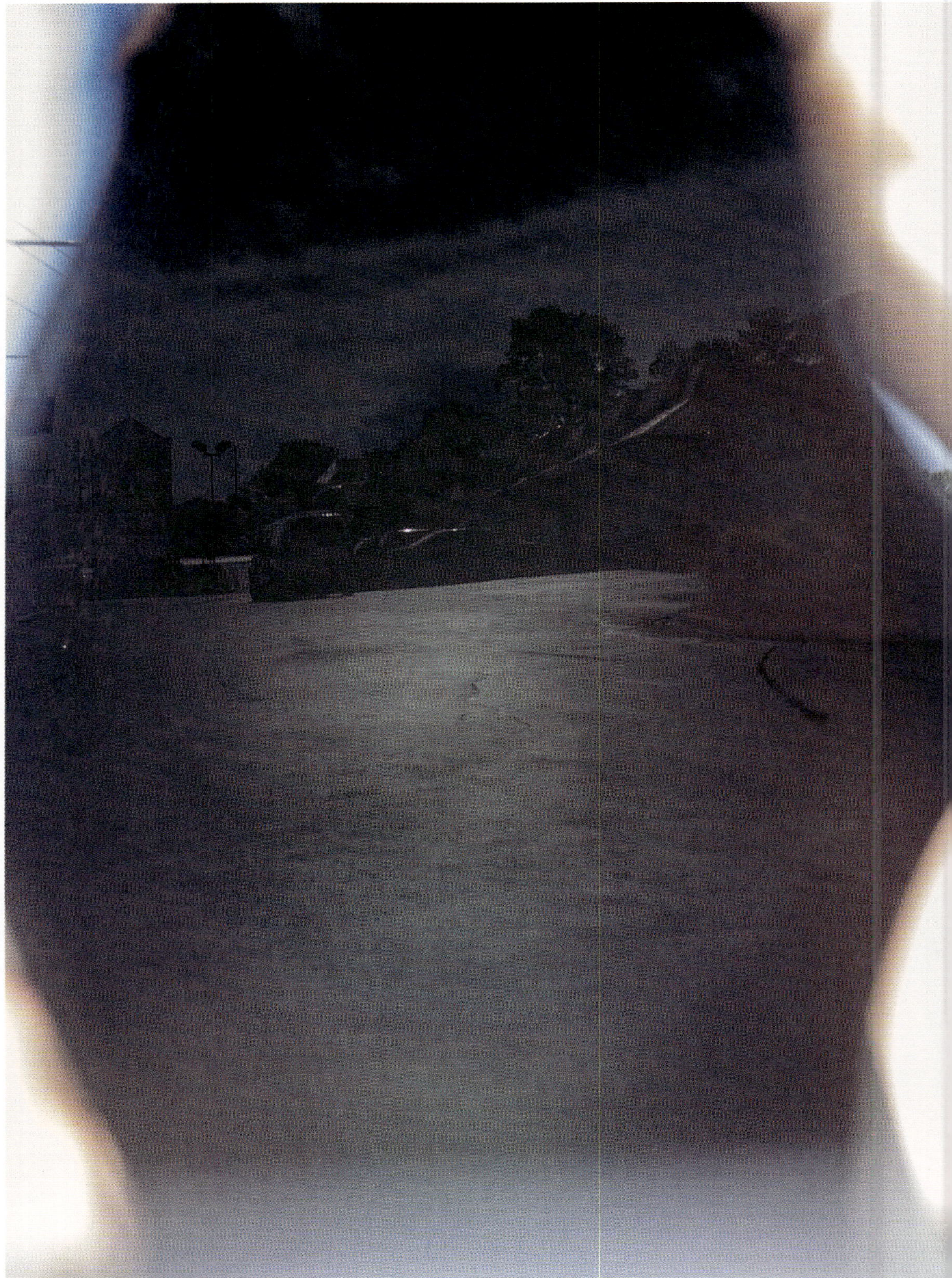

Gregory Halpern

North and South Carolina, USA

2017

A truly great photograph has the power to transport the viewer to wherever is being depicted, to make you feel as though you are there in the photograph itself.

This is exactly the feeling Gregory Halpern's mysterious photograph evokes: the image draws you in, it is as though you have blinked and opened your eyes only to find yourself in another place, although you do not know where.

The location is nondescript, geographically non-specific. It seems familiar and yet it is somewhere the viewer struggles to place. There is nothing tangible to grab onto, you sink into its infinite depths. Shadow engulfs the scene save for the areas touched by moonlight, which unsettle and disorientate. The result is beautiful and stark. Light seems to have leaked into the image; it is as though the landscape has caught alight and is melting away before your eyes.

The image is from Halpern's *Confederate Moons*, a series of photographs taken in North and South Carolina in 2017 during the month when a total eclipse of the sun occurred. Halpern has explained that initially the work was inspired by the eclipse itself but then became a meditation on the American South and on the current state of his home country, the United States. The strangeness of everyday life is a theme to which Halpern frequently returns and he is interested in making work where shades of discomfort and reassurance coexist. This is evident in this photograph, which lures you in with a reassuring air before throwing you off as soon as you consign yourself to it. It is not a photograph that can be easily or conveniently explained away, and there is discomfort in that too.

For Halpern, photography does not neatly frame reality, nor should it be expected to. He believes deception and tension are hardwired into photography and its relationship to truth is never clear cut. As he points out: '...it is said that photography is uniquely suited to "reflect" the world around us but what if our surroundings are complex to the point of being visually and verbally indescribable? That conundrum is the reality I want to reflect with the creation of a rightfully impenetrable thing.'

PHOTOGRAPHER BIO
American, b. 1977

GOOGLE THESE
A. The American Rust Belt, USA (2008–11), *ZZYZX. Los Angeles and vicinity, USA* (2008–15)

READ THIS
Go to theLensCulture website at: lensculture.com to read a feature on *Confederate Moons.*

Like This? Try These

- Jason Fulford
- Kata Geibl
- Adam Jeppesen

Sally Mann

Georgia, Untitled (Kudzu)

1996

Sally Mann is best known for her evocative photographs of her family, in particular her three children when they were young, but Mann's mystical and dreamlike Southern landscapes are equally beguiling. They usher us into their depths with the promise of secrets soon to be revealed, and, seduced by their exquisite, lustrous light, we follow eagerly.

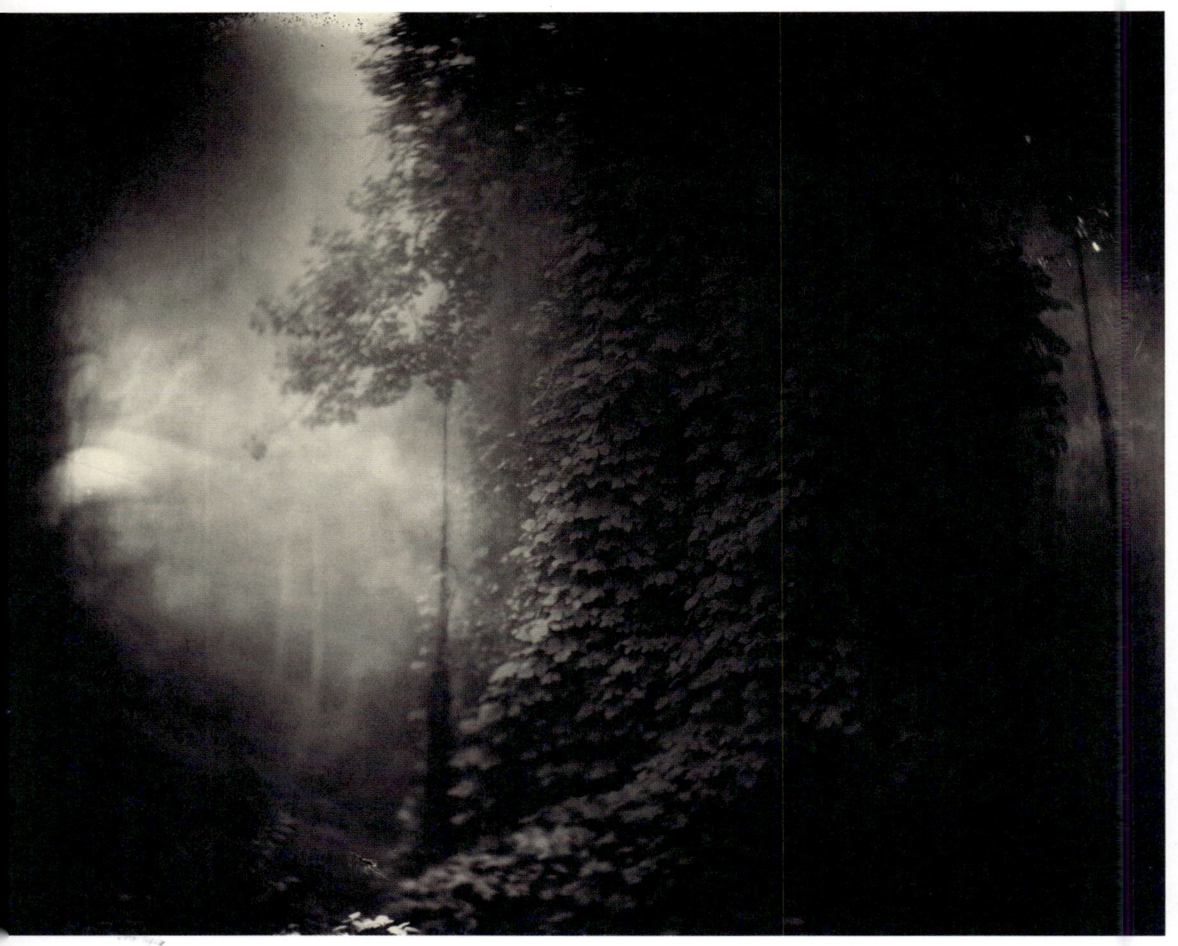

Although Mann made some landscapes in the 1970s before finding fame in 1992 with the release of her landmark series *Immediate Family*, she turned to photographing landscapes – her native Virginia, nearby Georgia and eventually much of the very deep South, especially Mississippi and Louisiana – with vigour as her children grew into adulthood. Using a large format camera and a selection of antique lenses, Mann immersed herself in the rural landscapes of the South, creating images that are as beautiful as they are unsettling. Imbued with history and at times the spectre of death, it is as though Mann's landscapes are from another time, which has much to do with the photographic process she uses; overexposed areas, vignetting and blur caused by the antiquated technology contribute to their 'old-fashioned' look, evident here. Awash with light, the image appears before our eyes as a photographic print emerges in darkness. It is as though we have just awoken from a dream and have not quite shaken off our slumber or adjusted to the new day.

Mann wields her chosen medium with the apparent ease of someone who has spent years carefully studying and translating their surroundings into photographic form, balancing light and dark to hint at what lies within the picture. Here, ethereal light spills across the scene, illuminating the kudzu-clad tree just enough to intrigue but to never fully reveal what we're looking at. Within this space between knowledge and not knowing, Mann invites us to wait awhile. It is here, too, that we might wonder if the landscape has a memory of its own, a question that has long fascinated Mann, and what it would tell if it could speak. This ancient tree has surely seen many things but in Mann's image it keeps its secrets like the photograph itself.

+ PHOTOGRAPHER BIO
American, b. 1951

+ GOOGLE THESE
Virginia, Untitled (Upper Field) (1993), *Deep South, Untitled (Checkmark Windsor)* (1998), *Battlefields, Chancellorsville (Reuer's Turn)* (2002)

+ READ THIS
Sally Mann: A Thousand Crossings (2018) by Sally Mann.

+ WATCH THIS
Blood Ties: The Life and Work of Sally Mann (1994), directed by Steven Cantor.

Like This? Try These

- Awoiska van der Molen
- Susan Derges
- Hiroshi Sugimoto

Rinko Kawauchi

Untitled

2007

How Rinko Kawauchi can make an ordinary staircase look like the stuff of dreams is anyone's guess. It is partly because of her exquisite handling of light for which she is admired, but also her sensitivity to the edges of the frame, specifically how they can be used to accentuate her chosen subject, in this case, four people travelling away from the viewer as though hypnotized or possessed.

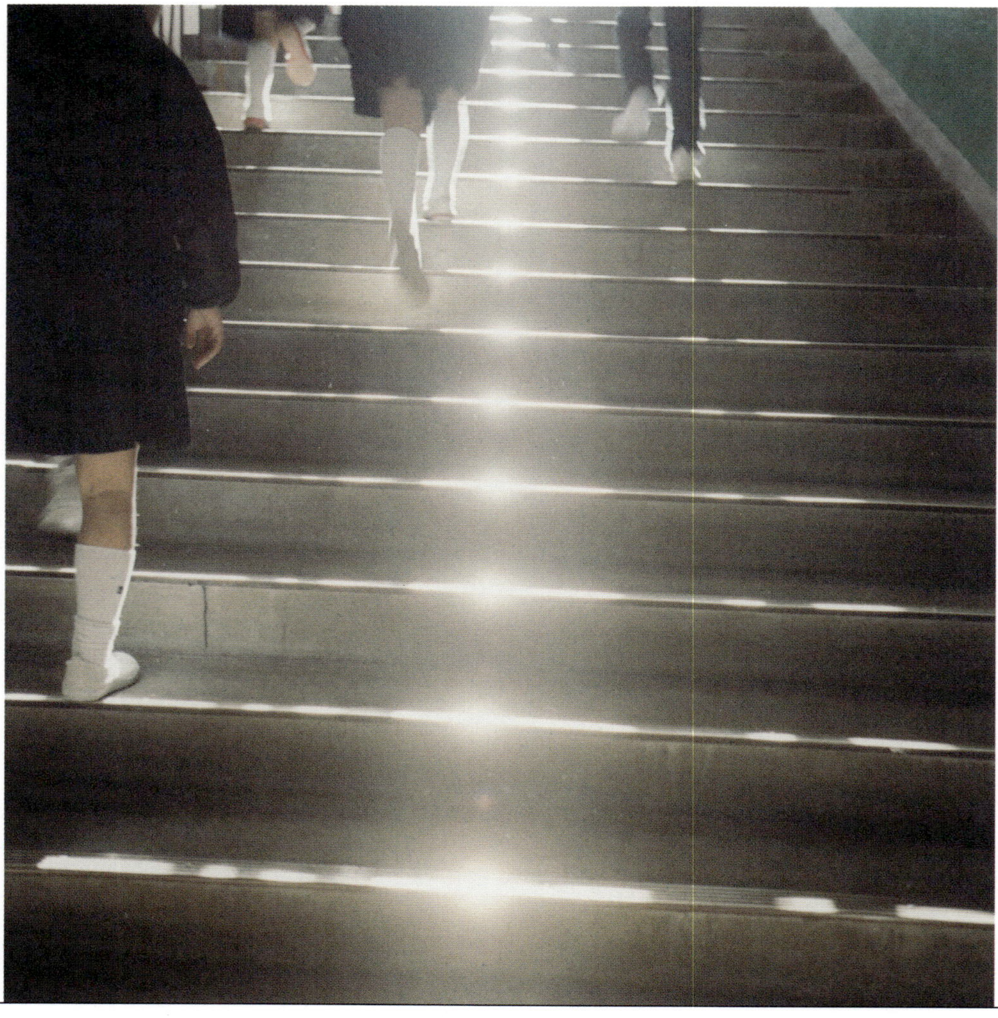

Kawuachi has framed her shot so that the heads of her subjects are unseen, along with most of their bodies. Yet what she chooses to show makes for a powerful composition. It seems as though the people are heading en masse to a promised land and the viewer is being invited to follow them. She prompts the viewer into letting his or her imagination run wild; perhaps her subjects are walking up a stairway to heaven or boarding an alien spaceship. But as much as the image is beguiling and entrancing, it also provokes a sense of unease and trepidation. There is no way of knowing what lies ahead – what is beyond the frame remains unknown, as she reminds the viewer of photography's fickleness. You are at the mercy of the image.

This photograph was published in Kawauchi's twelfth book, *Illuminance* (2011). Like many of her photographs, it evokes simultaneous feelings of wonder and apprehension. One of Kawauchi's great skills is her ability to allow myriad emotions to coexist in a single frame and across the sequences she creates in her books. The reader admires the most inexplicably beautiful of sights but at the same time feels ill at ease, swinging from melancholy to hope at the turn of the page or swipe of the screen. She reminds the viewer that hope and fear, joy and despair, beauty and the grotesque are never all that far apart. Ultimately, hers is an everyday mysticism, where transcendence seems but a step away. Kawauchi is a master of seeing, catching and communicating glimpses of the sublime in the commonplace in the most poetic of ways.

+ PHOTOGRAPHER BIO
Japanese, b. 1972

+ GOOGLE THESE
Utatane (2001), *Ametsuchi* (2012–13)

+ WATCH THIS
Kawauchi discusses her work in 'Rinko Kawauchi contemplates the small mysteries of life' on the San Francisco Museum of Modern Art YouTube channel.

+ READ THIS
The River Embraced Me (2016) by Rinko Kawauchi.

Like This? Try These

- → Mayumi Hosokura
- → Lieko Shiga
- → Gueorgui Pinkhassov

NASA

Pillars of Creation

2015

In 1995, the Hubble Space Telescope captured a sight that would be seared into minds for decades to come. It was the majestic *Pillars of Creation*, showing pillars of interstellar gas and dust in the Eagle Nebula, a star-forming region, 6,500 light years away from Earth.

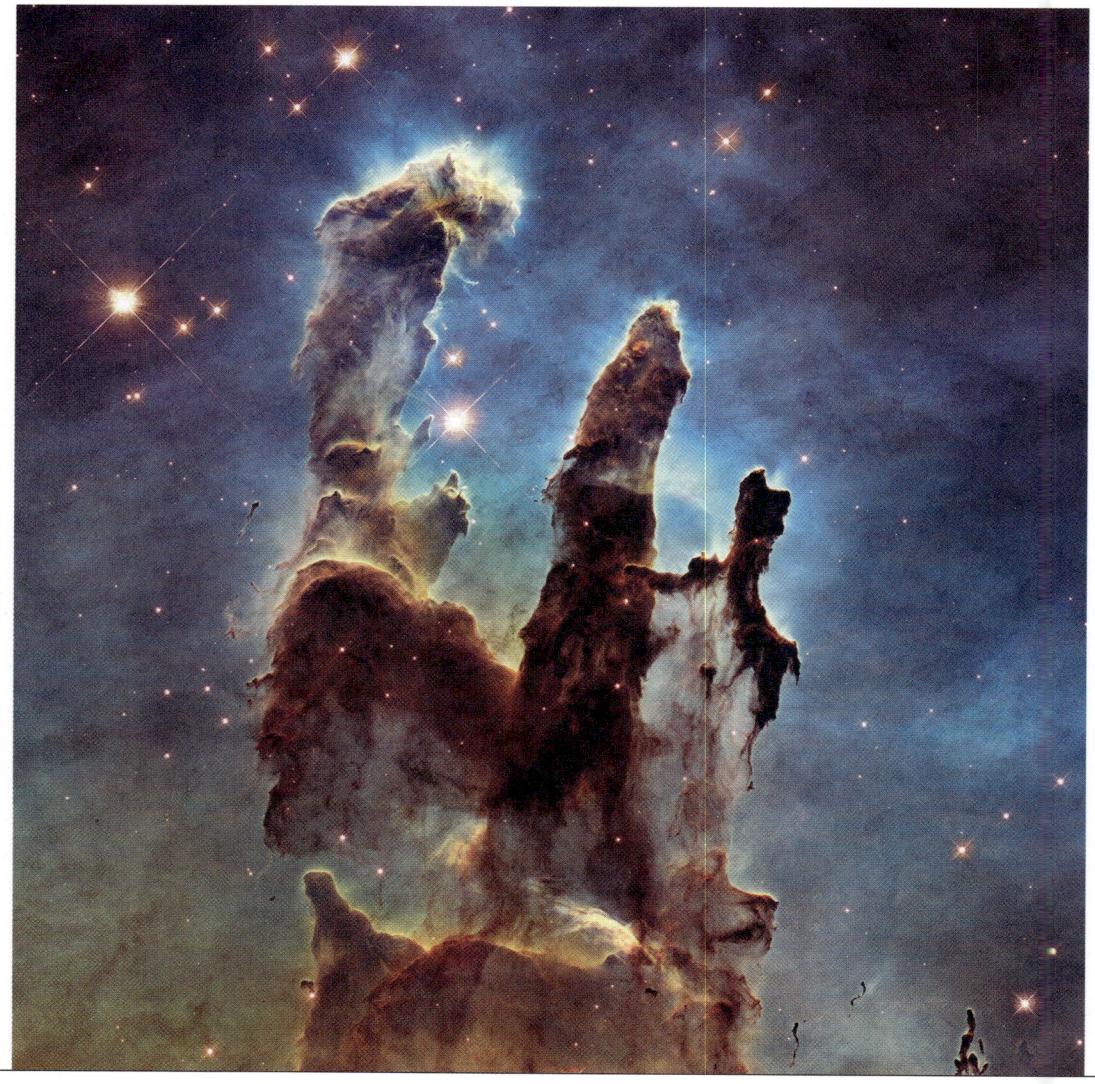

The image, which often appears in lists of top photographs, was a triumph of astronomical endeavour and has wowed audiences ever since its creation, its twinkling, dusty aesthetic perfectly calling to mind ideas of heaven or other spiritual worlds. Twenty years after the image was taken, in 2015, Hubble recorded the same region again on the occasion of its twenty-fifth anniversary, this time using Hubble's Wide Field Camera 3 installed in 2009. The result shown here was equally if not even more spectacular. With its rich, hazy spots of colour and undeniable presence, the updated version breathes new life into the most extraordinary of sights. The new image has better clarity, enabling astronomers to continue to study the changing state of this nebula in even greater detail. In this higher resolution view, light from oxygen, hydrogen and sulphur glows intensely blue, green and red respectively.

Despite its longstanding association with notions of creation, areas of the pillars are being eroded as the material heats up and then evaporates, and commentators have pointed to its new association with destruction. This image is one of the most compelling examples of photography's unrivalled ability to freeze its subjects in time: a mighty nebula shifting and evolving on its own terms, utterly oblivious to our humble planet, caught in a moment that will never happen again. It is tempting to over-philosophize such an image, reading it as a symbol of the transience of life or of mankind's insignificance. Nevertheless, the best images should take us out of ourselves and invite reflection on everything around us, which this picture certainly does.

+ GOOGLE THESE
NASA Earthrise (1968), *Astronaut Bruce McCandless Floats Above Earth, Untethered* (1984), *Ultraviolet Coverage of the Hubble Ultra Deep Field by The Hubble Space Telescope* (2014)

+ SEE THIS
Visit time.com for incredible images from the Hubble telescope: 100photos.time.com/photos/nasa-pillars-of-creation.

+ VISIT THIS
Visit NASA's YouTube channel for more incredible visuals.

Like This? Try These

- → hubblesite.org
- → robgendlerastropics.com
- → spacetelescope.org

Alessandra Sanguinetti

The Madonna, Buenos Aires, Argentina

2001

We are all likely to have dressed up and acted out plays at some point as children, allowing our imaginations to run wild. It is a way to learn who we are and our place in the world. So it is for Belinda and Guille in Alessandra Sanguinetti's celebrated series *The Adventures of Guille and Belinda and The Enigmatic Meaning of Their Dreams* (2003).

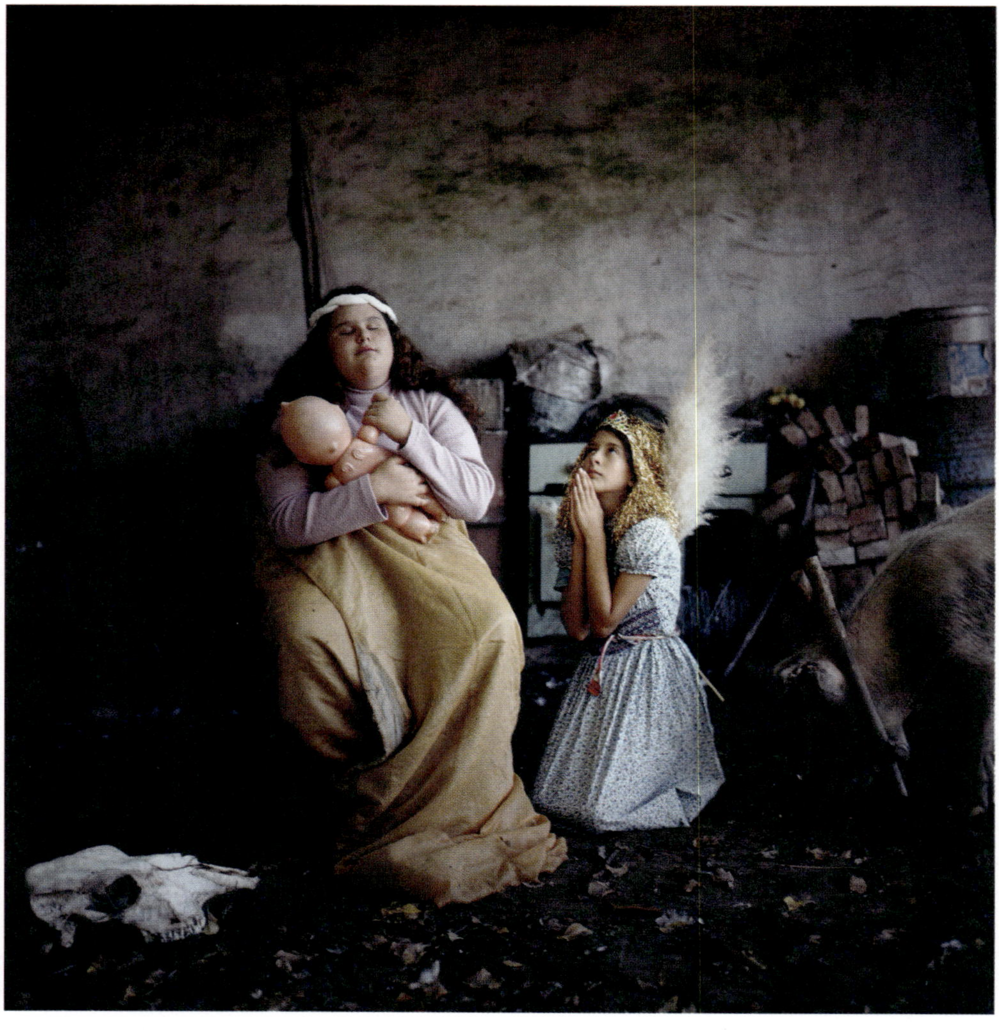

Together they act out what appears to be a scene from the Nativity. Sanguinetti met the young cousins at a remote farm outside Buenos Aires while she was working on a project about the relationship between animals and humans. She has said that the children were often around but it was not until the summer of 1999 when the girls were nine years old that she started paying attention to them. The girls were very close, and, intrigued by the way they were with each other, Sanguinetti began making photographs with them, suggesting ideas for scenes that they made their own. She photographed the cousins for five years, creating a remarkable body of work that lyrically and honestly paints a picture of the transition from childhood to adolescence and beyond.

In this image, as in others from the series, Sanguinetti perfectly captures a sense of of being carefree with a hint of childish awkwardness and earnestness, along with an impending sense of lost innocence. Of all the photographs in the series this is the one that most overtly blurs the boundary between fantasy and reality through its references to art and literature. It calls to mind the evocative and sometimes dreamlike portraits of British nineteenth-century photographer Julia Margaret Cameron, especially those that feature children acting out scenes from stories or dressed as angels. Cameron often drew on references from literature or painting, which she used to explore universal themes of life, love and death, and Sanguinetti does something similar here. Life and death, hope and faith, dreams and reality are bound up in the picture, sometimes literally so as with the presence of the animal skull. Guille with her eyes closed as though she is dreaming and Belinda's upward gaze accentuate the sense of being in between – between childhood and adulthood and between sleep and being awake – and we are reminded of the transience not just of childhood but also of life.

+ PHOTOGRAPHER BIO
American, b. 1968

+ GOOGLE THESE
Cecilia, Buenos Aires, Argentina (1995), *The Necklace, Buenos Aires, Argentina* (1999), *Ophelias, Buenos Aires, Argentina* (2001)

+ WATCH THIS
Go to icp.com to hear Alessandra Sanguinetti discuss her life and work as part of the International Center of Photography Lecture Series: icp.org/browse/archive/media/alessandra-sanguinetti.

Like This? Try These

- Julia Margaret Cameron
- Carla Kogelman
- Justine Kurland

Gregory Crewdson

Untitled

1998–2002

Gregory Crewdson's work is seldom discussed without reference to the cinematic. His use of light is always meticulously placed in the frame. He is known for his exceptional, almost obsessive, level of detail and everything – even the most seemingly insignificant item – is where it is for a reason. Another Crewdson hallmark is the uneasy atmosphere he creates in his work – there is a sense that something terrible is about to happen or has just happened. His eerily lit scenes are pregnant with possibility and dread.

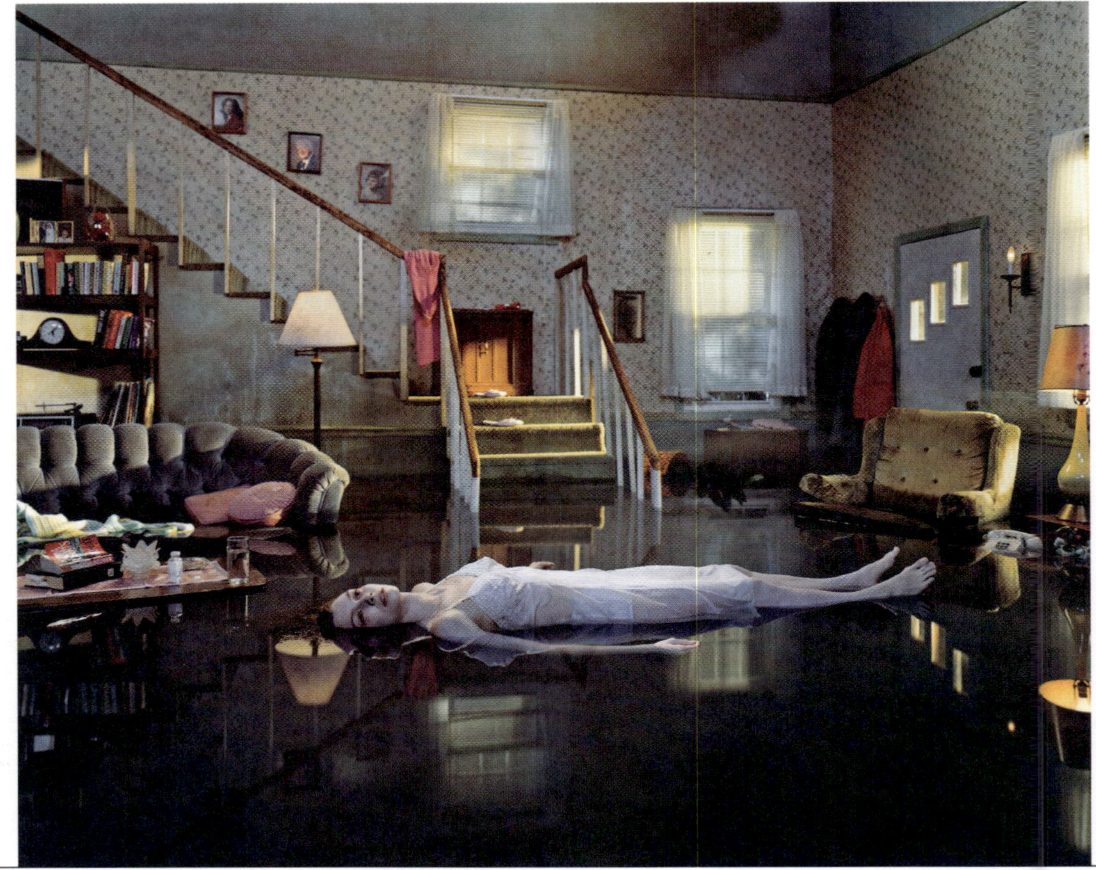

Crewdson often shoots his large-scale tableaux images at twilight. They evoke feelings of utter powerlessness. The sensation is as in a nightmare where we might desperately shout to get someone's attention in vain before disaster strikes, or inevitably wake up as we try to intervene. Likewise, in a Crewdson picture we always arrive too late and can only watch quizzically at what unfolds before our eyes. So it is with this image, which has obvious echoes of British artist John Everett Millais's *Ophelia* (1851–1852). But what on earth has happened?

Crewdson's images, which also channel Edward Hopper, David Lynch and Alfred Hitchcock, invite speculation but never offer answers. This photograph is no exception. As British art critic Adrian Searle said: 'It is almost impossible not to invent a story from Crewdson's scenes.' The catch is, there is no single story Crewdson is trying to tell, no obvious, absolute narrative to be deciphered. The woman is dead, we presume, but was she murdered, or did she take her own life? Is Crewdson trying to implicate the viewer? There is a strange sense of being in the scene and at the same time being a voyeur.

Crewdson's work draws on life in small-town America and what might lie behind closed doors. He is a master of staging scenes that are at once familiar yet mysterious, and real yet dreamlike. He has said that he looks to create something that feels ordinary and is tinged with beauty and terror. As is the case with Crewdson's finest images, such as this one, the more you look, the more you notice. Conversely, the less you really see or know. It is a conundrum of a picture that delights in its deliberate slipperiness.

+ PHOTOGRAPHER BIO
American, b. 1962

+ GOOGLE THESE
Natural Wonder (1992–1997), *Beneath the Roses* (2003–2008), *Sanctuary* (2009)

+ WATCH THIS
'Cathedral of the Pines' (2013–2014) on the Gagosian Quarterly at gagosian.com.

+ DISCOVER THIS
Crewdson's *Beneath the Roses* (2008) cost as much as a mid-budget movie, the *Guardian* reported in 2017, and four city streets were closed to make the shots that required rain and snow-making machines.

Like This? Try These

- Philip-Lorca diCorcia
- Hannah Starkey
- Jeff Wall

Trent Parke

Five-year-old Little Jack Watches 'The Simpsons' on Television in a Caravan in Cairns, Australia

2003

This photograph by Trent Parke belongs to his acclaimed series *Minutes to Midnight* made when he travelled 90,000 km (55,923 miles) around his native Australia in 2003.

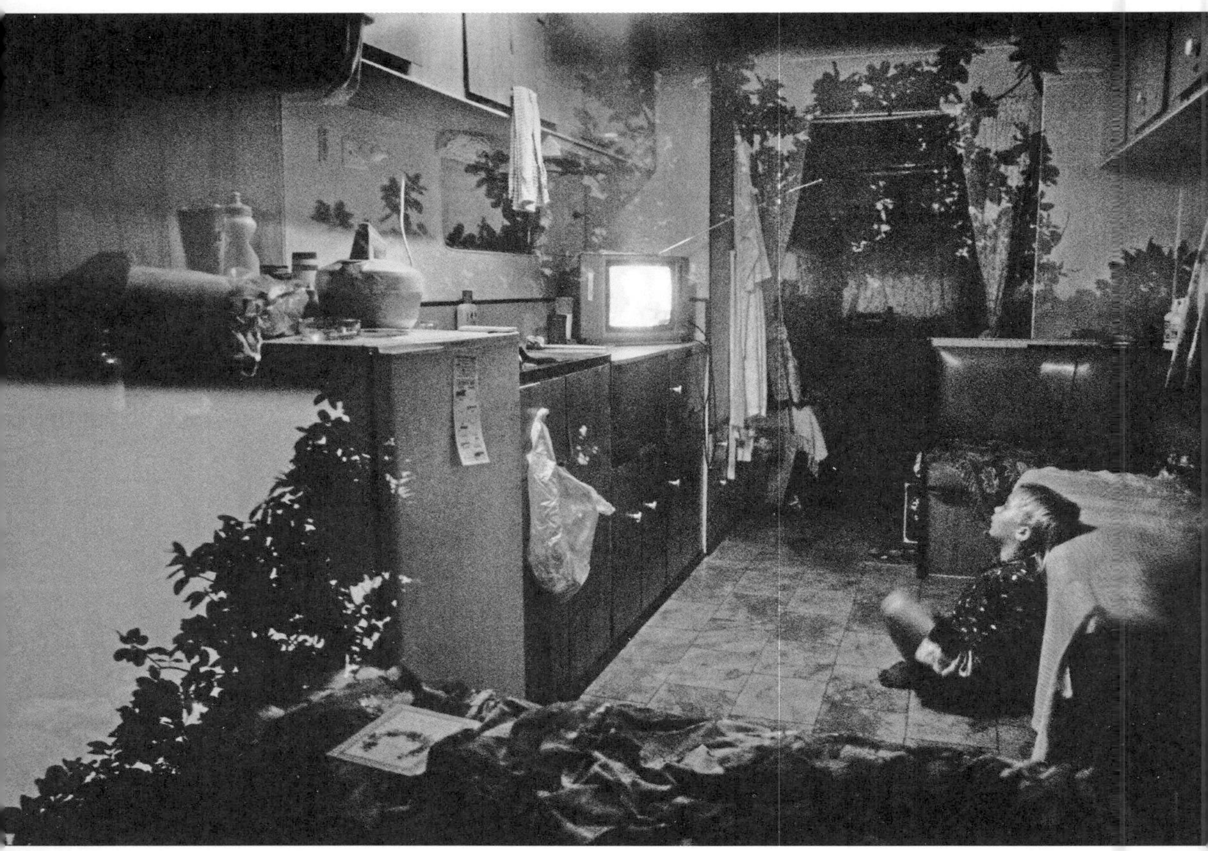

Much of the enjoyment this image provides comes from discovering elements that may not have come to light on a first look – tiny domestic details that gradually make themselves known and can be pieced together to form a jigsaw or a sketch, an impression of life. Simultaneously depicting inside and outside, the photograph invites us to pause and think about what might be going on. The shadowy silhouetted leaves and branches appear projected onto the scene, while the glaring, hypnotizing television set dominates. Together, they create a dreamlike feel. The interplay of light and dark transform what is an ordinary, unremarkable scene of a young boy watching television in a caravan into something far more sinister.

Can a picture tell a story or multiple stories? Parke's certainly can and do. He has spoken about his work being autobiographical: coming from his subconscious as well as from his experiences. The latter include witnessing his mother die from an asthma attack when he was thirteen years old. Perhaps we recognize a young Trent Parke in the child, unaware of the tragedy that is to come.

Parke has said he wants *Minutes to Midnight* to show what life was like in Australia. Consequently, we might read this image in many ways and trace many narratives. Possibly the claustrophobic scene depicted is a microcosm of a country trapped inside its own neuroses or sleepwalking into an uncertain future. Whatever we choose to take away from such a picture, Parke's masterpiece is a reminder that life plays out precariously between what we know and can control, and what we cannot.

+ PHOTOGRAPHER BIO
Australian, b. 1971

+ GOOGLE THESE
Moving Bus, Martin Place, Sydney (2002), *Caravan Park, Queensland, Australia* (2003), *Coober Pedy, South Australian Outback* (2004), *Wiluna, Outback Western Australia* (2004)

+ READ THIS
Minutes to Midnight (2005) by Trent Parke.

Like This? Try These

- Katrin Koenning
- Mary Ellen Mark
- Raphaela Rosella

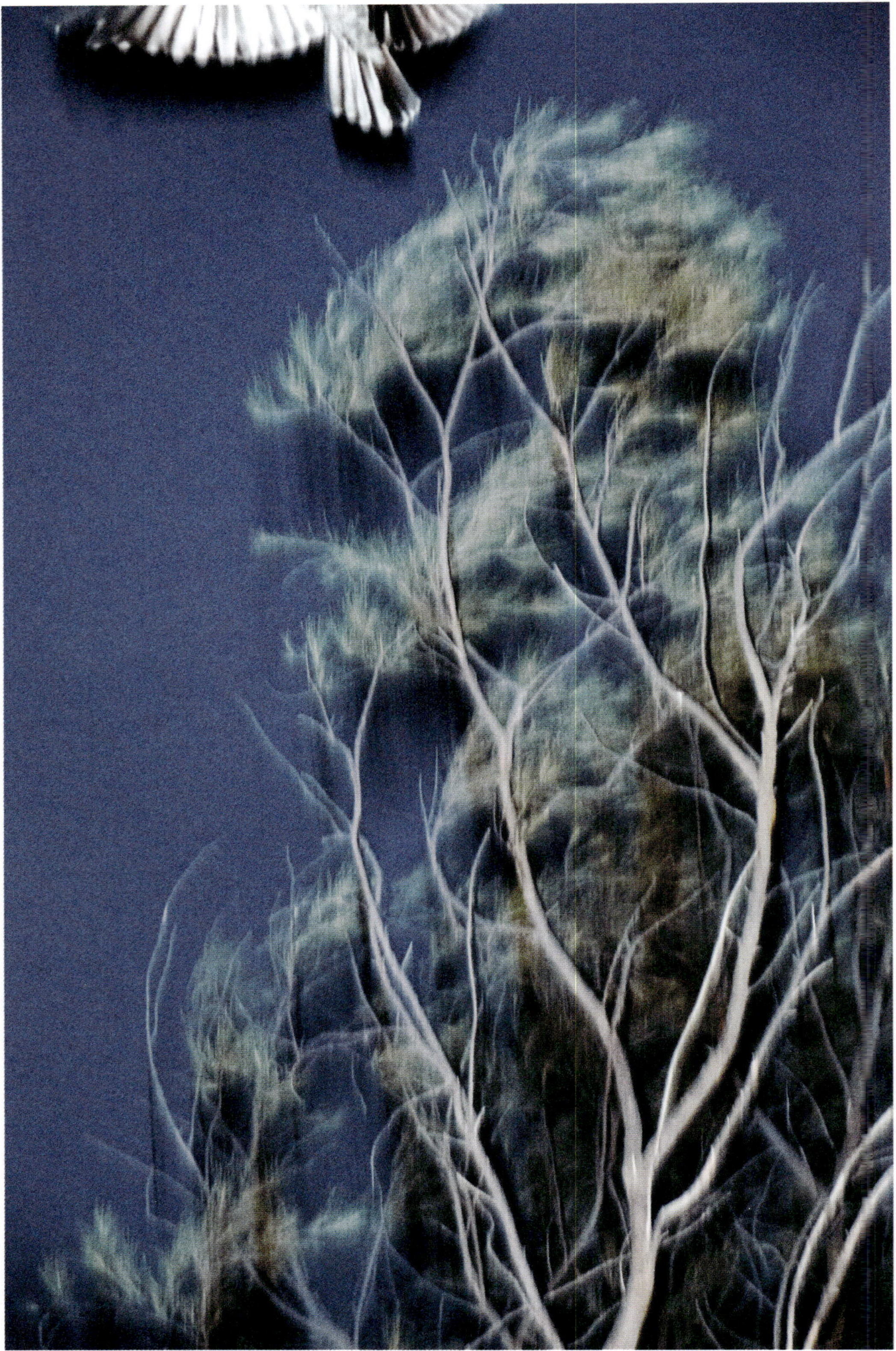

Sohrab Hura

The Crow that Escaped, India

2015

Perhaps the most fundamental way photography differs from film is in the depiction of movement. A photograph can only give an impression of motion of course, whereas film can record a moving subject in a more literal way. But within the boundaries of what it is possible to capture in a still image, the results can be visually striking, thought-provoking and deeply profound.

Indian photographer and member of the Magnum Photos cooperative Sohrab Hura regards stills as 'just a part of the larger idea of an image.' For Hura, images can be still, moving or even text and sound, and he has no problem mixing up and moving between these media. Even his stills appear to be moving. This dreamlike, evocative photograph is from his long-term project *The Lost Head & the Bird* (2014–18) that uses India's coastline as a lens through which to reexamine the nation's changing politics and society. Hura created an installation with a projection and soundtrack that played with movement and challenged the very limits of photography. From the sense of the wind in the swaying trees to the bird disappearing out of the frame and even the hint of light in the dark sky, everything is moving. It is a moment that is at once impermanent and everlasting.

Hura has said that what he was trying to photograph in the project as a whole is 'a pulse of the world that I was living in, here in India.' If you look through the images, which were taken along the Indian coastline, you will see that everything is alive, everything is fluid. In this work, Hura artfully blends reality and storytelling to give an impression of a country in political and social turmoil. He has said that the divisive politics, a surge in nationalism and terrible violence that was happening around him when he took the photograph felt 'unreal' and 'absurd', and this influenced the way he shot the pictures. We sense that unrest and uncertainty in this image, even though there are no people visible in it. As is often the case with Hura's images, there is a rawness to the photograph and, perhaps perversely, a quiet stillness too. This is a mysterious, magical image, which is incredibly visceral. It is as though the viewer has glimpsed behind a curtain into another world and what passes by is as in a dream.

+ PHOTOGRAPHER BIO
Indian, b. 1981

+ GOOGLE THESE
Tree Outside the House, India (2013), *Streetlight Outside the House, India* (2013), *The Bat and the Tree in Blossom, India* (2015)

+ LISTEN TO THIS
Photographer Ben Smith interviews Hura for the *A Small Voice* podcast.

Like This? Try These

- → Yoshinori Mizutani
- → Raghu Rai
- → Dayanita Singh

+ **PHOTOGRAPHER BIO**
Portuguese, b. 1977

+ **GOOGLE THESE**
Siloquies and Soliloquies on Death Life and Other Interludes (2016), *Family* (2016)

+ **READ THIS**
'Edgar Martins: Inside Out' on the British Journal of Photography website at: bjp-online.com.

Edgar Martins

Sometimes the Right Stuff is in Fact the Wrong Stuff

2019

What you see when dreaming is frequently topsy-turvy, nonsensical and muddled; it is almost real or familiar, but not quite, things are semi-recognizable and strange sights abound. Edgar Martins's image possesses a similar strangeness.

The viewer struggles to know to know what they are looking at and what it means. It is an image that deliberately evades comprehension, simultaneously unsettling, perplexing and absurd. The pendulum-like object looks as though it is part of the photograph, but on closer inspection, perhaps the circle has been added. The viewer wonders why and ponders whether Martins took the picture or if it is a found photograph. Whatever the truth, the image sparks myriad questions.

The photograph belongs to Martins's cryptically titled series *What Photography and Incarceration Have in Common with an Empty Vase* (2016–), which he made in collaboration with inmates from HM Prison Birmingham, their families and Grain Projects, an arts organization supported by Arts Council England and Birmingham City University. The project is complex and multifaceted as Martins examines the concept of absence and the consequences of enforced separation from a loved one through images, text, film, audio and installation. He presents an alternative view of what it means to be incarcerated

Martins's search to discover how you can picture something you cannot see, leads him to question the status of the photograph itself and the perception that it is a document of truth, which is unwaveringly trustworthy. Such questioning of the reliability of the photographic image is visible here: Martins has manipulated his subject to cast doubt over the scene so that we cannot trust that what the photograph is showing is real. The image explores absence as a concept by covering the subject's face. In doing so, Martins brutally severs any sense of connection or understanding we may have hoped to have with the subject. He plays with what is and is not seen, and consequently undermines photography's purpose. The more you look, the less you see, and at the same time your longing to see more, to know more, intensifies.

Like This? Try These

→ Laia Abril

→ Adam Broomberg and Oliver Chanarin

→ Clare Strand

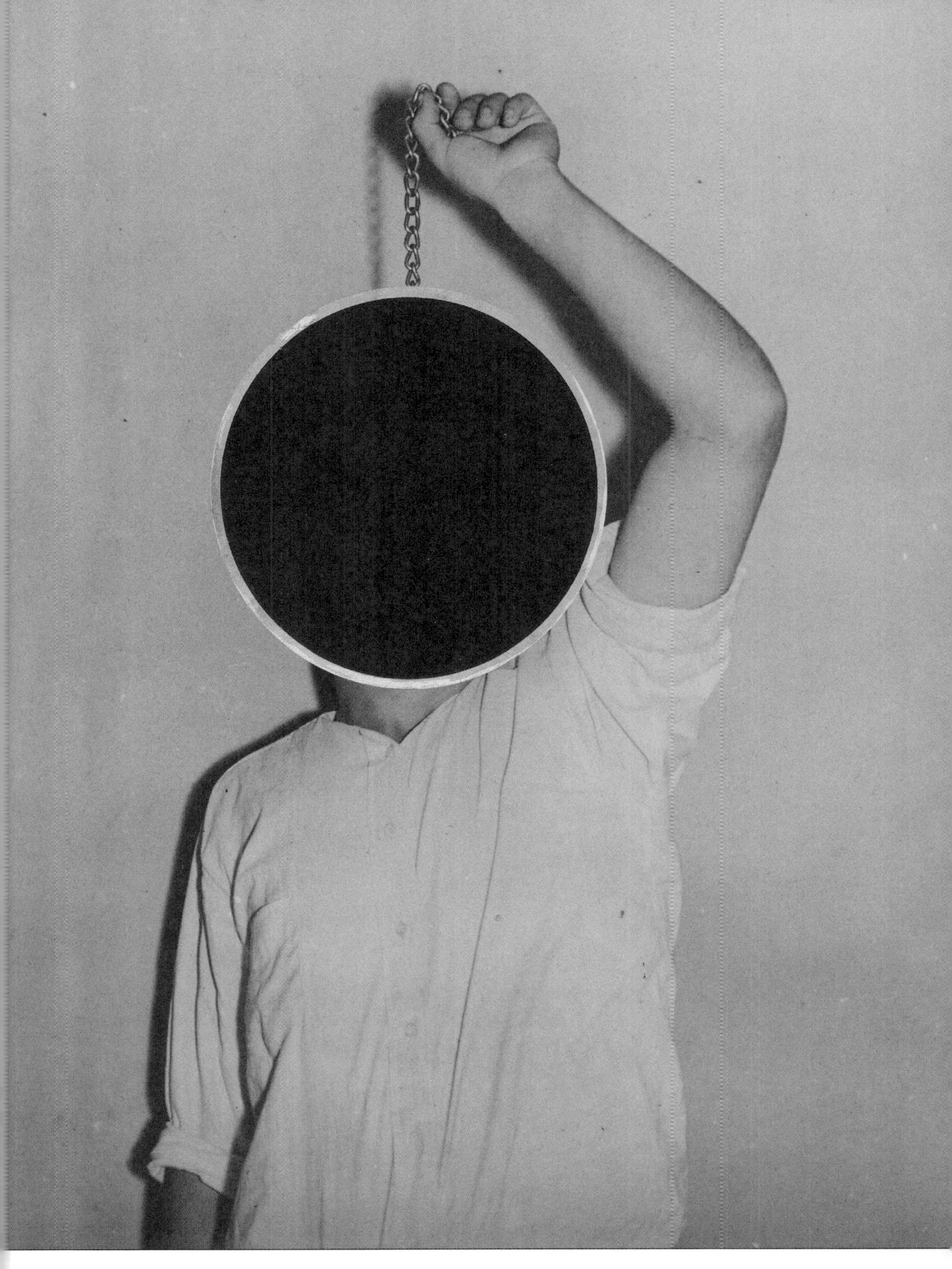

CHAPTER

7

REAPPRAISING THE EVERYDAY

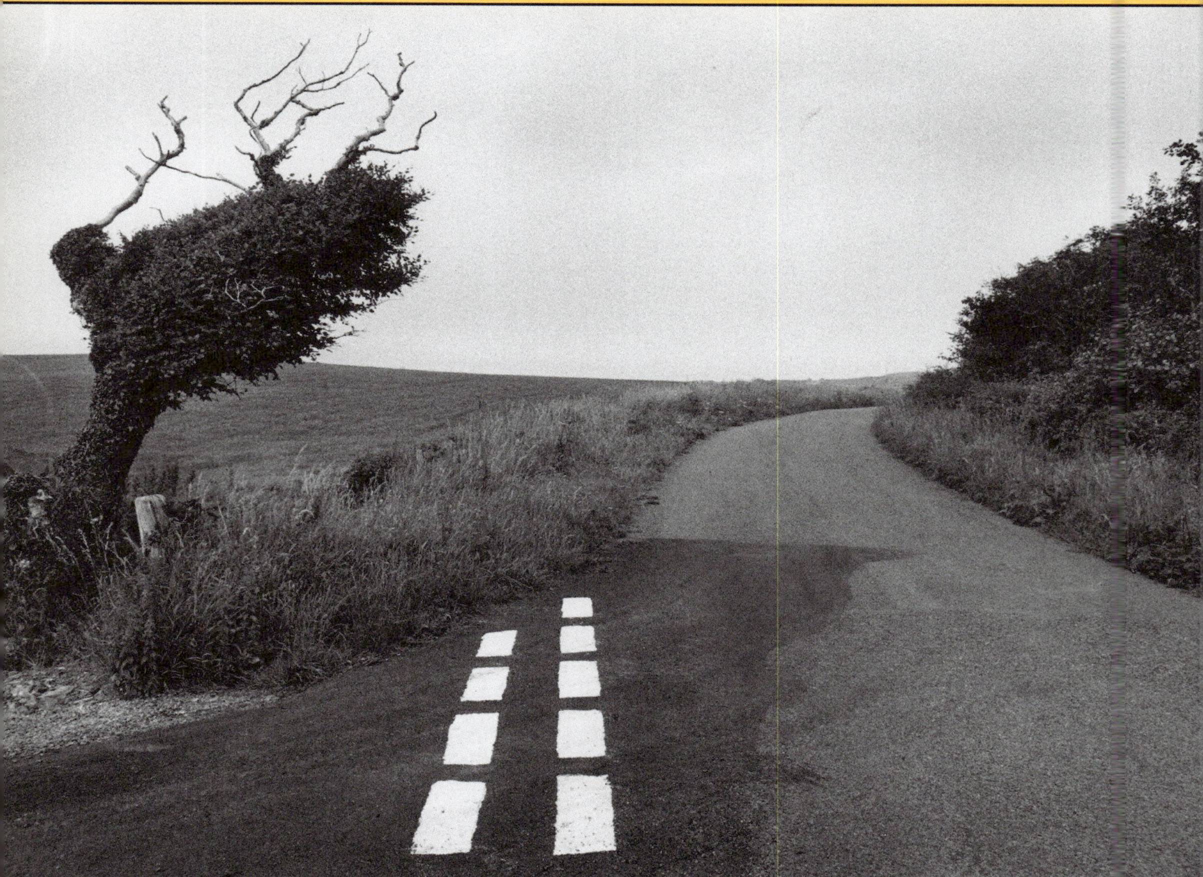

 Josef Koudelka—England

Josef Koudelka

England

1978

Among Josef Koudelka's most well-known works are the images he made of gypsies and Roma culture in then Czechoslovakia, and his photographs of the Soviet-led invasion of Prague in 1968. However, Koudelka's gift for creating images that are imbued with such natural visual poetry can be found in quieter works such as this unassuming photograph of a crooked tree and winding road in England.

Koudelka fled his native Czechoslovakia for England in 1970 where he sought political asylum. He was based in the country for some years although he frequently travelled to Europe, photographing whatever resonated with him in any given moment. He was formally stateless for a time and commentators often describe him as photographer who wandered or a displaced figure.

We can only imagine what made Koudelka pause and click the shutter at this precise spot on this day in 1978, perhaps during one of his wanderings. Yet to try to guess his motivation misses the point. It is more interesting to look at the photograph in a bid to uncover the visual resonances contained within. For there is much to take in and enjoy in a picture that some may consider unremarkable. There is a sense of restlessness in the picture that plays out not least in the presence of the road that metaphorically winds its way to an unknown, invisible future. There are hidden visual delights that help to knit the picture together, such as the echo between the shape of the tree and its spiky branches and tarmacked road. The individual components of a tree, road, sky and field are not especially noteworthy, but by bringing them together in the way he has, Koudelka elevates them to a higher plane, creating an image that is far greater than the sum of its parts.

+ PHOTOGRAPHER BIO
Czech-French, b. 1938

+ GOOGLE THESE
A Young Gypsy Suspected of Being Guilty Takes Part in a Murder Reconstruction, Jarabina, Czechoslovakia (1963), *Festival of Gypsy Music, Straznice, Czechoslovakia* (1966), *Invasion 68 Prague* (1968)

+ READ THIS
Sean O'Hagan's interview with Koudelka '40 years on: the exile comes home to Prague' on 24 August 2008 at Guardian.com.

Like This? Try These

- → Henri Cartier-Bresson
- → Bruce Davidson
- → Mario Giacomelli

Peter Mitchell

Untitled (Note 39)

2015

It is unlikely you have ever seen a scarecrow pictured like this. The anthropomorphic qualities and sense of motion are staggering. It is one of many Peter Mitchell photographed in his home county of Yorkshire from 1974 to 2015.

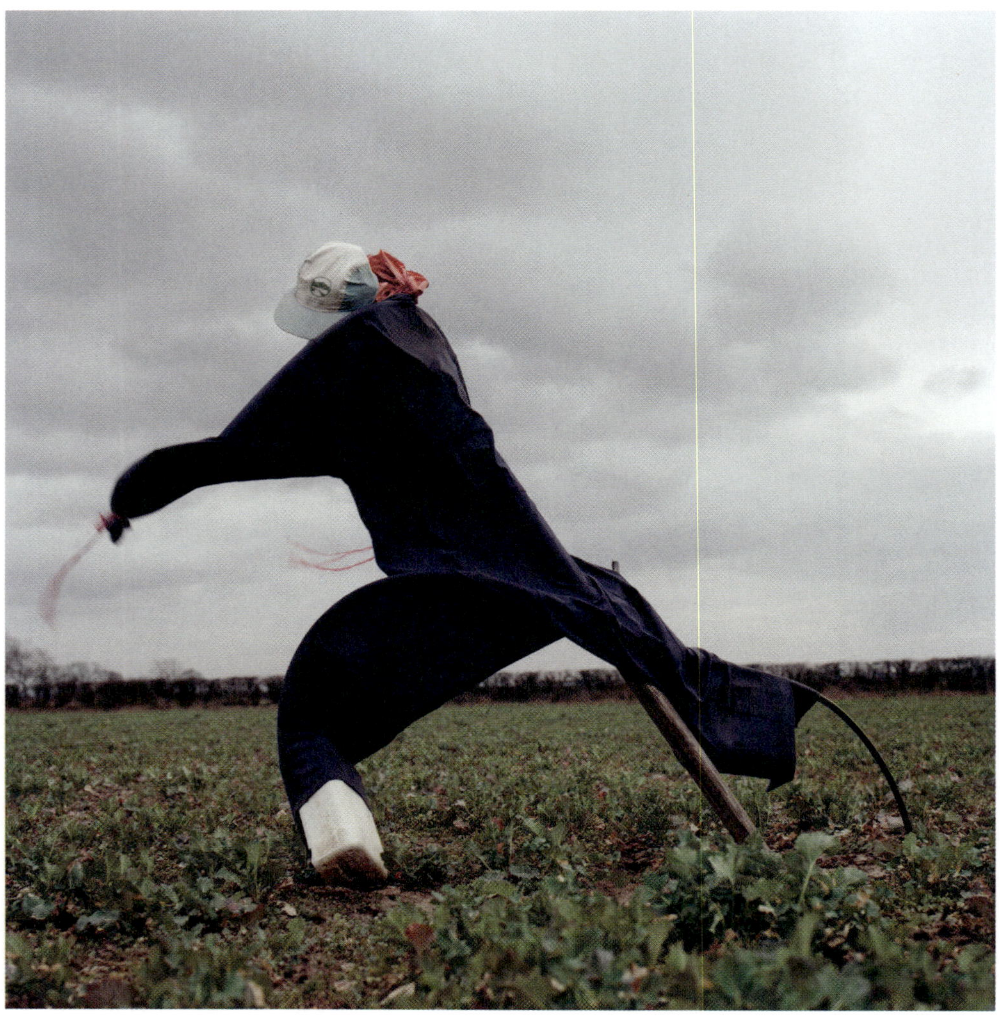

This well-dressed, eccentric scarecrow looks like it has places to go and people to see. Lurching across a field and out of the frame, his head down and arms outstretched, he does not have time to wait and is fixated on getting where he wants to go, wherever that may be. He will of course never reach his destination and instead remain pinned to the ground as if in a state of purgatory. Still, it seems he keeps trying, even though his actions are futile.

It is strange to speak about an inanimate object as though it is a person, but scarecrows are meant to resemble humans and this one seems more human than most others. The image was published in Mitchell's book *Some Thing Means Everything to Somebody* (2015), in which his uncanny knack of capturing the essence of each scarecrow's personality is evident. The book is also a visual autobiography in which photographs of Mitchell's most treasured possessions are interspersed with his portraits of scarecrows. A self-proclaimed collector of junk, Mitchell arranges the images chronologically as he builds the narrative of his life in photographic form. He has said the scarecrows allude to different aspects of his personality and this image is certainly the work of an observant if unconventional eye.

When English writer Geoff Dyer wrote about Mitchell's scarecrows for the *New York Times*, he said that a photograph can make you conscious of the thing in a way the thing itself never did, or rather, it can make you aware of the thing of which you were barely conscious. Mitchell's photograph does exactly that: suddenly we wonder why we have never noticed these hodgepodge creations before.

+ PHOTOGRAPHER BIO
British, b. 1943

+ GOOGLE THESE
A New Refutation of the Viking 4 Space Mission (1979), *Ghost Train, Francis Gavan, Woodhouse Moor, Leeds* (1986)

+ READ THIS
Some Thing Means Everything to Somebody (2015) by Peter Mitchell.

Like This? Try These

→ John Bulmer

→ Anna Fox

→ Martin Parr

Peter Marlow

Room of Kosovan Asylum Seeker Mehdi Saliuku, Walpole Bay Hotel, Margate

2002

This perfectly pleasant but very ordinary bedroom could belong to any number of British hotels. It just so happens to be room 22 in Margate's Walpole Bay Hotel, a family-run establishment that was built in 1914.

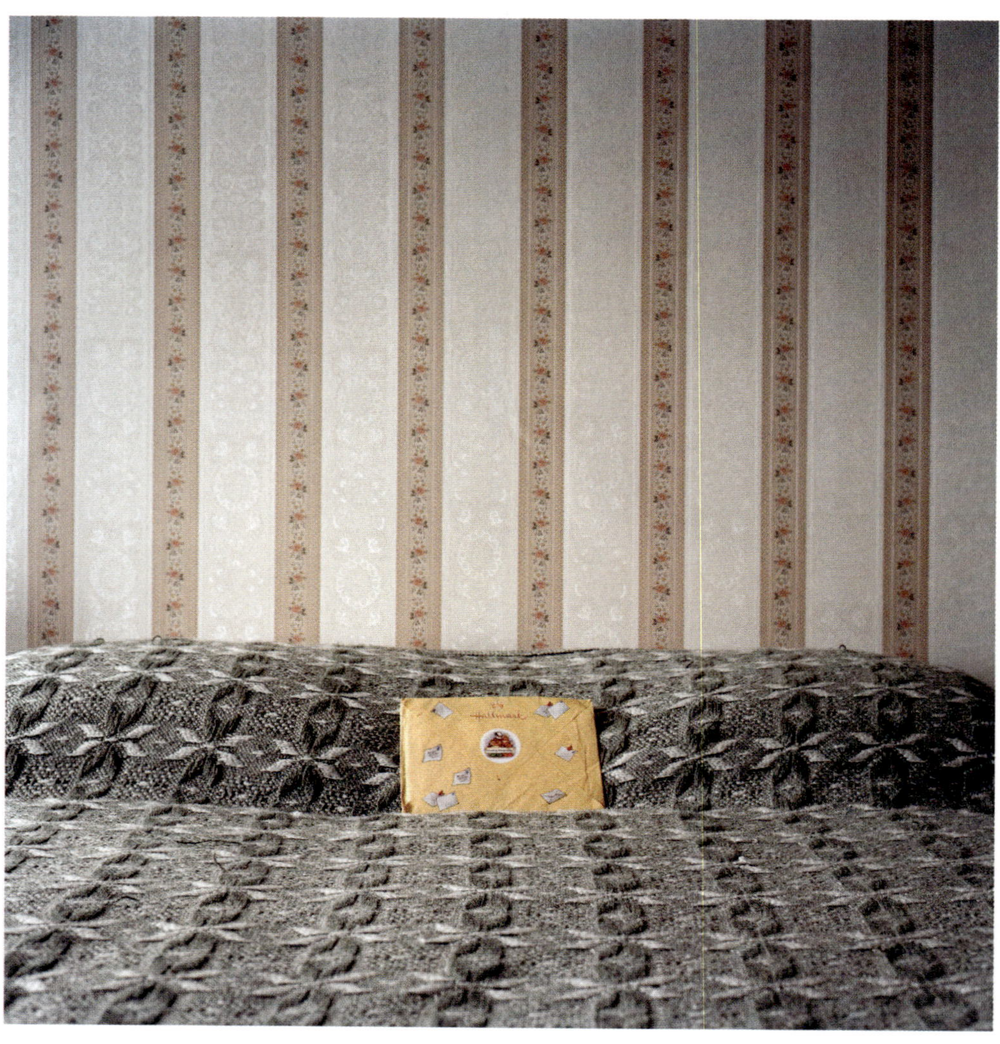

In Peter Marlow's photograph, nothing but part of the bed with its elaborate if slightly chintzy cover, the wallpaper-covered wall behind and what appears to be an envelope neatly propped up against the pillows are visible. At a glance, you may not think it to be a very photo-worthy subject, but Marlow saw potential and wielded his camera in such a way so as to make something of the scene.

The photograph with its delicate colours, beautiful soft light and expertly considered composition is interesting enough to look at and study from a purely aesthetic point of view, but there is more: at the time the picture was taken, the room was in fact home to Kosovan asylum seeker Mehdi Saliuku who came to England in 1998. When Marlow took the photograph in 2002, Saliuku had been fighting extradition since his arrival in the UK. An accompanying caption explains that he received help from the hotel's owners in this fight. Suddenly, what on the surface looks to be a very unremarkable scene takes on new significance. We begin to imagine what this man might have been like. Perhaps he had a family. What happened to make him travel to the UK in search of a new life? What had he been through? What or rather who did he leave behind? And now, years since the photograph was made, we might wonder, was he ever allowed to stay? We will likely never know.

The story, we can assume, begins and ends with this photograph. Such is the cruelty of photography, a medium that stops time in its tracks, that pulls back the curtain on a life or lives lived for just a moment, but ultimately leaves an incomplete narrative in its wake. That something as soulless as a hotel room could be home for a fellow human is a sobering thought. Marlow's haunting photograph, as deceptively simple as it first appears, is a reminder of photography's power to say so much through so little.

+ PHOTOGRAPHER BIO
British, 1952–2016

+ GOOGLE THESE
Liverpool – Looking Out to Sea (1982–90), *The English Cathedral* (2008–12)

+ LISTEN TO THIS
A recording of Marlow being interviewed by Adrian Arbib at the Pitt Rivers Museum in 2010, in 'Peter Marlow Interview' on the PittRiversound channel on SoundCloud, at soundcloud.com.

Like This? Try These

- → Peter Fraser
- → Mark Power
- → Alec Soth

Martin Parr

A Couple in a Café, New Brighton, England

1985

The awkwardness is almost unbearable, the silence deafening. You wonder if there is a point in every couple's life where they run out of things to say.

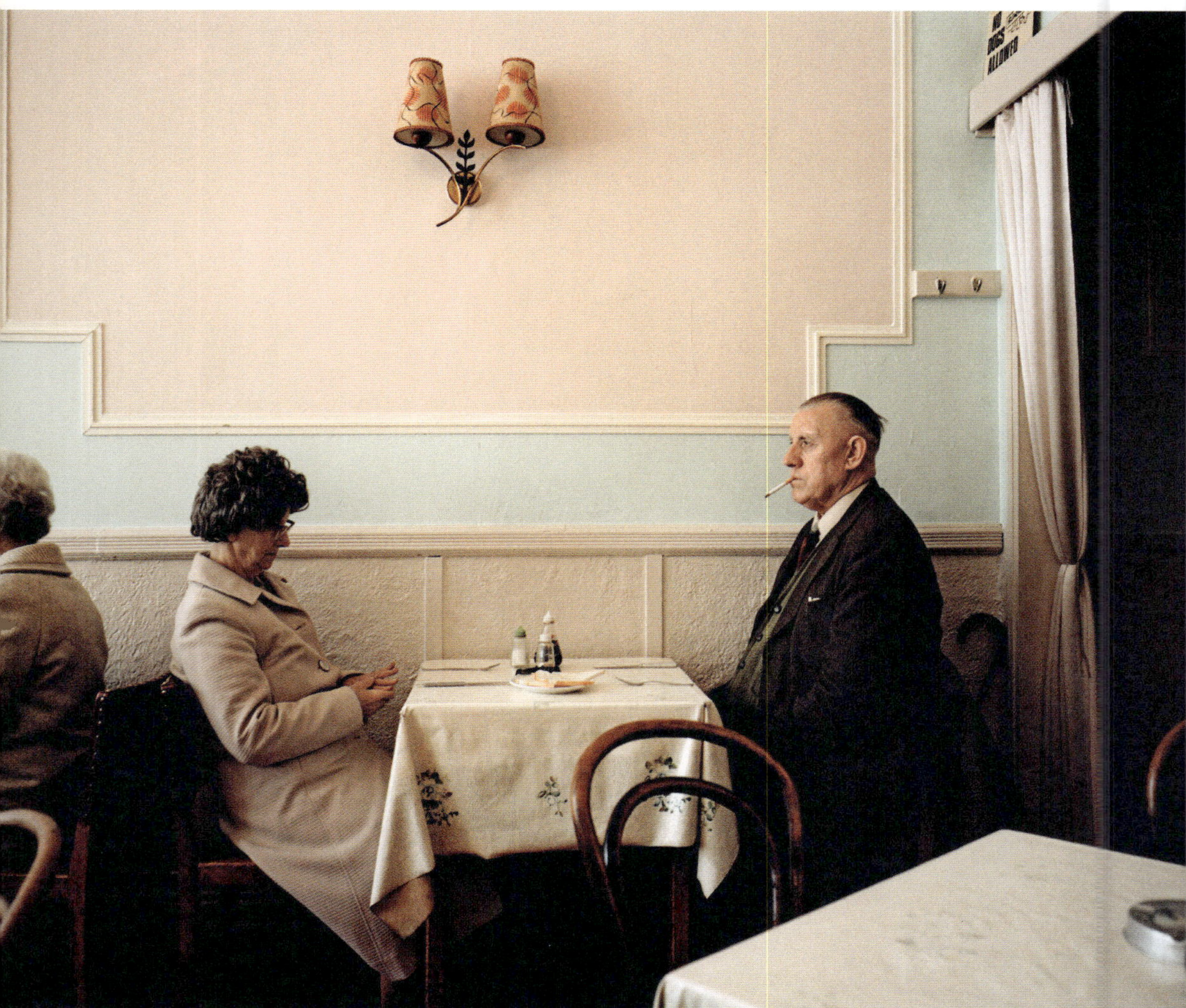

Few photographs comment so profoundly on the nature of disconnect as this one, which does so through the depiction of an ordinary occurrence: two people sitting in a café. Who would have thought such a scene could be the stuff of great photography? With the woman to the left chopped in half by the frame, the photograph presents a slice of life photographically and figuratively. We know nothing about the two protagonists, except that they are sitting in a café in New Brighton, Wirral, Merseyside, where no dogs are allowed. What has been said – or unsaid – we do not know.

Martin Parr is a master of the shrewd capture, a wry cultural commentator whose distinctive brand of observational photography divides opinion. His satirical photographs magnify tiny wrinkles. This has led some to criticize him for his ability to cruelly poke fun at his subjects and his voyeurism, while others praise his humour and perceptiveness.

This photograph belongs to *The Last Resort* (1983–1985), the series that helped to establish Parr's reputation. In this work he depicts life in the tired beach suburb of New Brighton in Liverpool at a time of economic difficulty in the Northwest of England. Parr said he wanted to show the decay of British society and this picture alone suggests the changing state of a nation that found itself rapidly unravelling.

+ PHOTOGRAPHER BIO
British, b. 1952

+ GOOGLE THESE
The Non-Conformists (2013), *Black Country Stories* (2014), *Ice-cream Van at Tenby Beach* (2018)

+ WATCH THIS
'Martin Parr: Photography is a Form of Therapy' on the Tate YouTube channel.

Like This? Try These

- Chris Killip
- David Moore
- Tom Wood

Paul Graham

Roundabout, Andersonstown, Belfast

1984

If ever there was an example of a photograph where nothing and everything is happening this is surely one. At first glance, the viewer sees an ordinary suburban roundabout that could be in any town in the UK. The sun is shining but there is not a lot going on. So why would anyone stop and take a photograph?

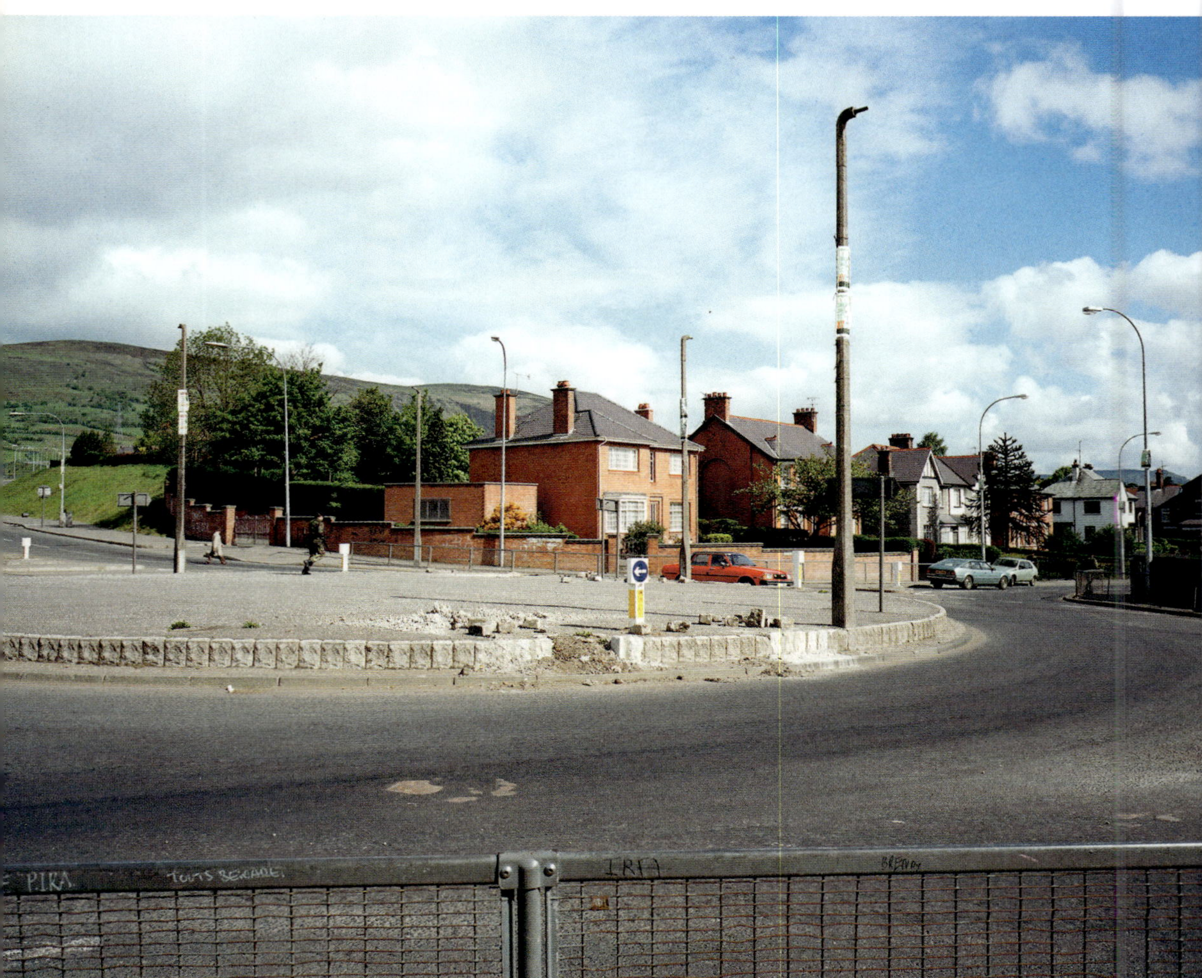

This is a view that the average British person will have seen a hundred times as a pedestrian and yet somehow the image invites closer inspection. Gradually details come to light: broken kerbstones and damaged street lights, nationalist graffiti on the railings in the foreground and three armed soldiers in camouflage gear walking away in the distance. Suddenly the scene does not look so innocuous.

Upon learning that the photograph is from British photographer Paul Graham's series *Troubled Land* (1987), which examines the charged landscapes of Northern Ireland in the 1980s, the image starts to make sense. This is Belfast, a place shaken to the core by conflict, where streets bear the visible scars of violence. Using available light, it seems as though Graham has approached photographing the scene in a documentary way, although there is something exceptionally considered about the photograph – every element is carefully positioned in the frame and woven tightly into the composition. He photographs a scruffy roundabout in an urban residential area with the kind of care normally afforded to a landscape. Vivid clouds and sky and rolling hills should lift spirits but offer little cheer here. The idea of the violence that has taken place is made all the more chilling by the bright jeering sun.

This is a quiet picture where time is as much a part of the photograph as the landscape depicted. The notion of time is an important one to Graham whose work engages with the world in deep and complex ways. Yet this is fitting given his attitude to photography: '…it has steadily become less important to me that the photographs are about something in the most obvious way. I am interested in more elusive and nebulous subject matter. The photography I most respect pulls something out of the ether of nothingness … You can't sum up the results in a single line.'

+ PHOTOGRAPHER BIO
British, b. 1956

+ GOOGLE THESE
Television Portrait (Cathy, London) (1989), *American Night* (2003), *A Shimmer of Possibility* (2007)

+ WATCH THIS
Graham discusses his work in 'Paul Graham: The Whiteness of the Whale', a video on the Pier 24 Photography channel on Vimeo.

Like This? Try These

- → Anthony Haughey
- → Kim Haughton
- → Paul Seawright

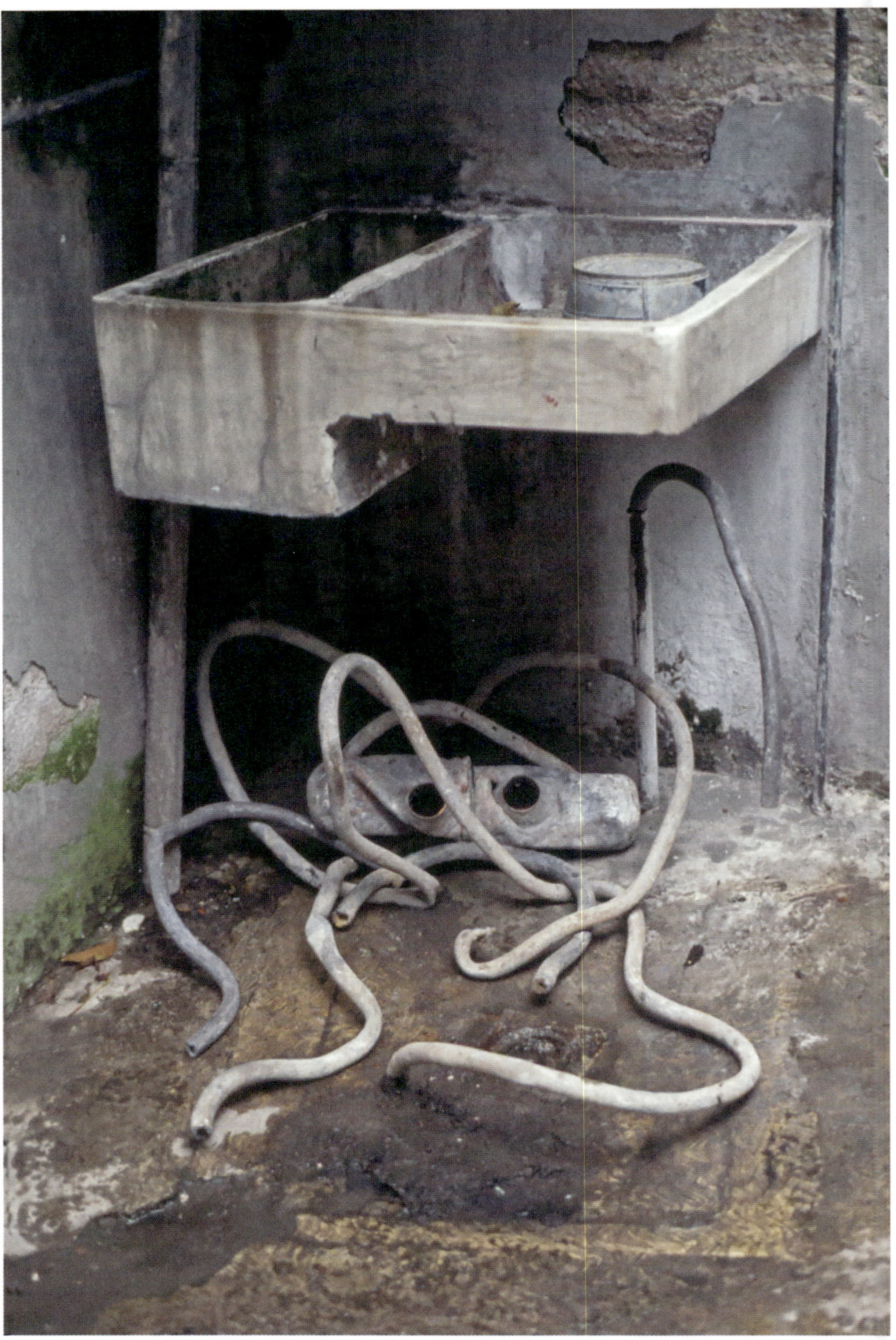

Gabriel Orozco

Octopus

1991

It is possible to be drawn into and to travel around Mexican artist Gabriel Orozco's photograph as you might a diagram, a blueprint or a map. The tangled pipes invite the viewer in and suddenly an insalubrious corner of a nondescript place becomes a site of fascination.

Orozco is a sculptor, photographer and conceptual artist known for responding to chance encounters with found objects or ready-mades. He photographs what he finds and sometimes also makes interventions. The ordinary is transformed in his work, as he imbues the apparently unremarkable with meaning in unexpected ways.

Among his interests is the lightening of mass – exploring how an object can be made lighter – and he has frequently used photography as a way to do this. As a two-dimensional object a photograph does not have mass in the same way that a three-dimensional sculpture does and, consequently, photography and sculpture remain locked in a dialogue.

For Orozco, who began using photography in his work in the mid 1980s, the camera is never merely a means to record or document. For him, the resulting photograph is always a composition in its own right. The photograph is the artwork. Spontaneity and a sense of play lie at the heart of all Orozco's work, whether he is working with sculpture, photography, installation, video or painting, and it is by remaining true to these principles that he is able to recast such apparently banal objects as items worthy of interest. That a tangle of old pipes should take the form of an octopus is testimony to Orozco's remarkable ability to see what others may miss. He does not only record what he sees, however, but enters into a dialogue with his subject that is dynamic, playful and in a sense, deeply profound.

– PHOTOGRAPHER BIO
Mexican, b. 1962

– GOOGLE THESE
Two Couples (1990–91), *Cats and Watermelons* (1992), *Ball on Water* (1994)

– WATCH THIS
Orozco discusses his work in a film on the Tate YouTube channel: 'Gabriel Orozco at Tate Modern'.

Like This? Try These

- Christian Boltanski
- Gordon Matta-Clark
- Richard Wentworth

Martin Roemers

Soviet Army Hospital, Jüterbog, former East Germany

1997

How do you photograph the aftermath of a conflict that never happened? This is the area of enquiry that Martin Roemers tackles in his epic project, *Relics of the Cold War* (1997–2009).

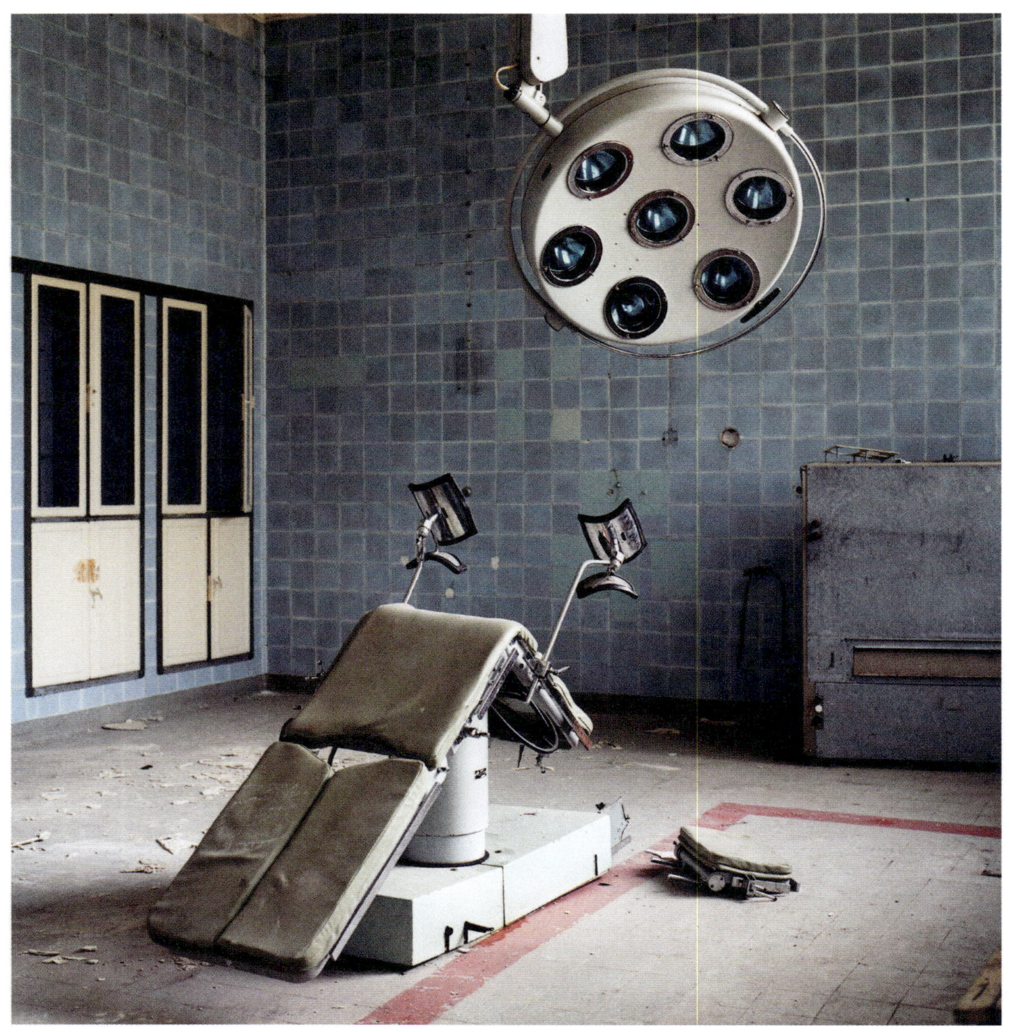

Roemers's project saw him visit ten countries including Russia, Poland, Germany and the UK as well as his home country of the Netherlands in his search for remnants of the Cold War (1947–1991) to photograph. He photographed everything from deserted army bases and military training areas to underground tunnels and rusty tanks. He also photographed inside an abandoned Soviet Army hospital at a military base in former East Germany as seen in this image. It is not immediately clear what we are looking at and Roemers does not give much away. The huge leering light, which draws our attention, looks like something from a science-fiction film. We could also be inside some kind of research facility at an aerospace agency. Although there are no people pictured in this eerie image of an abandoned site, a strong human presence remains. An uneasiness hangs in the air.

Roemers grew up during the Cold War, which was a period defined by division between Soviet Union and the United States and their respective allies, the Eastern Bloc and the Western Bloc. It was marked by mistrust, fear, hostility and an ever-present nuclear threat. He has spoken about how documenting the landscape of the Cold War allowed him to create a visual memorial to a conflict that never materialized. As time goes on, memories fade, and the process of decay takes hold as sites devoid of purpose are forgotten and left to rot. Superficially the photograph is not about much at all and yet there is a surreal beauty at work here, which calls us to pause and reflect on what might have been.

+ PHOTOGRAPHER BIO
Dutch, b. 1962

+ GOOGLE THESE
Trabant (1990–1991), *The Never-Ending War* (2004–05), *Metropolis* (2007–2015)

+ WATCH THIS
Martin Roemers discusses *Relics of the Cold War* on the Deutsches Historisches Museum YouTube channel.

Like This? Try These

- Sophie Ristelhueber
- Ambroise Tézenas
- Sara Terry

David Moore

from 'Pictures from the Real World'

1987–88

There is far more going on than initially appears in David Moore's slice-of-life masterpiece. It plays with notions of the frame, interior and exterior, near and far, and what it means to look, watch and see.

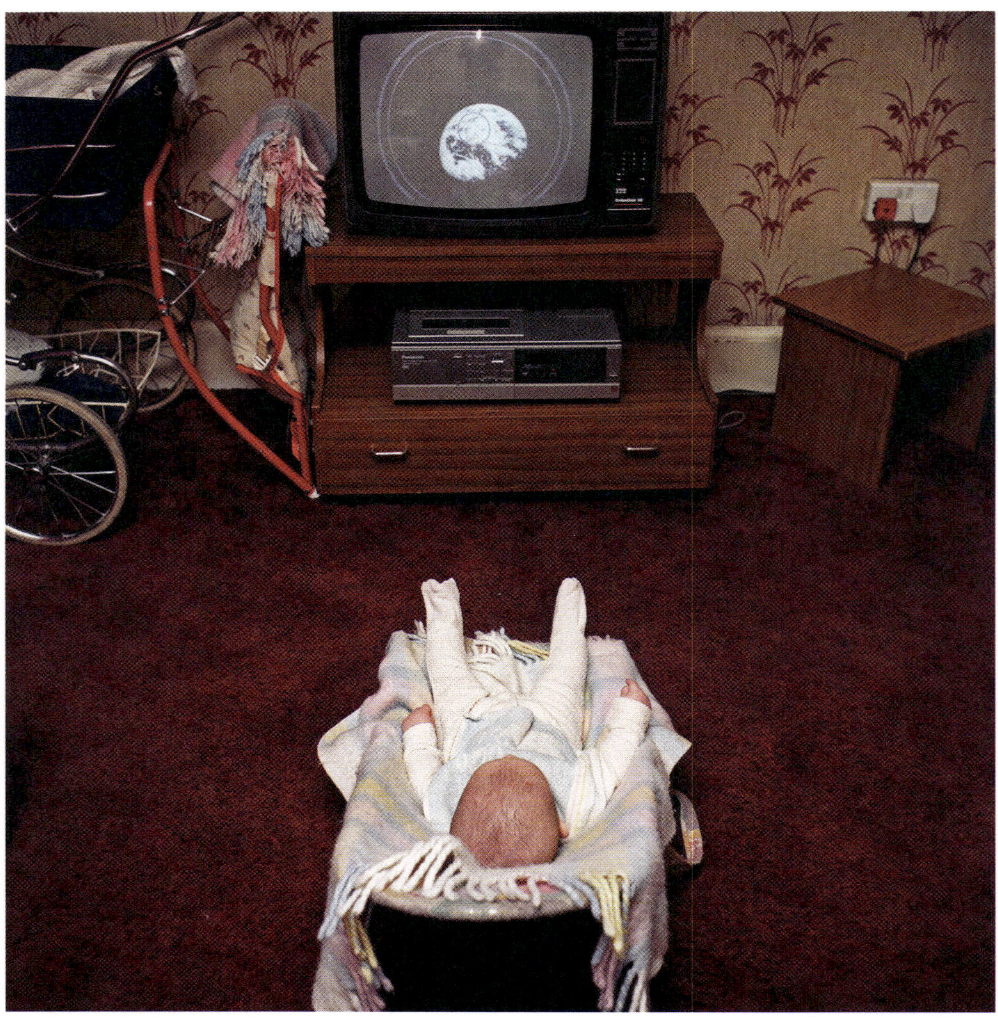

Moore took the image in a living room in Derby, England as a photography student in the late 1980s. He went to a housing estate and knocked on people's doors asking if he could take pictures, which yielded a stark series of intimate images of everyday, working-class lives that teeter on the edge of voyeurism. The viewer sees the baby through the photographer's eyes, who is watching what is on the television. At the same time, the viewer notices Moore's image reflected back on the screen, which is a reminder that the image is a construction; all is artifice even though this is a picture from the real world just as the title of his project, *Pictures from the Real World* (1987–88) says. There is a wonderful echo between the television screen, which frames reality, and the photographic frame, which does the same. Both point to humankind – or even life itself – personified here as the floating green and blue planet Earth and an infant with its life ahead of it. But what life might that be? Moore poses the question but leaves the viewer to find the answer.

In this cramped living room, feelings of claustrophobia are intensified by the deliberately tight crop, which seems to compress everything in the frame. Yet, like the child, the viewer looks out through the television screen, which serves as a portal into infinite space where we find Earth blinking back. It is a strange almost paradoxical series of realities that Moore collapses into a single frame: to be on Earth looking at an image of Earth, locked in a never-ending exchange. The viewer is in a kind of twilight zone made even more strange through the surreal-real setting. This is clearly no casual snapshot of a baby in a bouncer, although the snapshot aesthetic with its washed-out colours, informal composition and flash is nonetheless used to brilliant effect. Ultimately, Moore's image can be read as a comment on life for the poorest in Margaret Thatcher's Britain where a cheerless room becomes a microcosm of the harsh life that many working-class people had no choice but to endure.

+ PHOTOGRAPHER BIO
British, b. 1961

+ GOOGLE THESE
Civic Pride (1999), *The Last Things* (2008), *The Lisa and John Project* (2017)

+ READ THIS
Pictures from the Real World (2013) by David Moore.

Like This? Try These

→ Richard Billingham

→ Anna Fox

→ Paul Graham

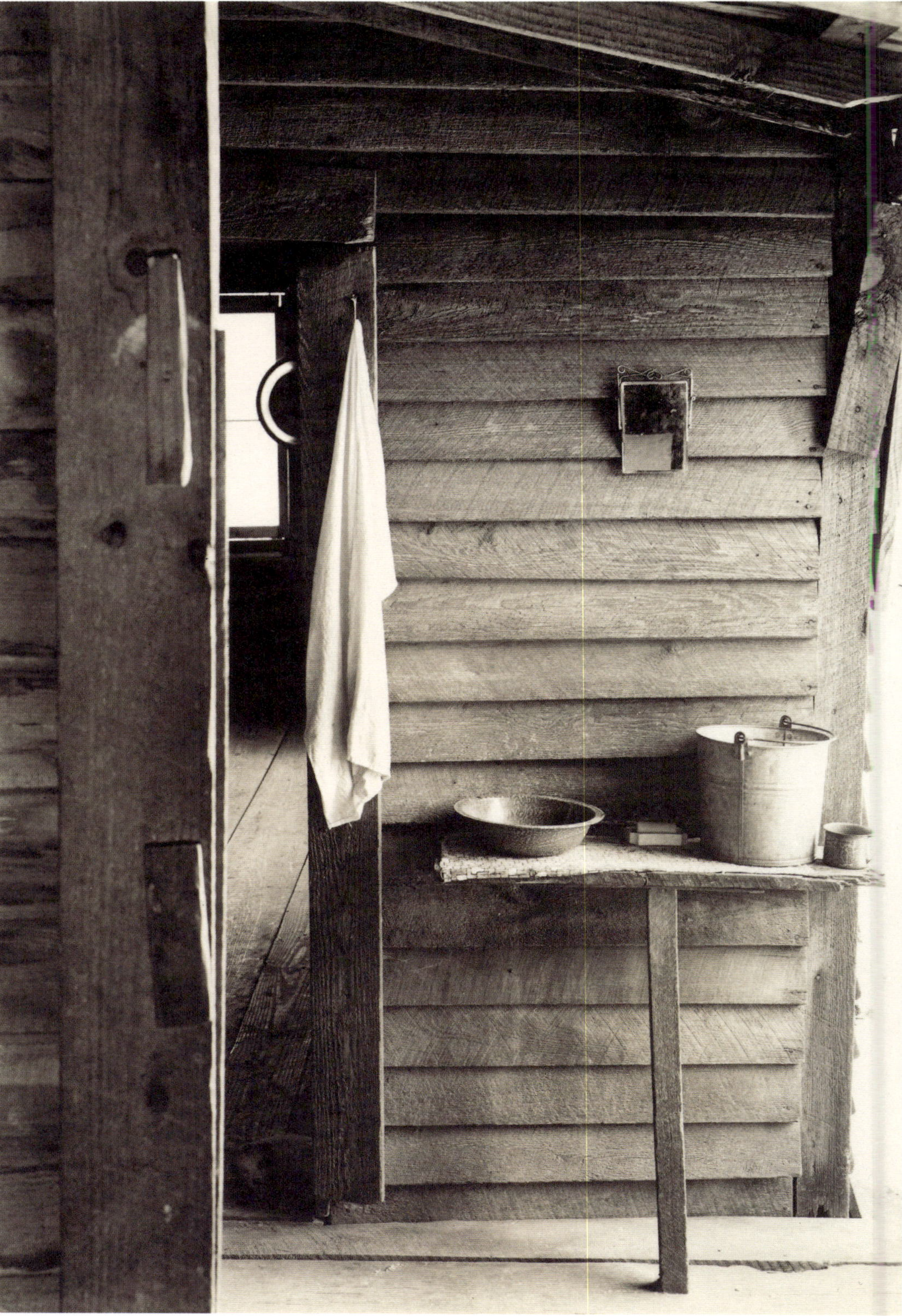

Walker Evans

Washroom in the Dog Run of Floyd Burroughs's Home, Hale County, Alabama

1936

Walker Evans studied and photographed everything that went before his lens with great care and attention to detail. As such, he created exquisitely composed images that elevate their subject matter to a higher plane and yet remain rooted in reality.

In this image, a humble washroom becomes a site of interest and intrigue. This is partly because of Evans's exemplary handling of natural light, which is perfectly balanced across the scene. He took the view that the elements of a picture were already there. As French historian and critic Gilles Mora said: 'rather than arranging the composition, the photographer's job, as [Evans] saw it, was to centre the existing configuration of visual surfaces offering themselves up to the eye – something that was already composed and had its own order.'

Evans took this contemplative image while working for the Resettlement (later Farm Security) Administration, a US Government initiative that offered aid to the people of rural America and documented people's lives through photography. There may not be any people in this photograph but there is a palpable human presence: the towel may have recently been returned to its hook, and the bucket and soap standing by it are arranged neatly. It is as though the occupant has popped out and will return any moment. Evans had a way of photographing interiors that paint a picture of their inhabitants even when they are nowhere to be seen.

This is an image pregnant with possibility and alive with poetry, a photograph that invites the viewer to take time looking at it and to enjoy poring over every detail from the crooked table leg and makeshift table to the enticing doorway in the middle distance. The small rectangular mirror is replete with connotations of looking and seeing, while the delightful repetition of shapes – the semicircles, circles and rectangles – adds a visual rhythm. All of these things are integral to the image and are knitted together carefully to give a comprehensive impression of a place, at this particular moment in time, as depicted by Evans with his 8x10 view camera.

+ PHOTOGRAPHER BIO
American, 1903–75

+ GOOGLE THESE
Corrugated Tin Facade of Contractor's Office, Moundville, Alabama (1936), *Alabama Tenant Farmer Wife (Allie Mae Burroughs)* (1936), *Post Office, Sprott, Alabama* (1936)

+ READ THIS
Walker Evans Photofile (2007) by Gilles Mora.

+ SEE THIS
Visit the J. Paul Getty Museum website at getty.edu and search for 'Walker Evans' to see a collection of Evans's work.

Like This? Try These

→ Dorothea Lange

→ Aaron Siskind

→ Ralph Steiner

Shannon Jensen Wedgwood

Makka Kalfar, Age 7, Walked Many Weeks From Igor

2012

A pair of shoes is about as everyday as it gets. You may cherish a pair of special heels for going out, but most people are lucky enough to own more than one pair and will take footwear for granted. This is not the case for the refugees in Jensen Wedgwood's award-winning series, *A Long Walk* (2012).

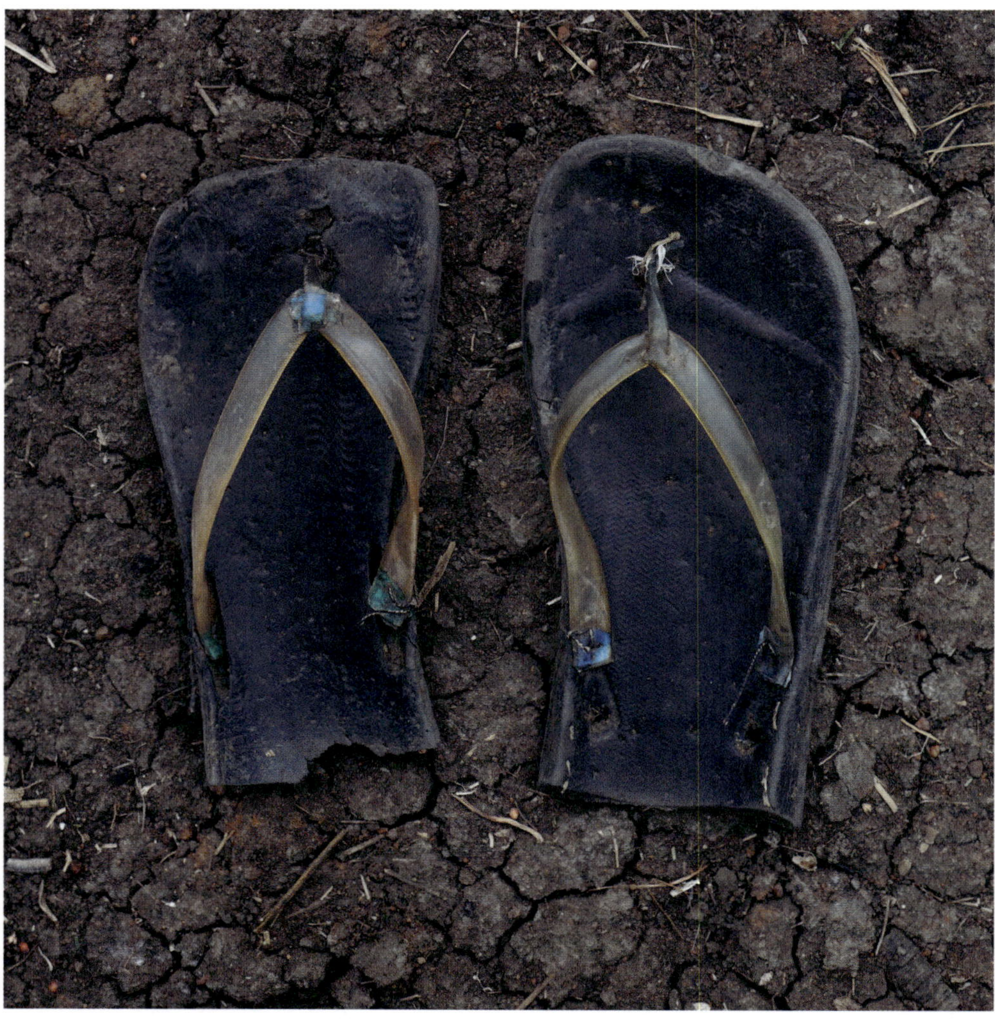

In 2012, documentary photographer Jensen Wedgwood travelled to South Sudan to cover the refugee crisis that was unfolding there. More than 100,000 people had fled the brutal fighting in neighbouring Sudan, walking hundreds of miles with the few belongings they could carry and their children in tow. Choosing to focus on what was happening on the border with Sudan's Blue Nile state, Jensen Wedgwood set about creating a photo story. But, with little interest from picture editors who claimed the story was not newsworthy, Jensen Wedgwood decided to change tack. Upon noticing the worn out yet treasured shoes the refugees were wearing or carrying, she realized that photographing people's shoes could be a way to get the media to take notice. By her own admission, what she was doing was 'not a typical documentary project' and the images are simplistic. Although they were simple to shoot, the shoes deliver a considerable emotional punch, telling stories not only of the terrible hardship endured by Sudanese refugees, but also their strength and refusal to give up.

Shot from above often against cracked ground, each image is a portrait of sorts. No person is present, nonetheless there is a strong sense of the person who owns the shoes. As Jensen Wedgwood explains: 'A fundamental goal of this work is to encourage a genuine human connection to someone else's experience … The viewer is asked to imagine the person whose feet were in these shoes.'

An accompanying caption gives just enough information: the name and age of the owner and the number of days they had walked, if known. In the case of seven-year-old Makkar Kalfar the owner of these cut-to-fit flip flops, Jensen Wedgwood says Makkar had walked from a place called Buk for an unknown number of days. Never was the expression to put oneself in someone else's shoes more apt.

+ PHOTOGRAPHER BIO
American, b. 1984

+ GOOGLE THESE
Southwood, Charlottesville, VA (2011–), *Bowl By Bowl, Tanzania* (2014), *Sewol Notes, Ansan, South Korea* (2014), *Witnessing the Death of a Syrian Refugee in Calais* (2015)

+ READ THIS
'A Sudanese Refugee Crisis, Photographed From the Ground Up' by James Estrin on lens.blogs.nytimes.com.

Other Compelling Photojournalists

→ Paula Bronstein

→ Gabriele Galimberti

→ Paolo Marchetti

CHAPTER

8

COLOUR IS KING

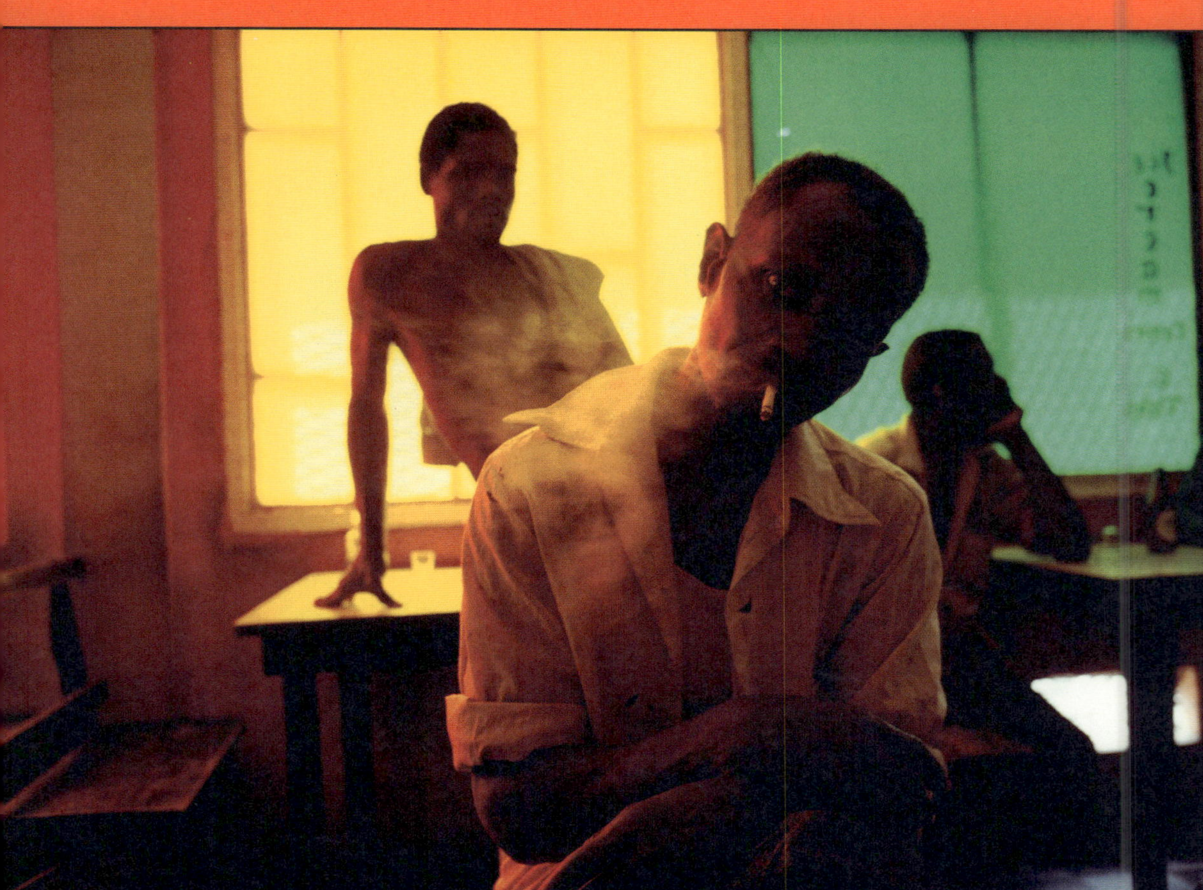

 Alex Webb—Grenada. Gouyave. Bar.

Alex Webb

Grenada. Gouyave. Bar.

1979

Heat radiates from the picture and if we close our eyes, we are there too. The smoke gets in our eyes and up our nostrils.

When Alex Webb took this photograph, he was just five years into his career as a professional photographer. Still only in his twenties, Webb was already shooting with maturity beyond his years. This is evident in this bold photograph, which is bold not just in the sense of its skilful and emotive use of framing, colour, shape and form, but also in terms of the photographer's resolve. It is easy to admire and praise the photograph's formal qualities as we look at it, but think for a moment about the making of the picture and its circumstances. Webb, a stranger, a foreigner, in a bar in the small town of Gouyave on the west coast of Grenada in the West Indies, spied these men, and, sensing there was a picture to be made, held his nerve, raised his camera to his eye and clicked.

He had noticed the men against what he describes as 'brilliant translucent windows'. He has said he watched them and they watched him – indeed, this is a picture as much about looking, watching, waiting, anticipating, as it is about colour, light and shadow. Although we cannot tell what the central figure is thinking, he meets our gaze resolutely, looking not only at us but also through us. We cannot escape his piercing and challenging stare. Photographer and subject, stranger and local, are locked in a silent exchange that Webb has the foresight to immortalize.

Webb is known for his evocative use of colour, which is vividly on display here. He has said that when he looks at a scene he does not just sense shapes and what appears to be happening, but also the relationship of the colours and 'their emotional and sensory resonances'. We see all this and more in an image that bristles with tension and mystery.

+ PHOTOGRAPHER BIO

American, b. 1952

+ GOOGLE THESE

Mexicans arrested while trying to cross the border to United States. San Ysidro, California. USA. (1979), *Children playing in a courtyard. Oaxaca State. Tehuantepec. Mexico.* (1985), *Cotton candy. Oaxaca. Mexico.* (1990)

+ READ THIS

Hot Light/Half-Made Worlds: Photographs from the Tropics (1986) by Alex Webb.

Like This? Try These

→ Cristóbal Hara

→ Fred Herzog

→ Constantine Manos

Bruce Wrighton

Glenwood Diner, Binghamton, NY

1987

A corner of a humble diner in Binghamton, New York does not immediately appear the stuff of beautiful photographs. Yet Bruce Wrighton elevates this most ordinary of scenes to the realms of poetry.

This is an image that implores the viewer to keep looking and rewards that investment of time: the colours become richer, the light more alluring and the setting increasingly attractive. Soon, the appeal of such a scene and why someone might want to take a picture of it becomes obvious even if it is a struggle to tell what the photograph is about. This begs the question whether photographs always have to be about something in an obvious way to be aesthetically pleasing. Perhaps assuming that Wrighton's photograph is focusing on something specific is a fruitless endeavour. Rather than trying to work out its meaning, perhaps it is best to accept Wrighton's invitation to experience his photograph before the desire to make sense of it kicks in.

Shortly before Wrighton died in 1988, he gave an interview where he discusses the ineffable nature of photographs. He talked about how images can have an 'initial power…that cannot be interpreted, that cannot be defined, that cannot be pinned down.' In his all too brief turn as a photographer Wrighton took many pictures that could be thus described. For two years before his death, he extensively photographed the people and places in and around his hometown of Binghamton with an 8x10 view camera. Ordinary passersby, cars and corners of bars, cafés, churches and other religious settings were his subjects and in Wrighton's hands become worth examining. Wrighton described the work he was making as 'representational, informational', showing 'what was in front of the camera'. In one sense his photographs are exquisite studies of form, light and colour that reveal his sophisticated understanding of how they could be brought together in a photograph. However, Wrighton's images are much more than formal studies. They are, as he said, 'beautiful in their own way… [born of] an unconscious kind of coming together' of elements. This is what makes a Wrighton photograph so special.

+ PHOTOGRAPHER BIO
American, 1950–88

+ GOOGLE THESE
Saint George and the Dragon (1986), *Dinosaurs and Dreamboats* (1987)

+ READ THIS
Read 'An Interview with Bruce Wrighton (1988)' at americansuburbx.com.

Like This? Try These

- → William Eggleston
- → Greg Miller
- → Richard Renaldi

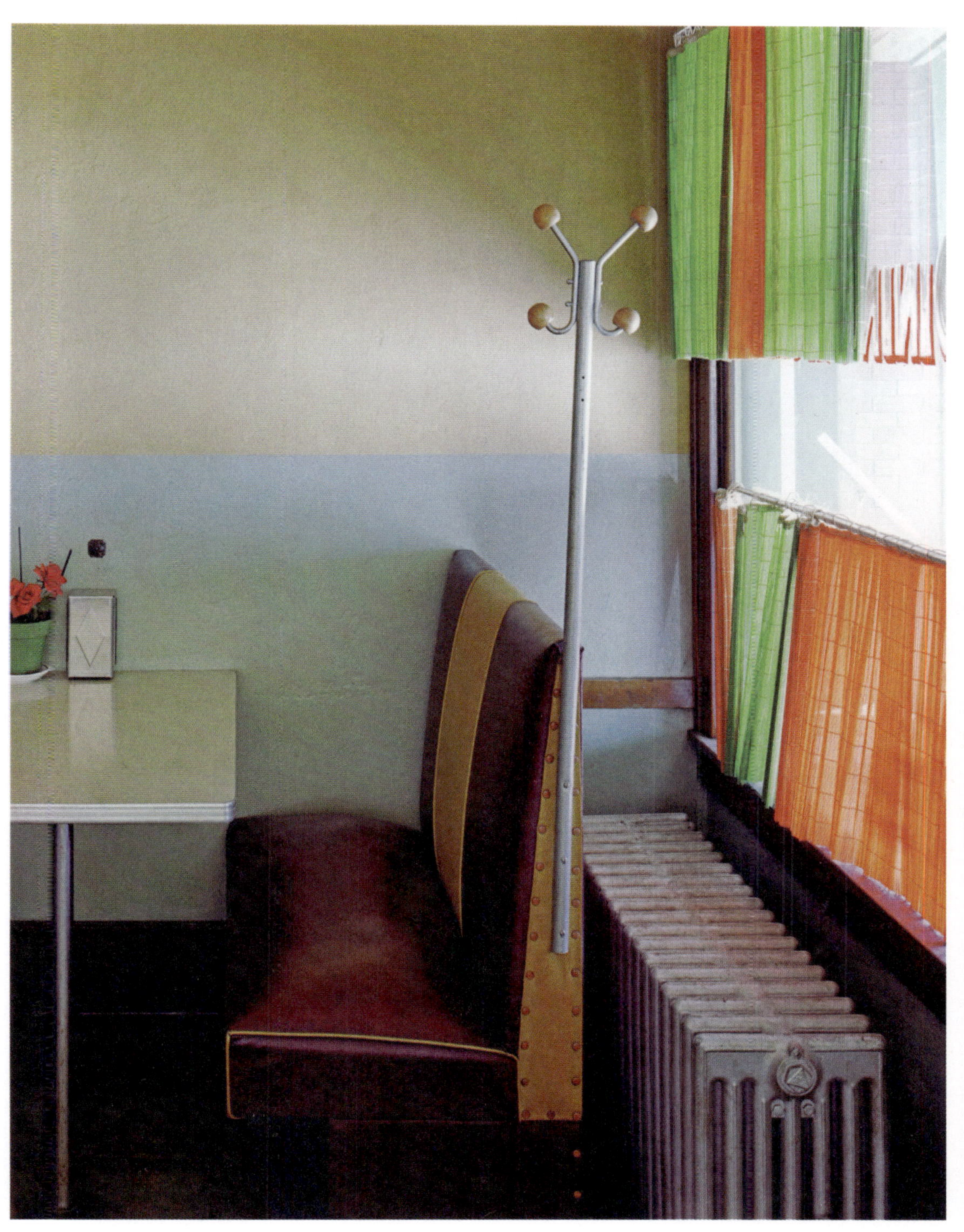

Carolyn Drake

Hotel Room, Zhetisay, Kazakhstan

2009

An open door, in photography as in life, is an invitation to look, to enter into, to experience. It beckons, entices, ushers and promises. It is no wonder that photographers have embraced the open door's metaphorical potential.

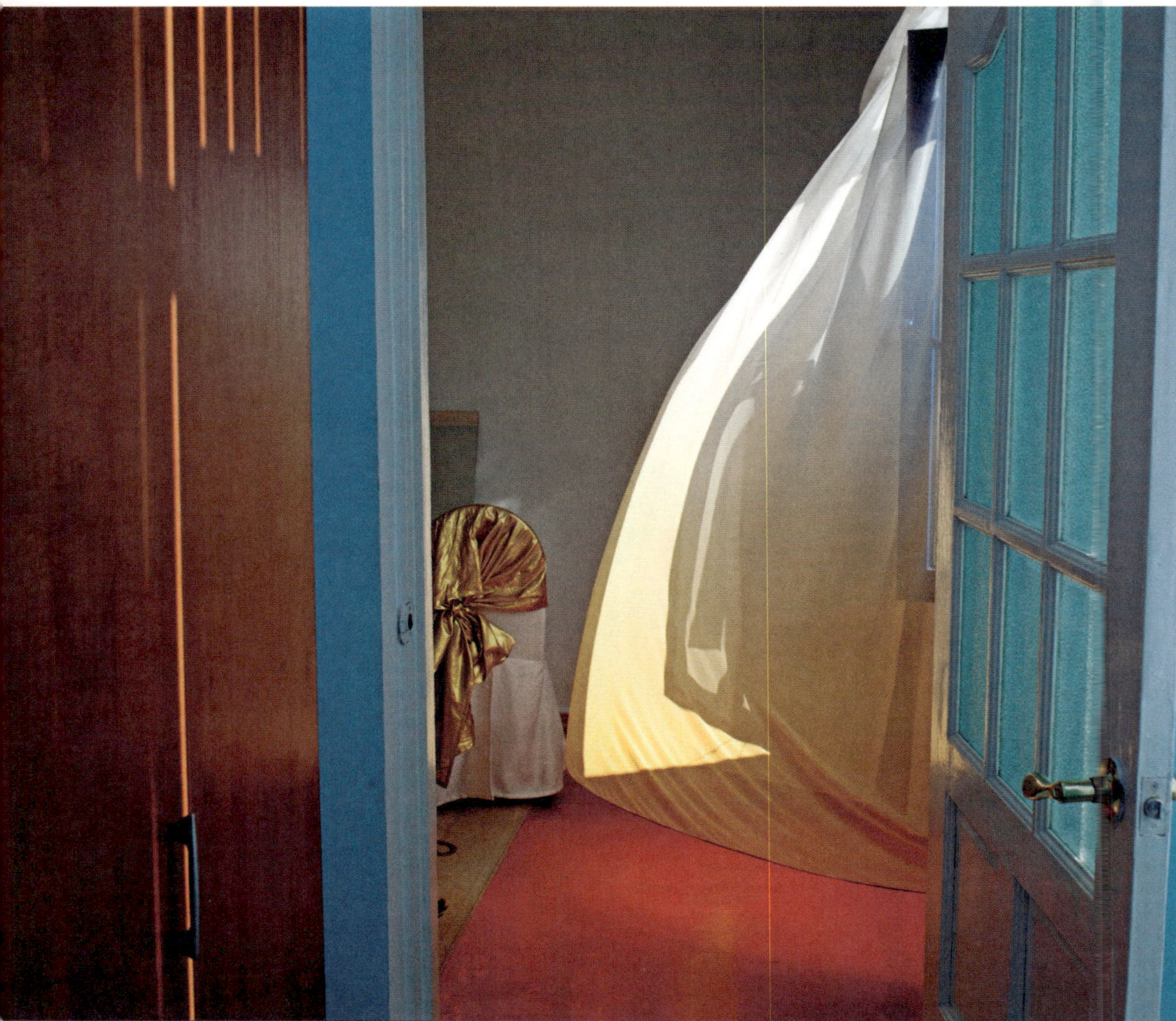

The two practitioners who have most famously exploited the idea of the door are British pioneer William Henry Fox Talbot in the earliest days of photography and American photojournalist Walker Evans. Carolyn Drake embraced the poetic power of the open door when she framed her photograph of a hotel room in Zhetisay, Kazakhstan, so that it stands at the centre of her composition. In Drake's image, which belongs to her series *Two Rivers* (2009), a photographic journey along the Amu Darya and the Syr Darya rivers in Asia, we wait with bated breath outside, pausing, anticipating what lies beyond the liminal space we inhabit.

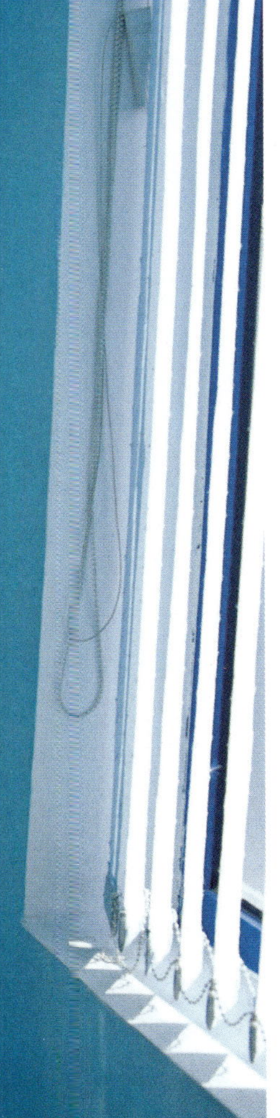

Her photograph is an exquisite celebration of line and blocks of space that interconnect perfectly and pleasingly. The door plays an important role in neatly framing the curtain inside as it gently blows back and forth in a breeze from a nearby window. An open door, open window, the look-through, inside-outside, a threshold and the many intriguing metaphorical associations we might make regarding such pictorial elements are obvious, but the real star here is the colour. Such a combination of complementary colours, vibrant blues, gold, reds, oranges, is a gift to a photographer and Drake does not waste the opportunity. In his book *Looking at Photographs*, American photographer, critic and curator John Szarkowski talked about how 'photographers who are concerned with the ephemeral flow of things' might 'collaborate with luck'. He was discussing a photograph by Mario Giacomelli, but his remarks might apply to Drake: she did not pre-plan these magnificent hues but embraces and runs with their poetic potential, just as she embraces an open door that invites us to enter.

+ PHOTOGRAPHER BIO
American, b. 1971

+ GOOGLE THESE
A Coal Miner in the Locker Room fter his Work Shift at Progress Mine in the Town of Torez, Ukraine (2006), *Oksana with a Leaf of Cabbage from the Garden of the Internat where She Lives in Isolation with more than Sixty Girls and Women Categorized as Disabled, Petrykhiv, Ternopil, Ukraine* (2016)

+ LISTEN TO THIS
British photographer Ben Smith interviews Drake on his podcast, *A Small Voice*, at bensmithphoto.com.

Like This? Try These

→ Jonas Bendiksen

→ Bieke Depoorter

→ Harry Gruyaert

Duffy

Birdcage

1977

In the age of photo-editing software and digital imaging it is easy to create almost limitless effects after taking an image. However, in the late 1970s, when Duffy created this famous photograph for cigarette brand Benson & Hedges, photographers had to use every trick they could to bring their ideas to life.

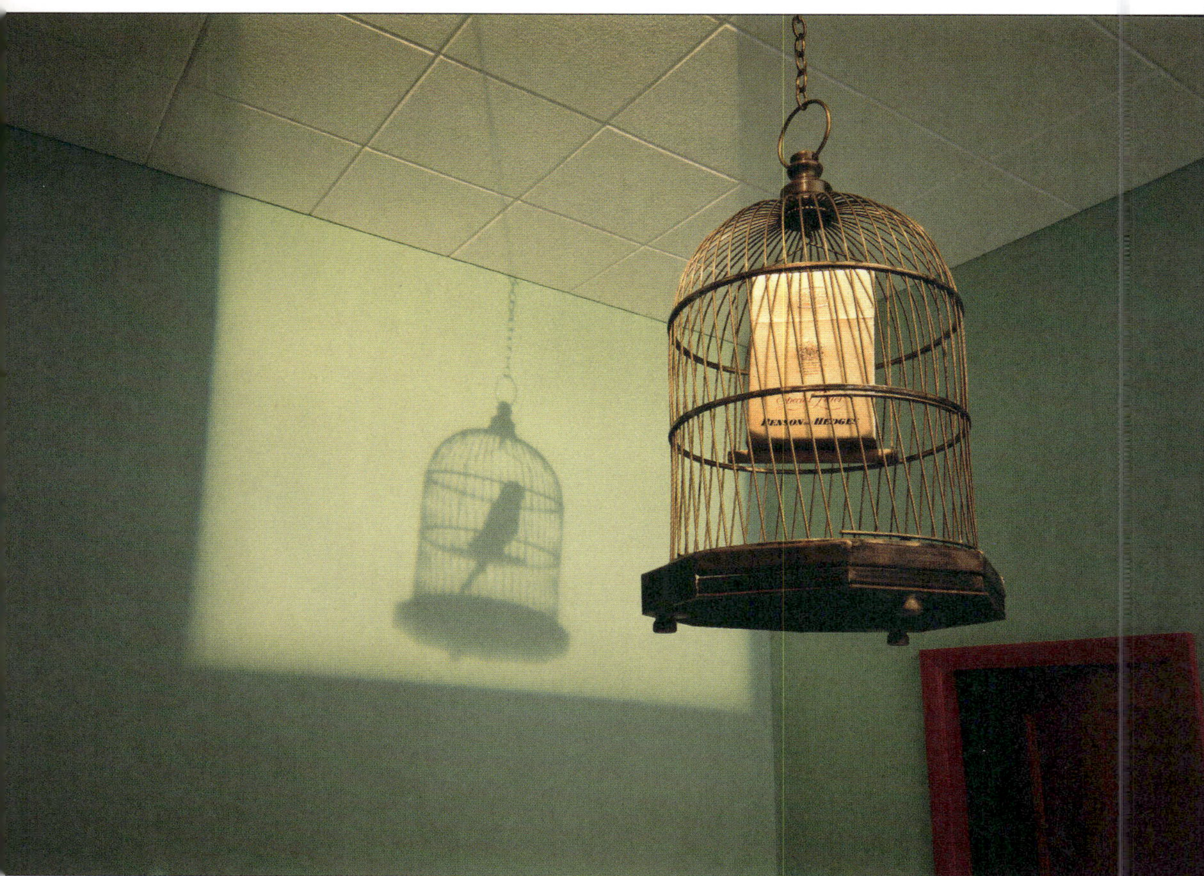

Duffy, who, along with David Bailey and Terence Donovan tore up the worlds of fashion and celebrity portraiture in the 1960s, was no stranger to innovative thinking. He had been working successfully on advertising assignments since the early 1960s. Technically proficient and with a creative vision to match, Duffy was well placed to bring the concept sketched out by influential advertising agency Collett Dickenson & Pearce to life.

This was the second of four images Duffy made to promote the cigarette brand in 1977. An especially creative approach was needed since people were not allowed to be shown in advertisements for tobacco products. The idea put forward had a surrealist slant and involved playing with viewer expectations. Viewers did not see what they expected in an image – in this case a bird in the cage – but saw a packet of cigarettes. Here, the set is bathed in what looks to be late-afternoon sun and Duffy projected an image of a bird onto the far wall. It is a strange sight made even more so by the unusual perspective and mishmash of lines and angles. Yet the real hero of the scene, as to be expected in an advertisement, is the product itself, which glows gold against the soft green interior. Suspended from above and positioned just off centre, the birdcage and its prize contents are elevated to another level. We are left in no doubt regarding what to think and how to respond; this glorious vision is to be praised, worshipped and admired.

As clever and sophisticated as Duffy's handling of perspective and scale are, it is the rich colours that make the photograph. Everything in this illusory image is judged perfectly and has been assembled by the photographer's skilful handling of colour. As Duffy said in 2009, his images for the campaign were 'not phoned in from the coast, it's all done in the camera'. Knowing the skill that went into creating this image makes such a sight all the more impressive.

Like This? Try These

- Ilka & Franz
- Catherine Losing
- Scheltens & Abbenes

+ PHOTOGRAPHER BIO
British, 1933–2010

+ GOOGLE THESE
Snail & Eye (1956), *David Bowie, Aladdin Sane, Classic* (1973), *Mousehole* (1977), *Smirnoff Skydivers* (1978)

+ WATCH THIS
'Duffy: The Man who Shot the Sixties' on the DEVELOP Tube Photography Video Channel on YouTube.

Horst P. Horst

Dinner Suit and Headdress by Schiaparelli

1947

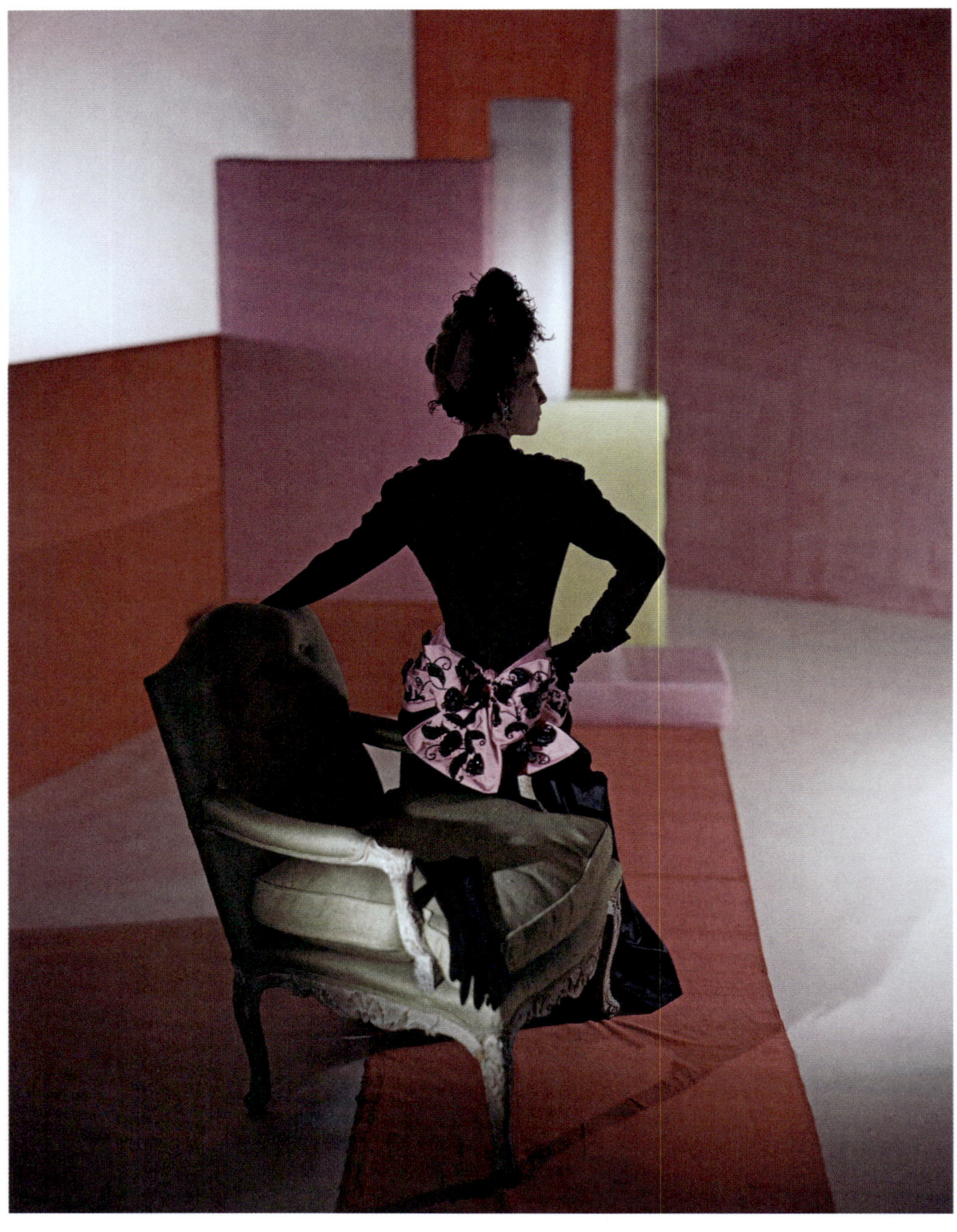

Whether or not you believe fashion photography is art, Horst P. Horst's work makes a convincing case. Equally at ease working in black and white and in colour, Horst was a master of using light.

His career lasted sixty years and saw him shoot countless fashion stories for *Vogue*. He used his talent for lighting to create images that depict the clothes he photographed in sumptuous ways, but also possess a timeless elegance, beauty and grace. This beautifully lit image of a model wearing a dress by Italian fashion designer Elsa Schiaparelli is one example. Used in *Vogue* on 15 February 1947, it demonstrates how skilful Horst was at using colour, light and form to craft compositions that are more than fashion pictures. Every element is there for a reason, from the placing of the arms and the model's slightly downward-looking eye-line to the haughty straight-backed pose and blocks of colour that fall away into the distance. His bold use of planes of colour calls to mind early twentieth-century Suprematism artists whose abstract paintings privilege basic geometric forms. Indeed, Horst had developed an appreciation for avant-garde art at an early age and experimented with avant-garde techniques in many of his photographs. Such is the richness of colours on display this could be a high-society portrait or even a royal and Horst's artistry is comparable to that of sixteenth- or seventeenth-century portraitists.

Horst was technically proficient and was quick to embrace and master new colour photographic processes when they became available in the late 1930s. It was an exciting time to be working in fashion publishing because of the possibilities for creative image-making that such technical advances afforded. Horst's fashion photographs may be strong contenders for portraits in their own right, but his eye remained firmly fixed on making sure the clothes never got lost in the picture. He always thought about every picture as a whole. This is demonstrated here by the carefully illuminated lavish pink bow that is complemented by the pinks of the background and the striking silhouette of the bodice.

+ PHOTOGRAPHER BIO
German-American, 1906–99

+ GOOGLE THESE
Salvador Dalí's Costumes for Leonid Massine's Ballet Bacchanale (1939), *Mainbocher Corset* (1939)

+ READ THIS
'Horst P. Horst an Introduction' on the Victoria & Albert Museum website: vam.ac.uk/articles/horst-an-introduction

+ WATCH THIS
'Horst in Colour' on the V&A YouTube channel.

Like This? Try These

→ Cecil Beaton

→ Erwin Blumenfeld

→ Clifford Coffin

Harry Gruyaert

Baie de Somme, Fort Mahon, France

1991

Dip into most areas of Harry Gruyaert's extensive oeuvre and you will be met with colours of all kinds: rambunctious reds and garish oranges, pastel pinks and aquamarine blues and greens. Gruyaert has worked with colour for decades and understands how to use it to deliver what he wants from a scene and accentuate it.

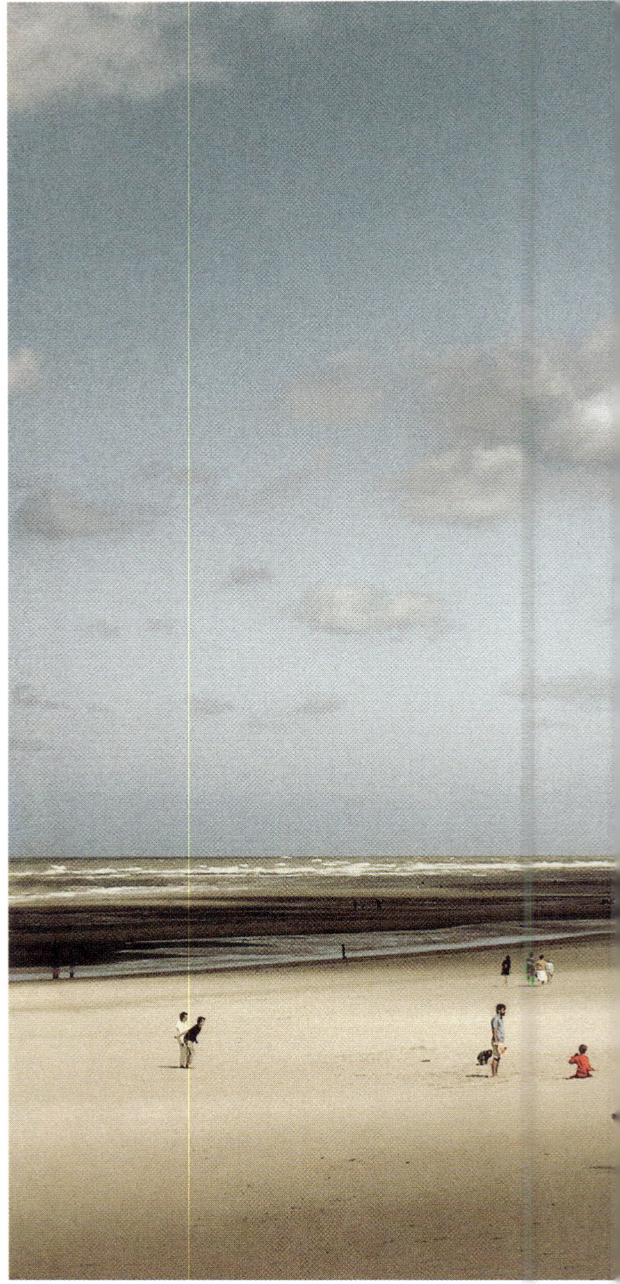

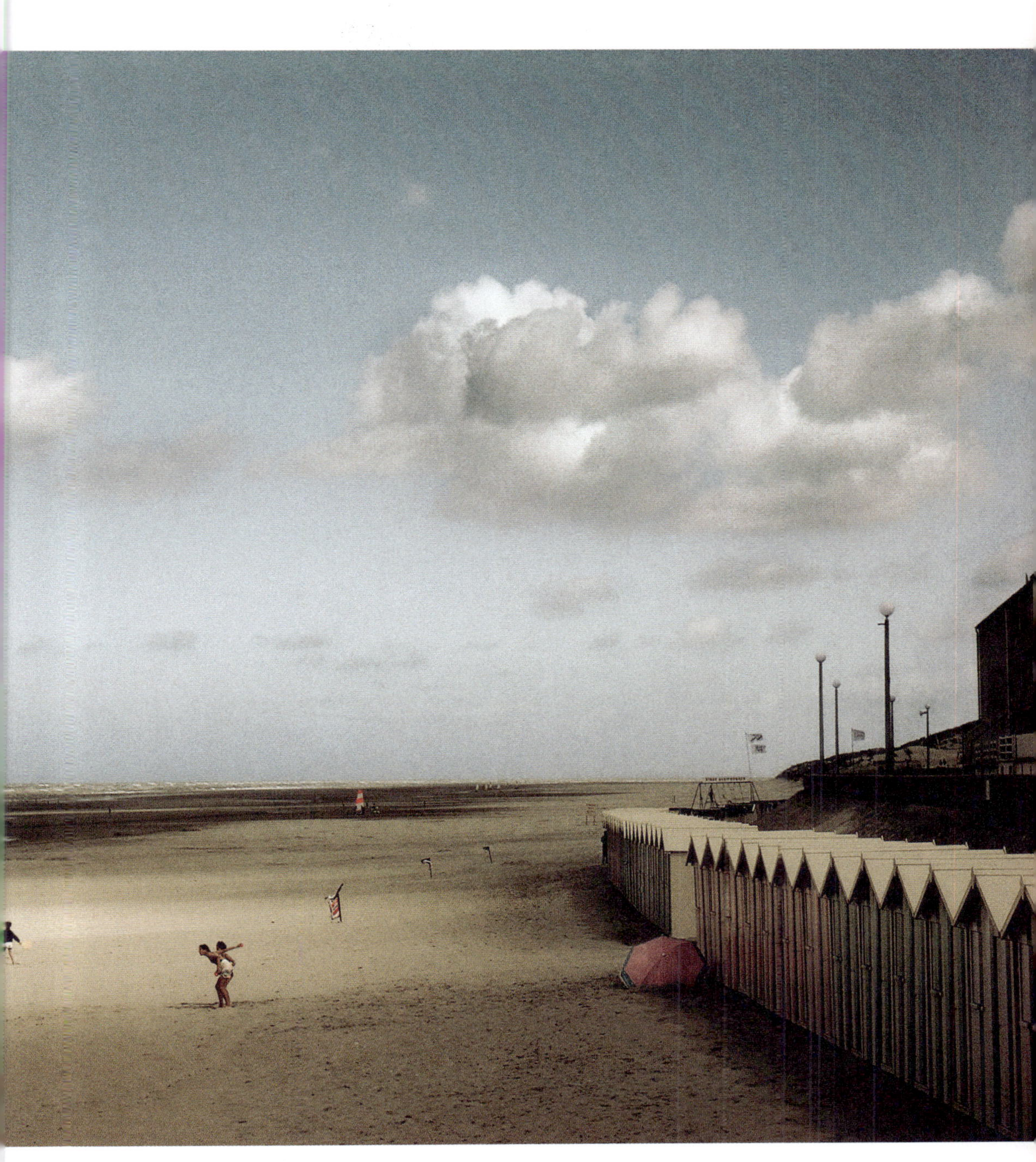

+ PHOTOGRAPHER BIO
Belgian, b. 1941

+ GOOGLE THESE
Quarzata, Morocco (1986), *Boom, Belgium* (1988), *Berck Beach, Nord-Pas-de-Calais, France* (2007)

+ WATCH THIS
Gruyaert discusses his photographic practice and career on the *Masters of Photography* website at mastersof.photography/harry-gruyaert.

In Gruyaert's hands, colour resonates deeply. It is not just the means; it is the raison d'être. In many of his finest photographs, colours are often bold and loud, but in this photograph of the seaside resort Fort-Mahon-Plage in northern France he uses it with a delicate touch. Using natural light to bring out the scene's colours, Gruyaert transports the most commonplace and universal of pastimes to another realm. One of the ways the photograph succeeds is the way it combines the sublime of landscape photography with the feel of a nineteenth-century *tableau vivant* (living picture), although the characters are not posed and the scene is not staged. The clouds look like cotton wool and could belong to a photograph by nineteenth-century French photographer Gustave Le Gray. The tiny figures, so perfectly positioned, could be actors on a giant stage or set, yet they are just ordinary people, holidaymakers perhaps, enjoying an afternoon at the beach. In addition, the way the light falls on the scene and the muted colours are reminiscent of a painting by English artist L. S. Lowry, who was famous for his works depicting scenes of life in industrial areas.

Gruyaert's colours come together perfectly: the pink of the child's bat echoes the pink parasol and the figure in red helps to anchor the picture. There are many such details to enjoy. The figures call out to be studied like the creations of an Impressionist master, and even the beach huts with their soft greens, yellows and pinks are noteworthy. Gruyaert could not have planned for such colours and small dramas to be present on the day he took this photograph, there was an element of luck. However, he saw the possibilities they afforded. That he watched and waited for the scene to play out the way he wanted before firing the shutter is the mark of a virtuoso.

Like This? Try These

→ Luigi Ghirri

→ Simon Roberts

→ Massimo Vitali

Sanne De Wilde

Untitled #2

2015

+ PHOTOGRAPHER BIO
Belgian, b. 1987

+ GOOGLE THESE
The Dwarf Empire (2011), *Samoa Kekea* (2013), *Land of Ibeji* (2018) with Bénédicte Kurzen

+ WATCH THIS
Exploring the "Island of the Colour Blind" with Sanne De Wilde' on the Nikon Europe YouTube channel.

Most people take seeing in colour for granted. It is one of the fundamental ways people engage with and understand the world. But for those with achromatopsia, a rare genetic condition that causes colour blindness and hypersensitivity to light, the world is rendered in shades of black, white and grey.

An estimated one in 30,000 people are affected by the condition worldwide, but on Pingelap, a tiny atoll in the Pacific Ocean, approximately one in ten islanders have achromatopsia. It is the most colour-blind place on Earth. The prevalence stems from the eighteenth century when the island was engulfed by a typhoon, leaving around twenty survivors. The ruler carried the recessive gene that causes the condition. After a few generations, most of the inhabitants were related to him. De Wilde uses photography to examine the role genetics play in people's lives and how this shapes communities. In 2015, she travelled to the atoll to explore how the Pingelapese affected with achromatopsia see the world. Her journey formed the basis of her series *The Island of the Colorblind* (2015). She took black and white images, but also used a camera fitted with an infrared lens and a colour filter, which resulted in luminous, surreal images like this one. Some individuals with achromatopsia say they can see slight variations of colour and De Wilde says photographing in this way was a 'metaphorical attempt to envision how people with achromatopsia see the world'.

In this image, De Wilde shows families return to the mainland after a picnic on an uninhabited island nearby. Her photographic approach accentuates the lushness of the setting. It is is breathtaking, as if a mystical utopia, a land that promises abundance and tranquillity. In one sense, the image harks back to the hand-coloured photographs of the nineteenth century. However, as De Wilde has said, it also calls to mind images found in the twenty-first century of refugees desperately trying to reach a place of safety. Most of all, the photograph raises questions regarding ways of seeing: how humans see and how the camera sees. De Wilde uses colour as a device to remind us that there is no singular way of seeing and that the vision of a camera is as varied as that of any individual.

Like This? Try These

→ Kisei Kobayashi

→ Bénédicte Kurzen

→ Maria Lax

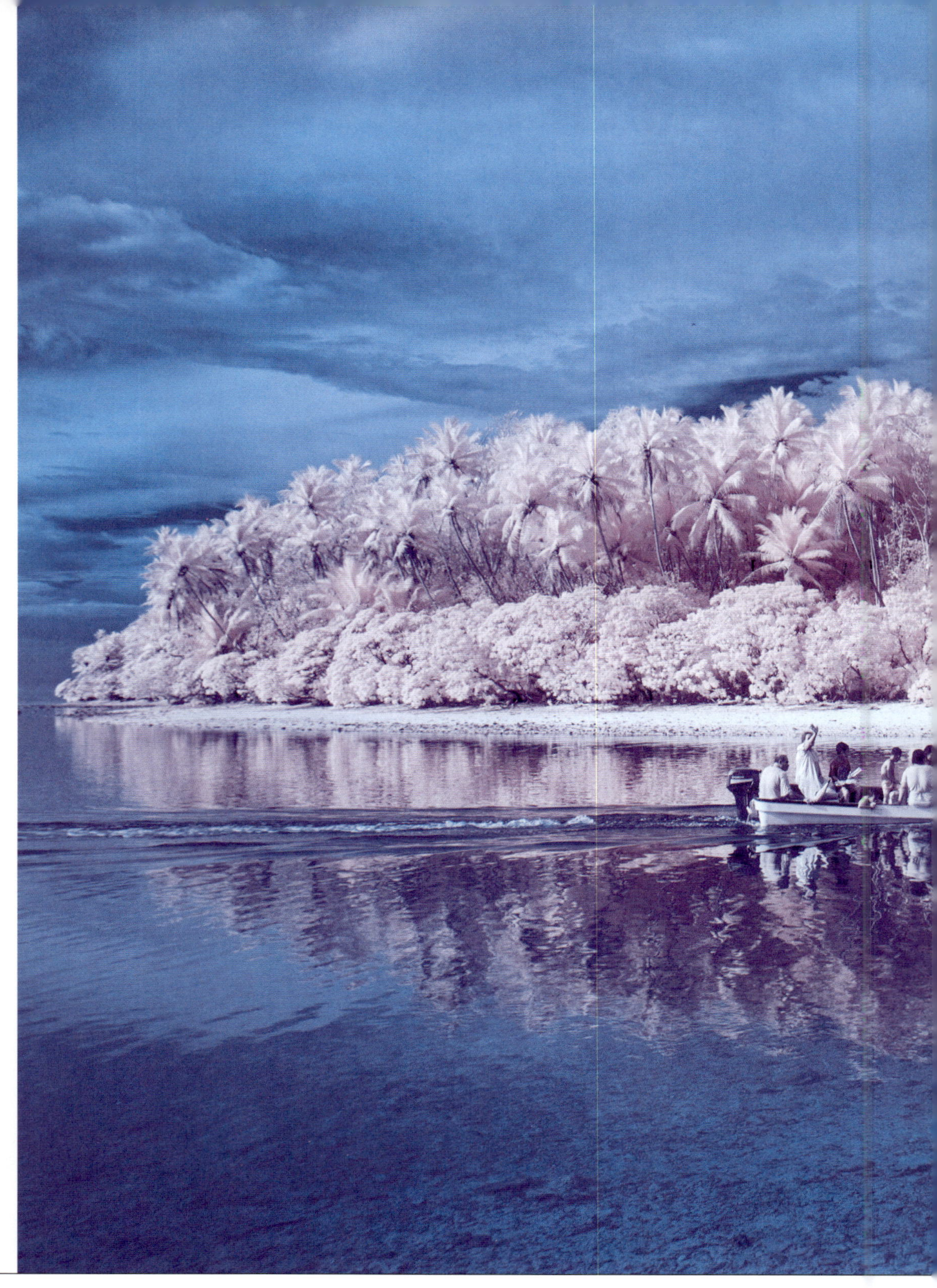

 Sanne De Wilde—Untitled #2

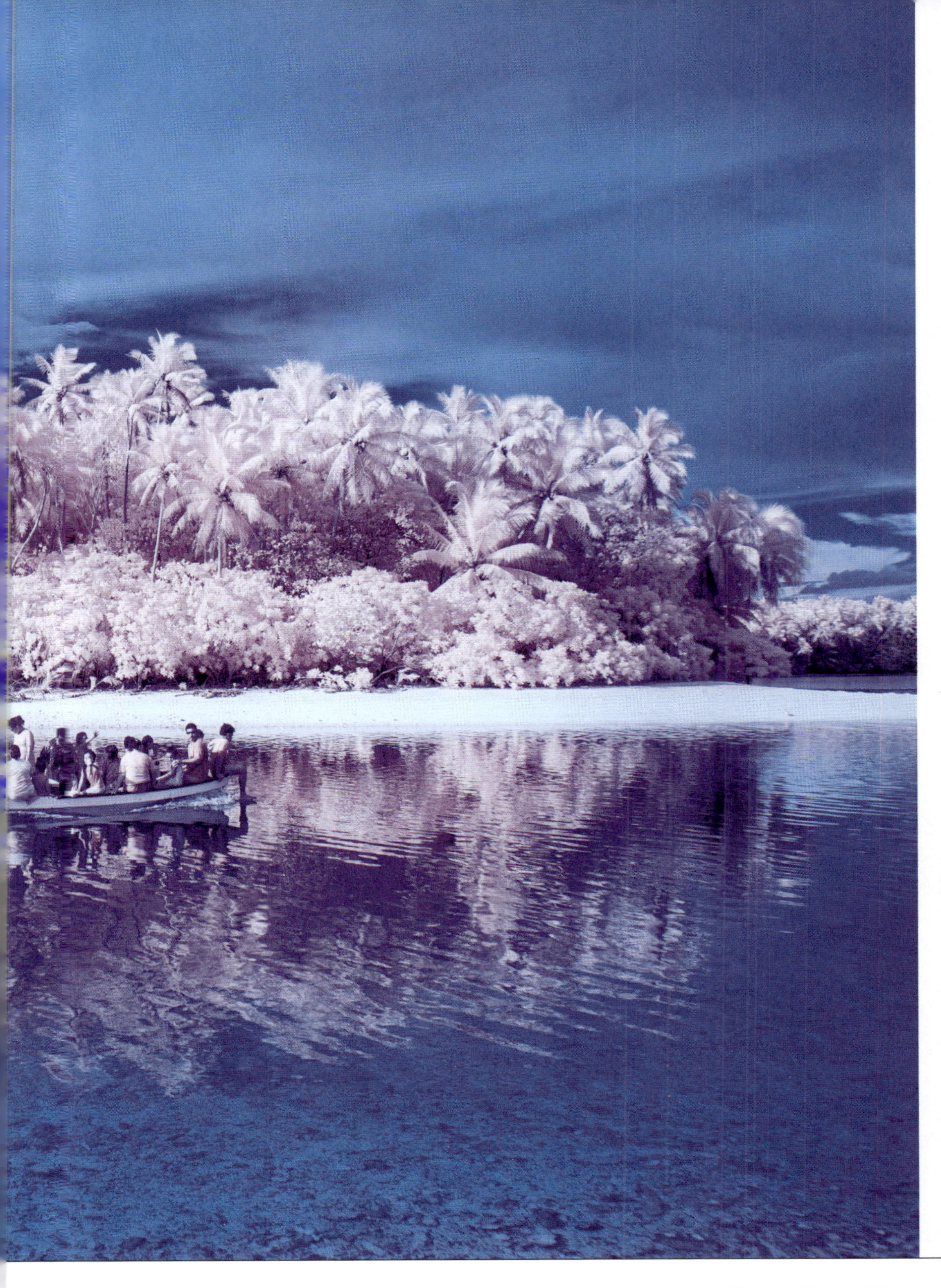

+ PHOTOGRAPHER BIO
German, b. 1968

+ GOOGLE THESE
Plant life, c (2013), *paper drop Oranienplatz, d* (2017)

+ WATCH THIS
Tillmans discusses his practice on the Tate YouTube channel in 'Wolfgang Tillmans – "What Art Does in Me is Beyond Words"'.

Wolfgang Tillmans

Palm tree, sun burst

2015

Like a burst of sun on a gloomy day or a firework in the night sky, the exotic-looking plant in Wolfgang Tillmans's photograph explodes with colour, life and energy. It lights up the room.

By framing the shot with his subject almost edge to edge and in the centre, Tillmans makes it difficult to look anywhere other than at the colourful plant. If your eyes wander, they are quickly brought back to the central spectacle. Tillmans encourages you to work your way around his subject, carefully studying each perfectly imperfect illuminated spike, and if you pull back to take in the plant in its entirety, it appears to take on a character of its own. The unremarkable interior resembles an office and seems an odd setting for such a resplendent sight. You wonder where and what this place is (it is Tillmans's studio) yet the longer you look, the more the plant seems to be exactly where it should be. It might even be sprouting from a desk, but somehow such a possibility seems perfectly normal.

Tillmans's great gift as a photographer is his ability to turn ordinary objects into items both of beauty and endless fascination. He creates photographs that are really interesting to look at. It is not that he goes out of his way to make pictures that are 'random and everyday', as he told The Guardian in 2017; rather, his images are 'calls to attentiveness'. He is simply asking that people look around them.

Among the many topics Tillmans explores in his work is the ability of digital cameras to render subjects in great detail, how the viewer might question what they see by looking at subjects from different angles, and how a three-dimensional world might be translated into a two-dimensional picture. His images span portraiture, still life and much more. They are often playful and incredibly detailed, and sometimes he blows them up to a large scale. His photographs frequently question what it means to make pictures, especially in a modern world that is awash with images. He has said: 'I'm always interested in the question of when something becomes something, or not, and how do we know'. There is a sense that has happened here, although the viewer can only imagine what was going through his mind as he clicked the shutter having realized that this plant could be made to look so magnificent.

Like This? Try These

→ Peter Fraser

→ Jörg Sasse

→ Manfred Willmann

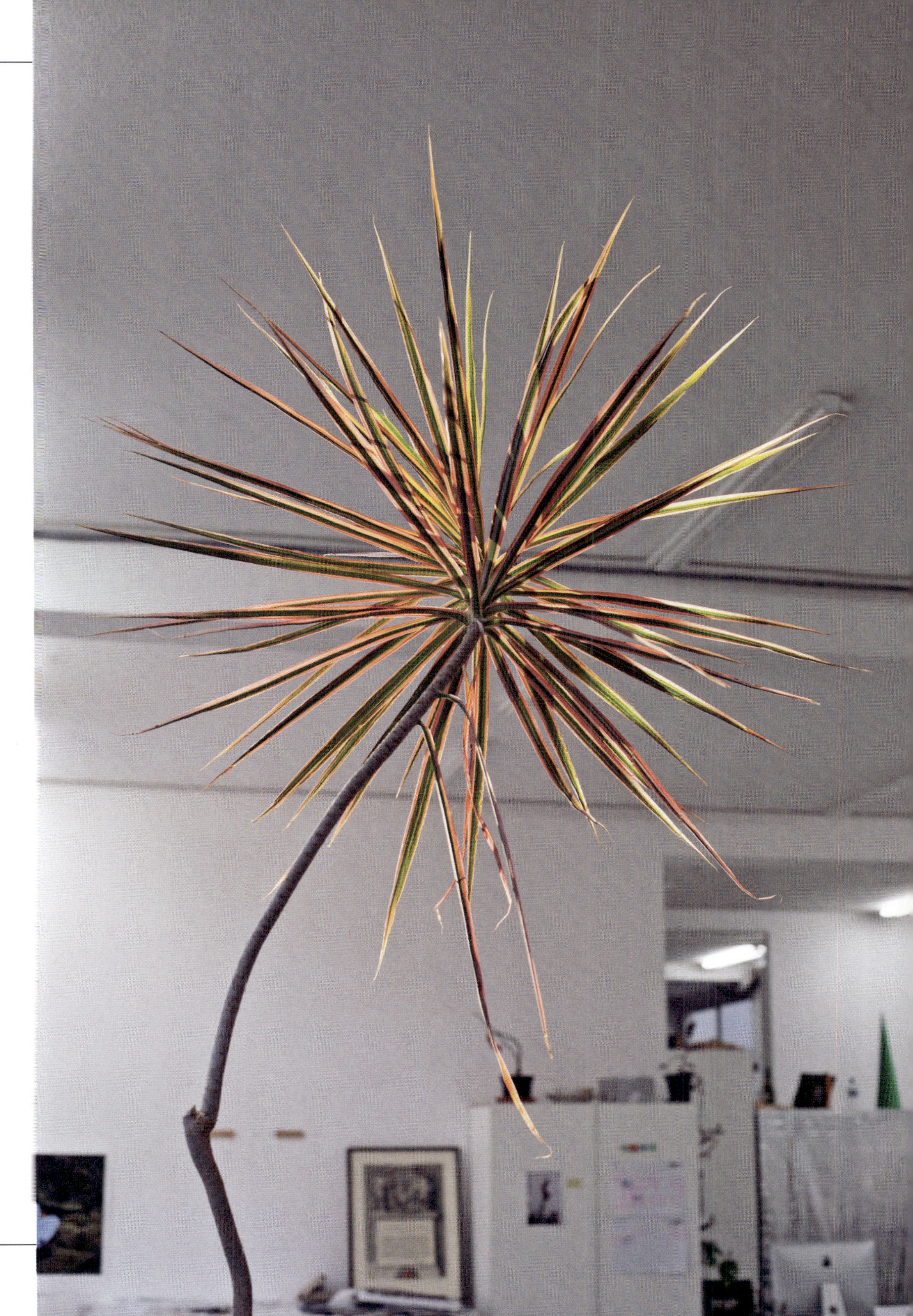

Constantine Manos

Fort Lauderdale, Florida, USA

2000

'Anything can happen in public', says Constantine Manos, who is hugely respected for his vivid and often surreal colour photographs of the everyday lives of Americans. With a Manos picture anything can happen and his are images that catch you off guard.

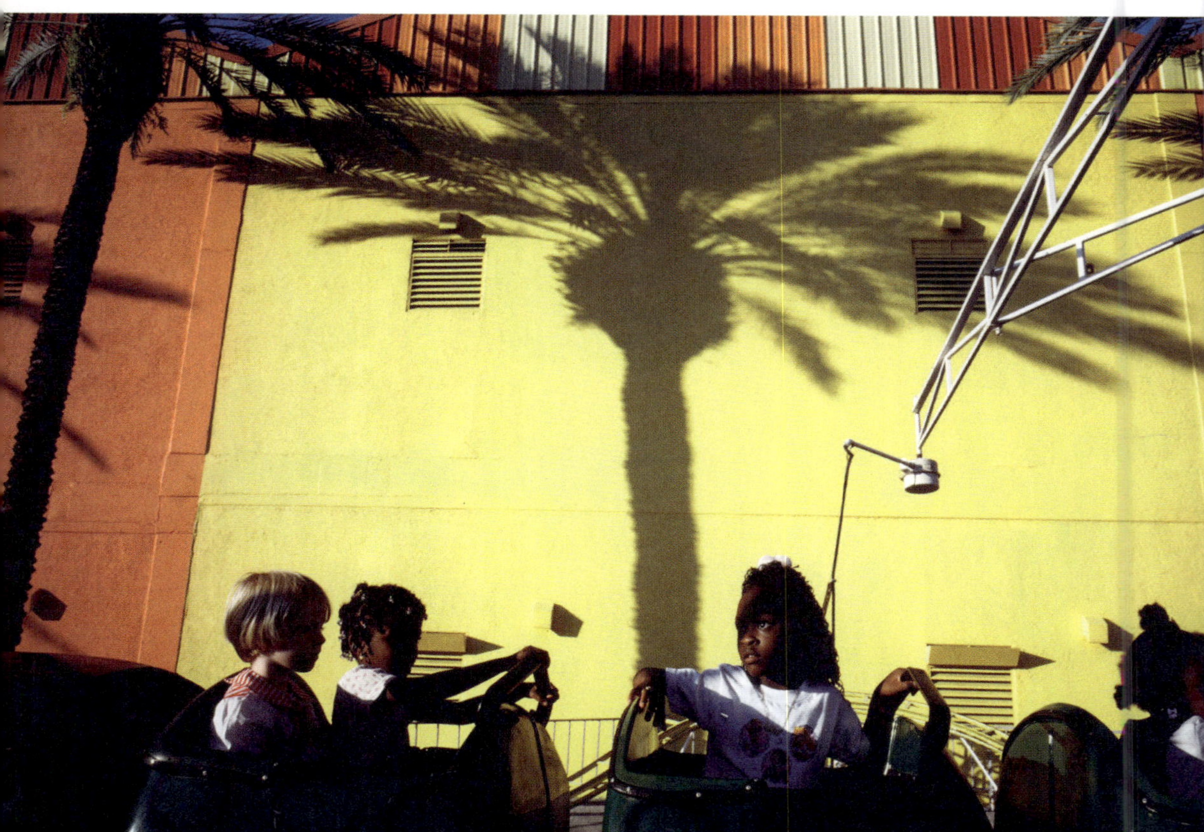

Odd shapes may loom large in the frame as colours vie for your attention, protagonists casually wander in and out of the picture while shadows obscure and tease. Manos began his photography career shooting in black and white, but in the early 1990s he turned to colour and began the project for which he is best known, *American Color* (1995). Photographing across the United States in places such as Daytona Beach in Florida and Venice Beach in Los Angeles, on beaches and along promenades, at fairs and parades, Manos captured glimpses of ordinary Americans as they went about their lives. The images present a snapshot of what life was like in the United States at that time, although they were never intended to be historical visual accounts or serve as documentary photographs. Nevertheless, they are noteworthy for their clever use of colour, light and shade. A Manos picture stretches across the entire frame and the subject matter continues to the edges. The viewer can travel through each image, reflecting at every turn on what might be going on.

Manos is interested in asking questions and 'presenting problems to the viewer', and stays true to the idea here. The viewer wonders who this little girl is and what has captured her attention. It is she who draws in the viewer but beyond assumptions about her background and age the photograph gives little away. You can attempt to read and decipher the rest of the picture on a superficial level noting that the children appear to be on a fairground ride and are in bright sun, but there is little other information. Despite this, Manos's uncanny image, a masterclass in style, mood and the power of colour, hooks in the viewer. His photograph surprises and hypnotizes, and continues to do so the longer you look at it.

+ PHOTOGRAPHER BIO
American, b. 1934

+ GOOGLE THESE
A Greek Portfolio (1975/1999), *American Color* (1995), *American Color 2* (2010)

+ WATCH THIS
'Constantine Manos – 5 Photographs and the Stories Behind Them' on the Leica Society YouTube channel.

Like This? Try These

→ Andrea Hernández Briceño

→ Matt Stuart

→ Alex Webb

Saul Leiter

Taxi

1957

Saul Leiter was never in a great hurry to make his photographs. He was happy to listen to music, drink coffee, and take pictures when the desire to do so arose.

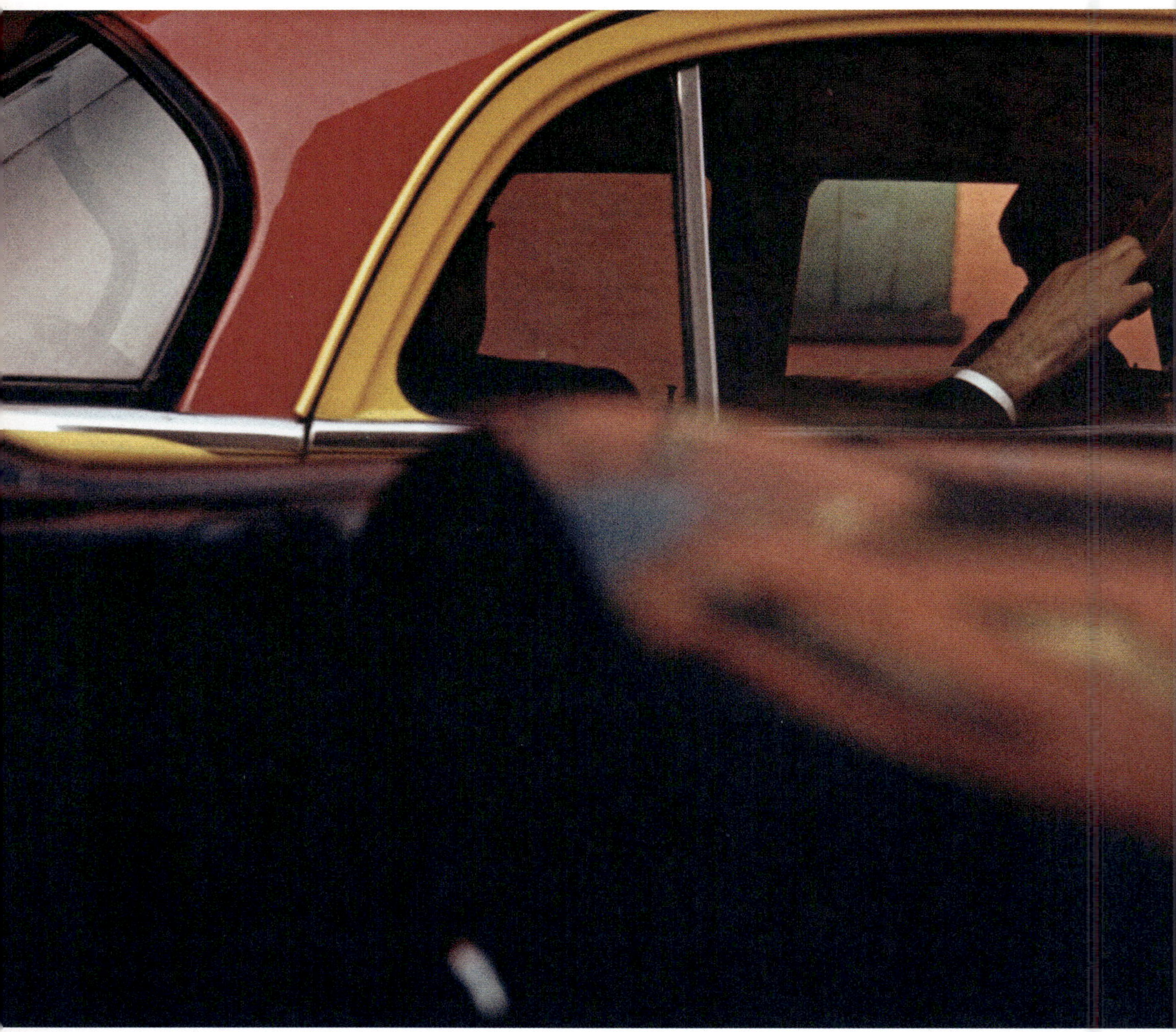

Yet when Leiter did photograph, he made it count. Quite often he would photograph the comings and goings on the streets around his home in Manhattan in New York, relishing the rich hues of the Kodachrome slide film he used. He started out in black and white but turned to colour in the 1950s, creating immaculately composed studies of the world as he saw it. A world that was awash with colour and made up of glimpsed interconnected shapes and sights. His photographs hint at something but never completely reveal what is going on. 'Painterly' is the adjective often used to describe Leiter's approach. This is unsurprising given that he pursued painting before he was encouraged to take up photography by the American Abstract Expressionist painter Richard Pousette-Dart. He used the camera to almost paint his photographs into existence. His immense skill lay in using planes of colour to construct his photographs. Their slightly compressed perspective means that they appear to have more in common with abstract painting than photography. Leiter loved to incorporate reflections, shoot over or around obstacles, and through gaps and windows. He would often fill the frame with colour, although shadow was important too.

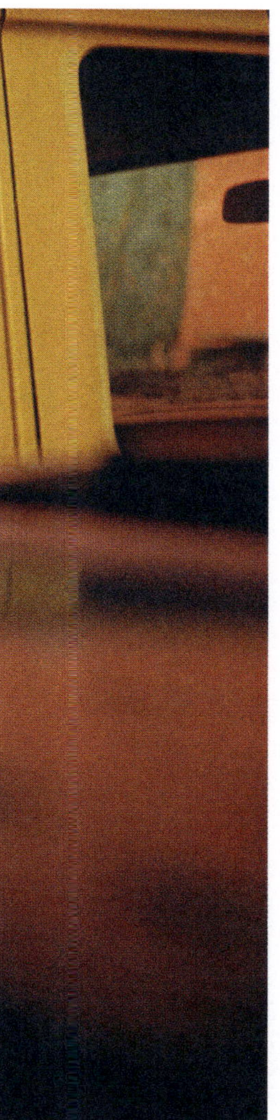

In this image the negative space of the bottom left third of the photograph is as integral to the overall composition as the areas of red and yellow. Shadow extends through the pictorial space, helping to glue everything together. Even the tiny patch of light has a part to play in the composition: cover it for a moment with the tip of your finger and the photograph loses its sense of balance and rhythm. Imagine what this photograph would look like in black and white – there would only be a combination of incoherent shapes. Leiter knew how to use colour to make his photographs soar.

+ PHOTOGRAPHER BIO
American, 1923–2013

+ GOOGLE THESE
Through Boards (1957), *Canopy* (1958), *Jay* (1958), *Snow* (1960)

+ WATCH THIS
The documentary *In No Great Hurry: 13 Lessons in Life with Saul Leiter* (2013) by Tomas Leach. It can be found here: watch.innogreathurry.com.

+ READ THIS
Saul Leiter: Early Color (2006) by Martin Harrison.

Like This? Try These

→ Ernst Haas

→ Fred Herzog

→ Vivian Maier

CHAPTER

9 A WONDERFUL WORLD

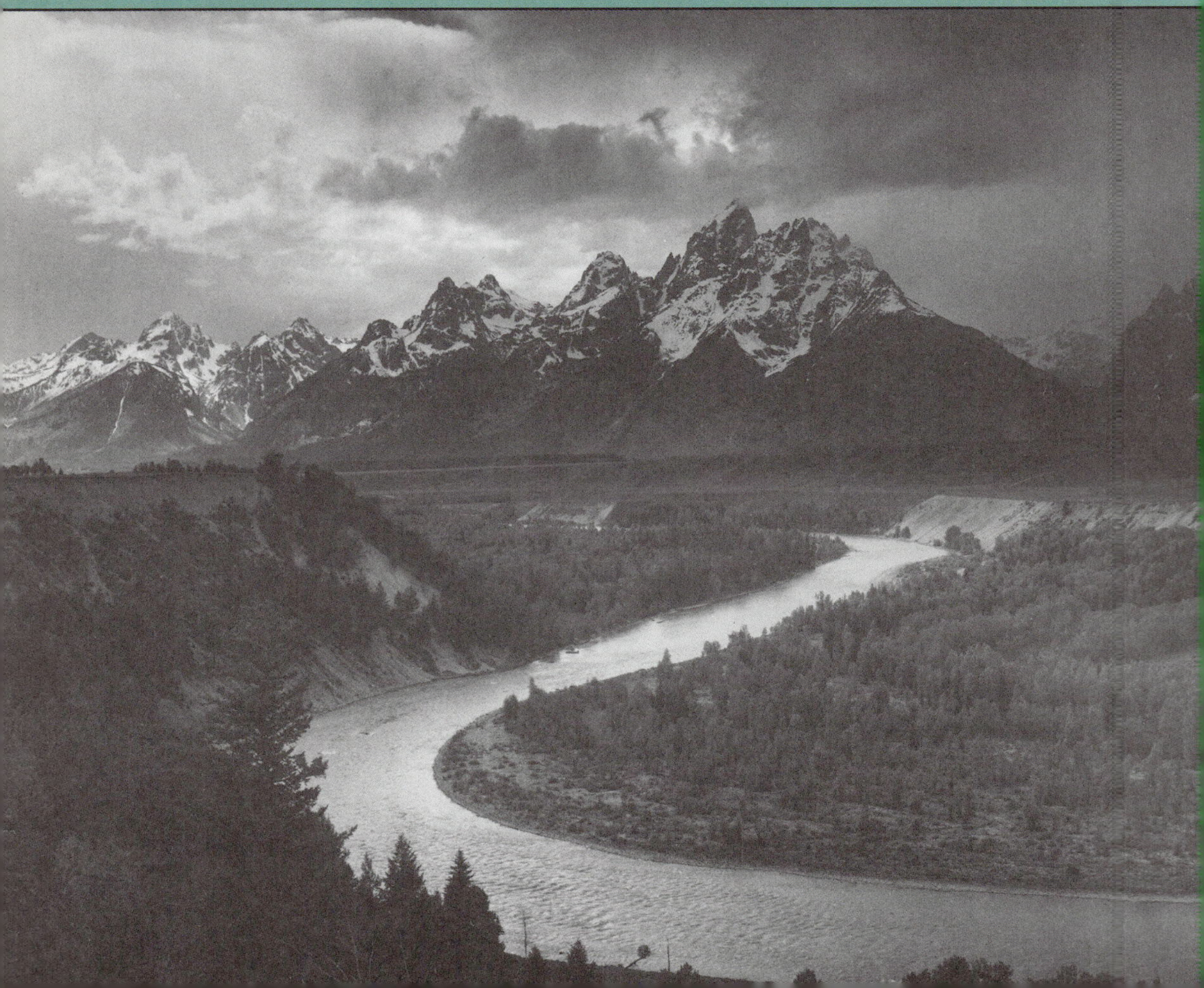

Ansel Adams

The Tetons and the Snake River, Grand Teton National Park, Wyoming

1942

Chances are you will have seen an Ansel Adams photograph before, even if you did not realize it. The American photographer is frequently cited as a forefather of photography, and his photographs of the American wilderness are mass-produced globally.

By the time Adams took this photograph of the Teton Range of the Rocky Mountains he had been making photographs in his beloved wild America since his teenage years, having regularly visited Yosemite National Park since 1916. Linger over any Adams photograph and you will see how expert he was at rendering landscapes in subtle and exquisite tones of black, white and grey. He developed and used something called the zone system to help him achieve tonal balance across every image. Adams was an advocate of 'straight photography', which privileges sharp focus and detail. However, he is renowned for capturing how a subject felt to him and he visualized how he wanted a picture to look before taking it thanks to a technique known as visualization. He wrote in his autobiography: 'The visualization of a photograph involves the intuitive search for meaning, shape, form, texture... The image is formed in the mind – is visualized – and another part of the mind calculates the physical processes involved in determining the exposure and development of the image of the negative.'

The tonal balance and contrast of this photograph is exemplary. The light dances lightly on the water's surface while the sun's rays begin to break out from behind dark clouds and tickle the tops of the mountains. As Adams's business manager and biographer William Turnage wrote, his images 'sought an intensification and purification of the psychological experience of natural beauty'. This is what happens here. In an age where the natural world is being destroyed at a devastatingly rapid rate you can look to Adams's photographs as reminders of how wonderful and precious the world is.

+ PHOTOGRAPHER BIO
American, 1902–84

+ GOOGLE THESE
Frozen Lake and Cliffs, Sierra Nevada, California (1932), *Moonrise, Hernandez, New Mexico* (1941), *Moon and Half Dome, Yosemite National Park, California* (1960)

+ READ THIS
'Ansel Adams: 10 Things to Know' feature on the Christie's website, at christies.com.

+ DISCOVER THIS
This photograph was one of 115 images included on The Voyager Golden Records carried by the Voyager spacecraft in 1977. The records contained sounds and images used as examples of human life and culture should any inquisitive extra-terrestrial life want to know.

Like This? Try These

→ Henry Hamilton Bennett

→ William Henry Jackson

→ Carleton E. Watkins

Alec Soth

USA/Canada, Falls 34

2005

Alec Soth is one of contemporary photography's greatest chroniclers of American life. He says his interest in photography lies in the sequencing of images so that each resonates with those around it rather than in what he has called the 'incredible image or the iconic moment'.

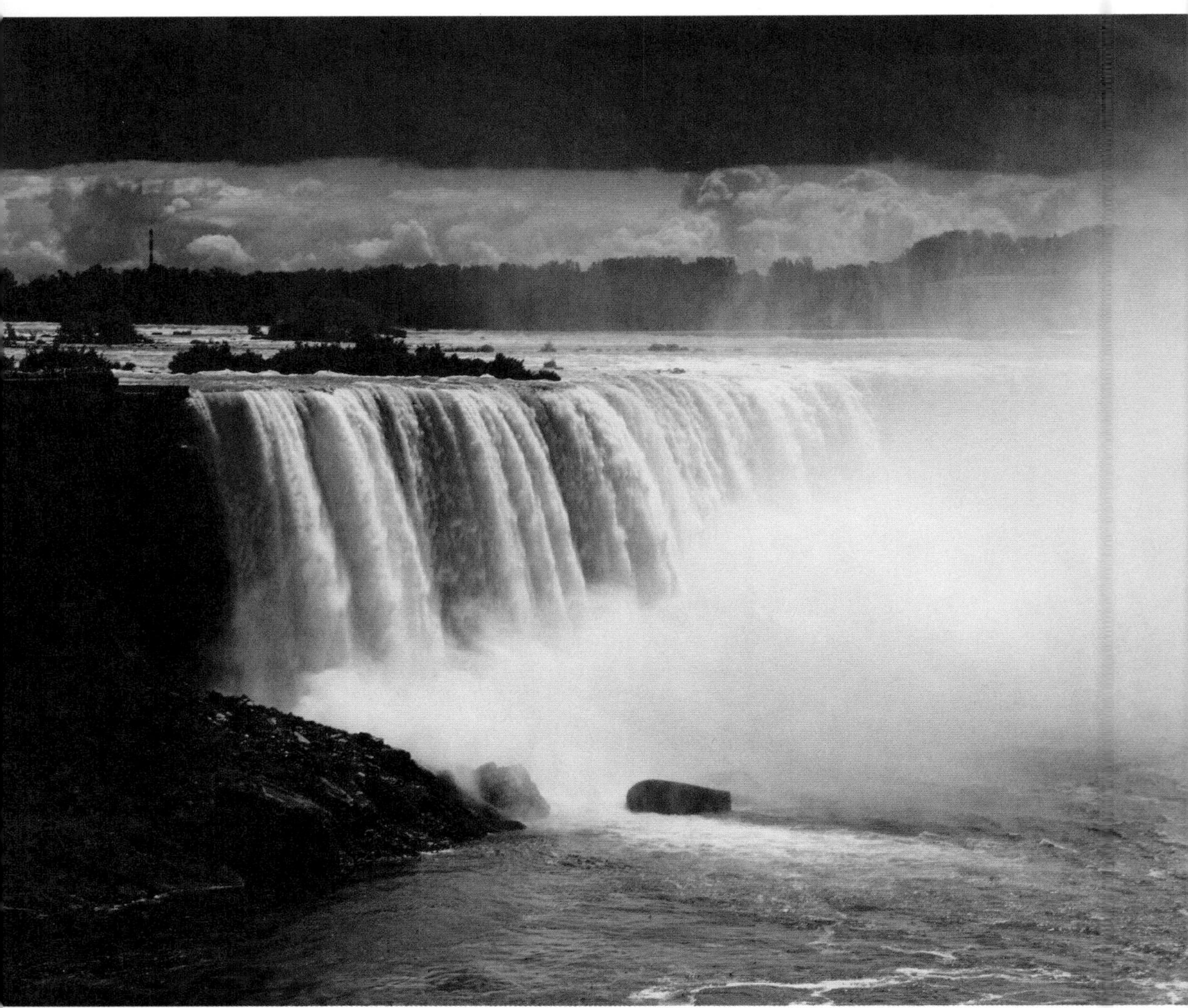

Delve into any of his major series including *Niagara* (2004–2006) to which this photograph belongs, and you will see the care taken in this regard. But while Soth is a master of using the photographic sequence as 'a form of extended narrative' as British journalist Mick Brown says, you can begin to understand how he uses photography to speak about what it might mean to be human by looking at a single picture, even one without people.

It is testament to Soth's skill as an image-maker that in his depictions of the American landscape, including this majestic almost celestial view of Niagara Falls, you find a similar nagging sense of the underlying melancholia present in many of his portraits. As you look out across the tumbling misty water, it recalls the work of nineteenth-century American landscape painters of the Hudson River School such as George Inness, Thomas Cole and Frederic Edwin Church. This is unsurprising given that Soth tried his hand at painting before turning to photography.

Niagara Falls, often referred to as a symbol of the American conservation movement, is one of the most painted and photographed landscapes in North America. It is a popular tourist destination particularly for newlyweds, and a place that has come to embody a sense of hope, romance and love. In Soth's version, one of several images of the famous falls in *Niagara*, you share his viewpoint as he stands back and surveys the light across this great expanse and tinkers with the exposure and framing before making his picture. The beauty of Soth's photograph, which seems to pay homage to the sublime in landscape painting, is breathtaking, but the image resonates on a deeper level: humans may live and die but the cascading water keeps moving.

+ PHOTOGRAPHER BIO
American, b. 1969

+ GOOGLE THESE
Kym, Polish Palace, Minneapolis, Minnesota, USA (2000), *Charles, Vasa, Minnesota* (2002), *Rodeo Dance, near San Antonio, Texas, USA* (2013)

+ WATCH THIS
Alec Soth - A Film by Ralph Goertz on the channel iksmedienarchiv on YouTube.

Like This? Try These

- → Jack Latham
- → Bryan Schutmaat
- → Vanessa Winship

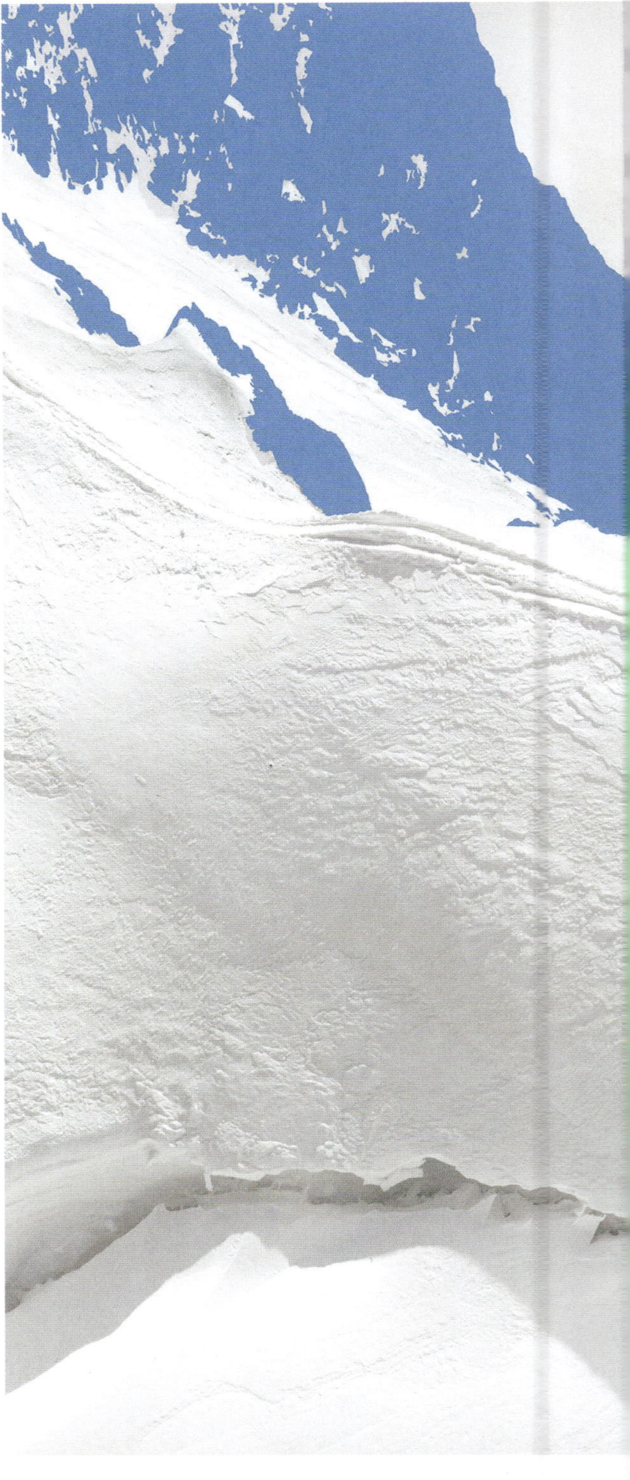

Olivo Barbieri

Alps – Geographies and People #5

2012

It is impossible to talk about Olivo Barbieri's photographs and not mention the words 'spectacle' and 'sublime'. His images, shot all over the world from the air, are spectacular in terms of their clarity of vision, technical precision, aesthetic clout, epic sense of scale, and dazzling depictions of nature and the built world.

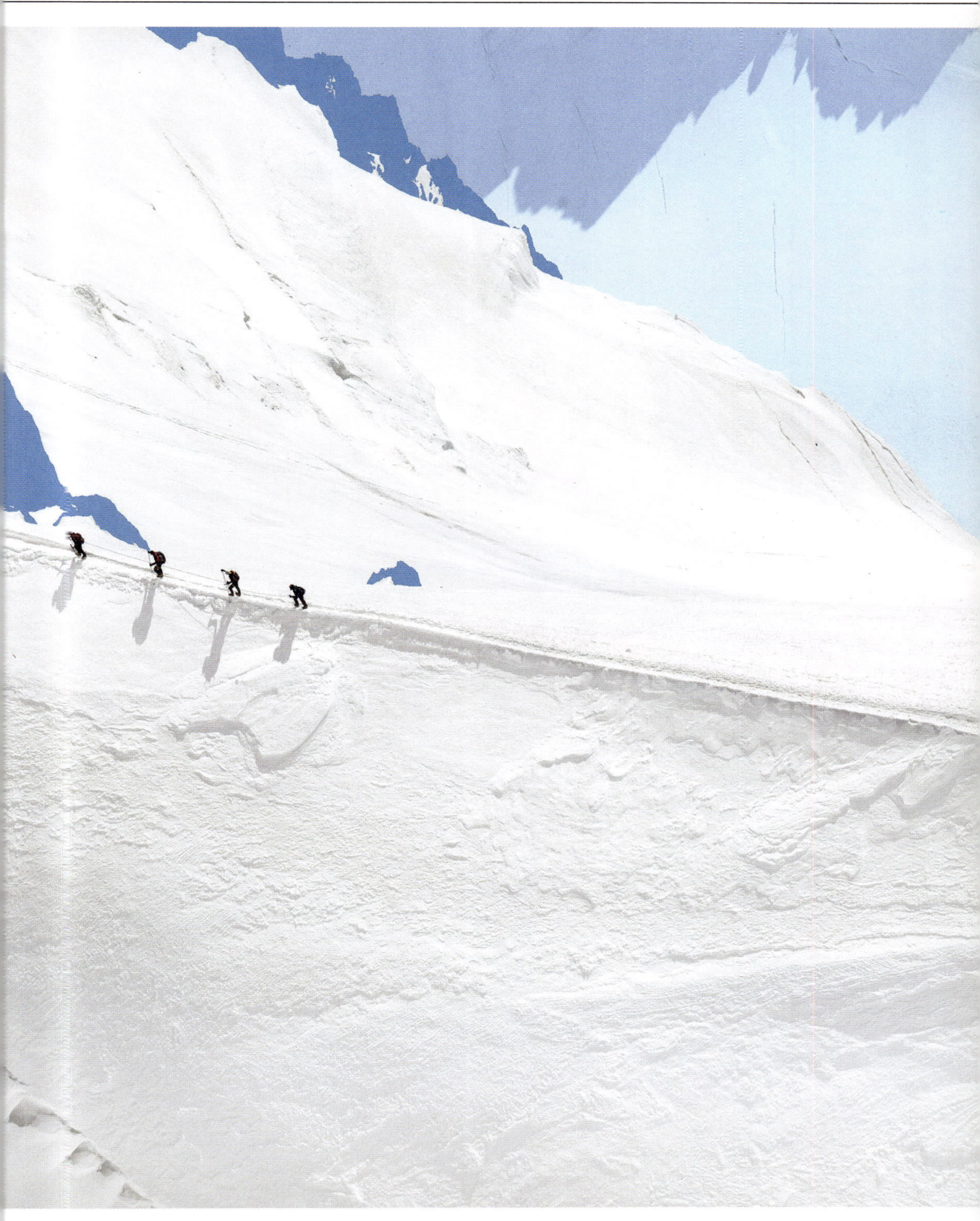

+ PHOTOGRAPHER BIO
Italian, b. 1954

+ GOOGLE THESE
Site Specific (2003–12), *The Waterfall Project* (2006–07), *Dolomites Project* (2010)

+ READ THIS
Visit Aperture's website aperture.org to read Christopher Philips's essay on Barbieri's series *Site Specific*.

Barbieri came to prominence with his tilt-shift photographs of Italian cities, which selectively focus on parts of the scene below, a technique he used in many places from São Paulo to Istanbul, Bangkok, Mexico City and more. This image, from a series he made over the Alps from a helicopter, continues along similar lines in the way it delights in playing with scale to distort reality. However, rather than using the selective focusing of tilt-shift as the principle device, Barbieri employs a technique he calls 'solid colour', which involves erasing and selectively whiting out parts of the mountains, to accentuate the mountains' expansiveness and in turn draw attention to the diminutive size of the climbers. Paradoxically, although the adventurers appear as tiny dots in the landscape and as such their faces are not visible, their courage and determination is heightened. This is humankind against nature where nature is stripped back to its sparsest elements. By diminishing the landscape's geographical specificity Barbieri renders it rootless. It is in such disorientating spaces, which the photographer refers to as a 'blank maps', that the viewer loses themselves.

The image could be read as a metaphor for human toil and strife in the face of great uncertainty. Moreover, Barbieri eloquently points to photography's inherent artifice and malleability, its potential for twisting reality, and demonstrates how its visual language can be pushed far beyond what you might expect. He demonstrates his showmanship in the process, which spars with his restless desire to reveal how phantasmagorical the world is.

Like This? Try These

→ Luigi Ghirri

→ Luca Locatelli

→ Massimo Vitali

+ **PHOTOGRAPHER BIO**
German-Russian, b. 1994

+ **GOOGLE THESE**
A traditional horse race of the Tuvinese National Festival Naadym in the steppe, at 43 degrees (2018), *Former ballerina Sofia has been dancing in the striptease club for six years after an injury kept her from dancing in the Krasnoyarsk State Theatre* (2018)

+ **WATCH THIS**
Heitmann discusses her work in 'LOBA Winner Newcomer 2019: Nanna Heitmann' on the Leica Camera YouTube channel.

Like This? Try These

→ Mitch Epstein

→ Kevin Faingnaert

→ Joel Sternfeld

Nanna Heitmann

Minusinsk, Yenisei River, Russia

2018

What is it about forests that captivates people? Childhood stories about woods, bears, wolves and witches travel with you, subconsciously at least, into adulthood when you begin to shake off such childish things. Yet, it is surely impossible to enter a patch of woodland anywhere in the world and not be moved to some degree.

In a similar way with this image German-Russian photographer Nanna Heitmann transports you back to the fairy tales of childhood where magic and fantasy reign supreme and good and bad battle it out ad infinitum. She was intrigued and inspired by Slavic folklore when she made the series *Hiding from Baba Yaga* (2018) to which this photograph belongs. Her mother is Russian and what she knew of the country came mostly from Russian fairy tales and children's films. Keen to experience something of the country for herself, she set out to photograph along the Yenisei River, the fifth-longest river in the world, which stretches from the Mongolian border through Siberia and into the Arctic Ocean. As she journeyed downstream, Heitmann had in her mind Baba Yaga, a mischievous witch in Slavic folklore who lives in the middle of a forest and appears in the work of Russian painters and illustrators such as Ivan Bilibin and Mikhail Vasilyevich Nesterov.

However, as much as Heitmann's work explores the region's mythology, it is really about what life is like for the people who live in this most desolate of regions. Themes from social and physical isolation to the inhabitants' relationship to the land pervade the project. Yet among the many intimate portraits are several landscapes, including this atmospheric image taken close to the town of Minusinsk. Wildfires are not uncommon in such densely wooded areas, and Heitmann has said that in the summer of 2018 there were a large number in Siberia partly because of the previous dry and warm winter. Something about the soft light and the way it falls on the feathery foliage gives the scene a dreamlike quality and for some a degree of melancholy. At the same time, the smoke adds a sinister air. Heitmann's quiet but powerful image is suspended between a fairy tale and the realities of a changing world, and stands as a beautiful if stark reminder of the fragility of nature but also its resilience and timeless beauty.

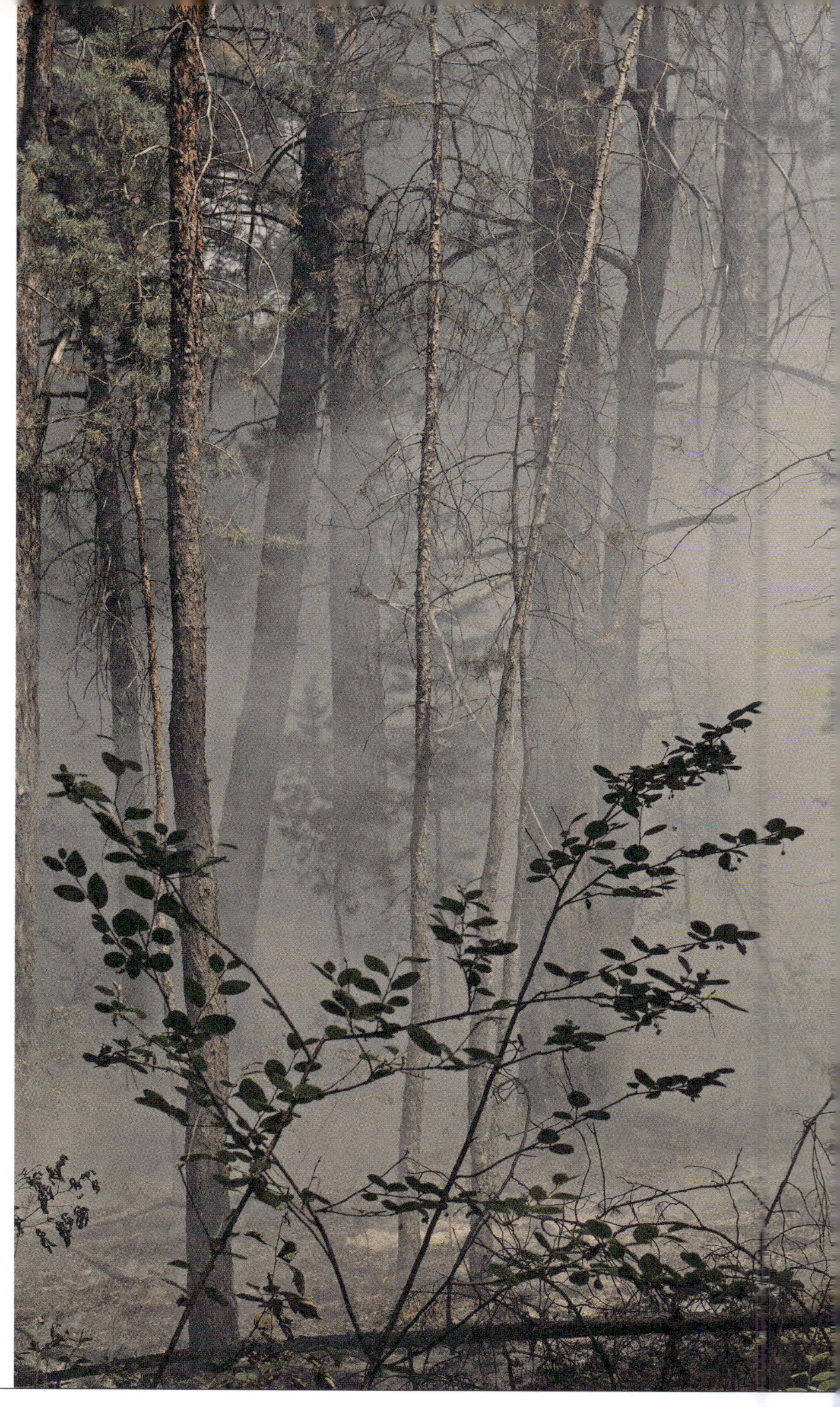

 Nanna Heitmann—Minusinsk, Yenisei River, Russia

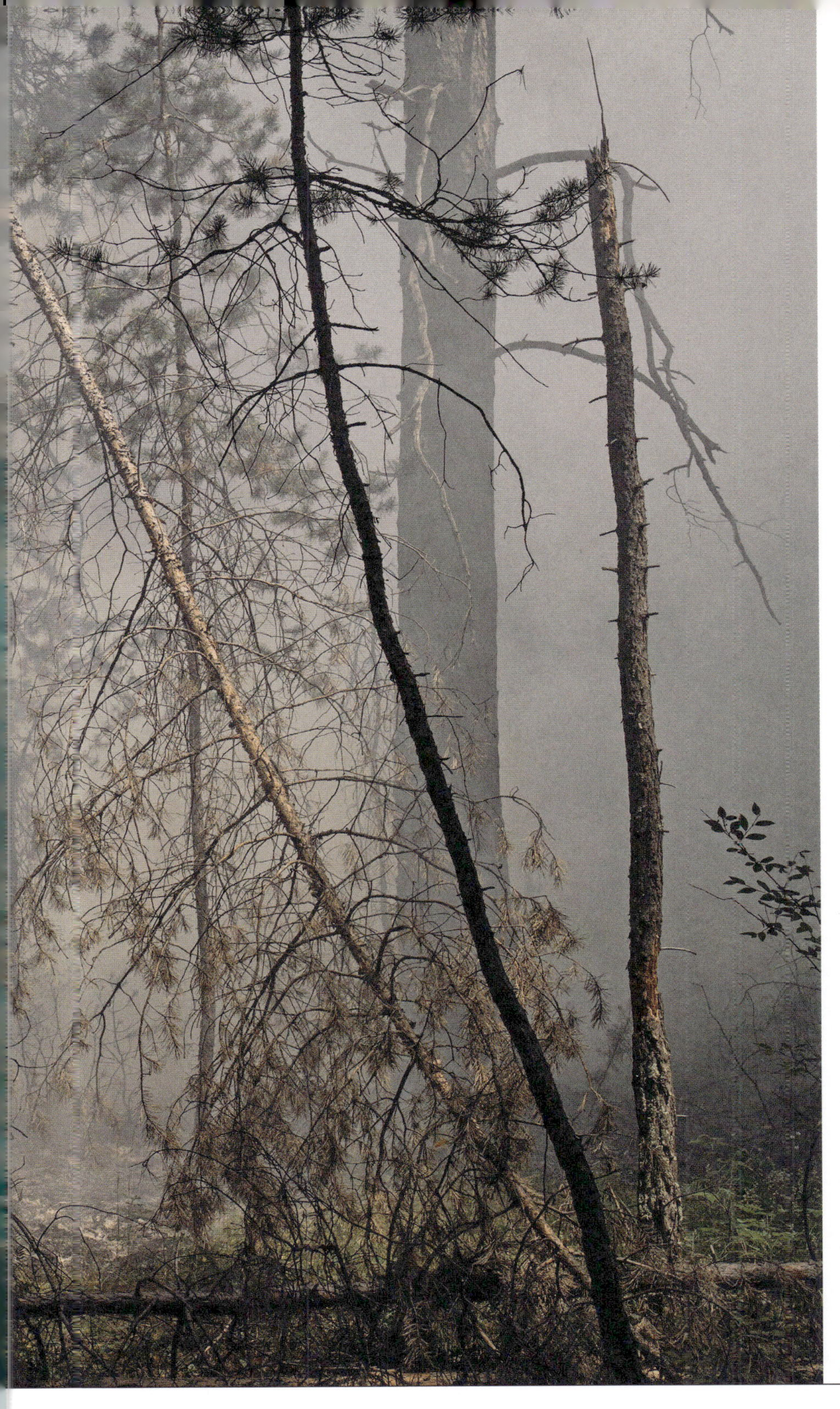

Georg Gerster

Watering Place, Western Australia

1989

Today people are used to seeing the earth from above. Most people have smart phones with cameras and think nothing of taking a picture through the window of an aeroplane to capture the view below. But the aerial photographs of Georg Gerster have a particular power.

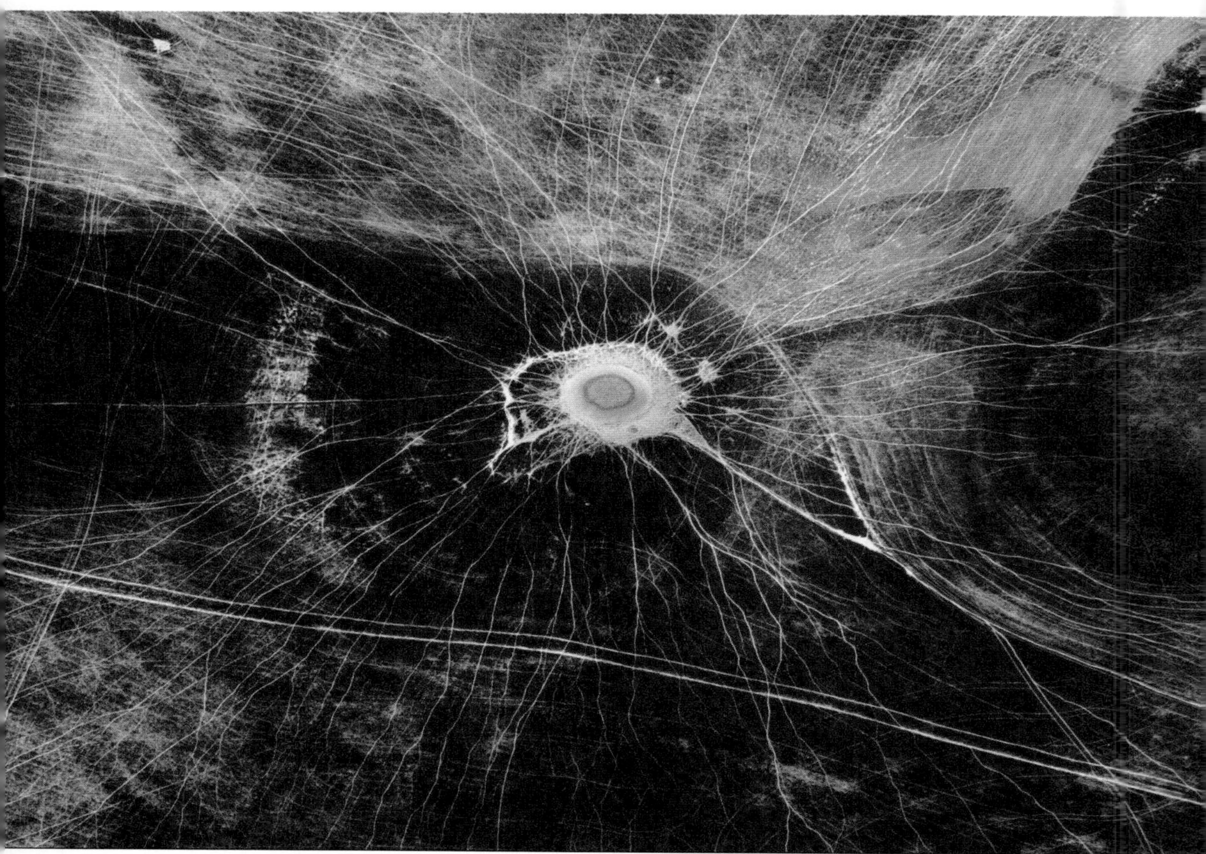

Photographers and flying enthusiasts have been making aerial photographs since 1858, so when Gerster started photographing from the air in the early 1960s, the genre of aerial photography was already well established. However, Gerster took the genre to a new level through his commitment to elevating aerial photography to something more probing, contemplative and ultimately artistic. He said height provides overview, which facilitates insight and in turn generates consideration and respect. If aerial photographs before Gerster offered a new perspective, his images gave a greater understanding of the world by picturing it in ways not seen before. He was a former magazine science editor turned freelance journalist with a focus on science reporting and aerial photography who photographed in more than one hundred countries during his career. His subjects were both natural and man-made landscapes, and much of his work focused on the impact of humans on the natural world.

Like many of Gerster's greatest aerial photographs, the view shown here is at first disorientating and there is nothing to give a clear sense of scale. The photograph is so abstract that at a glance it could be a gunshot hole in a pane of glass. It is a naturally forming watering place used by sheep at the foot of the Stirling Range of mountains in Western Australia. Gerster's caption to the image reveals that water collects in the soak and the groundwater level is high. He also poetically describes the tracks that lead into the hollow as 'silver threads'. One wonders what Gerster felt or thought looking down at such a scene from a great height. It must surely have been a mixture of emotions and thoughts ranging from awe and wonder to more sombre reflections on the preciousness of the natural world and the threat posed by human activity. Gerster made making images that inspire respect for the natural world his life's work and he never lost sight of his desire to create photographs that deliver an emotional punch.

+ PHOTOGRAPHER BIO
Swiss, 1928–2019

+ GOOGLE THESE
Harvest Pattern in the Pampas, Argentina (1967), *Drainage Patterns at Lake Natron, Tanzania* (1984), *Movable Market in Veracruz, Mexico* (1997), *Paradise Lost: Persia* (2008)

+ READ THIS
The Past From Above (2005) by Georg Gerster.

Like This? Try These

- → Yann Arthus-Bertrand
- → Edward Burtynsky
- → Bernhard Edmaier

Mark Power

View From the Bridge, Icebreaker 'Fennica', Bay of Bothnia, Finland

2002

It is not immediately clear what this disorientating image is. Perhaps it is a cloud-covered moon or a searchlight lighting up the night sky. It is a light but one that is beaming out across ice-covered waters.

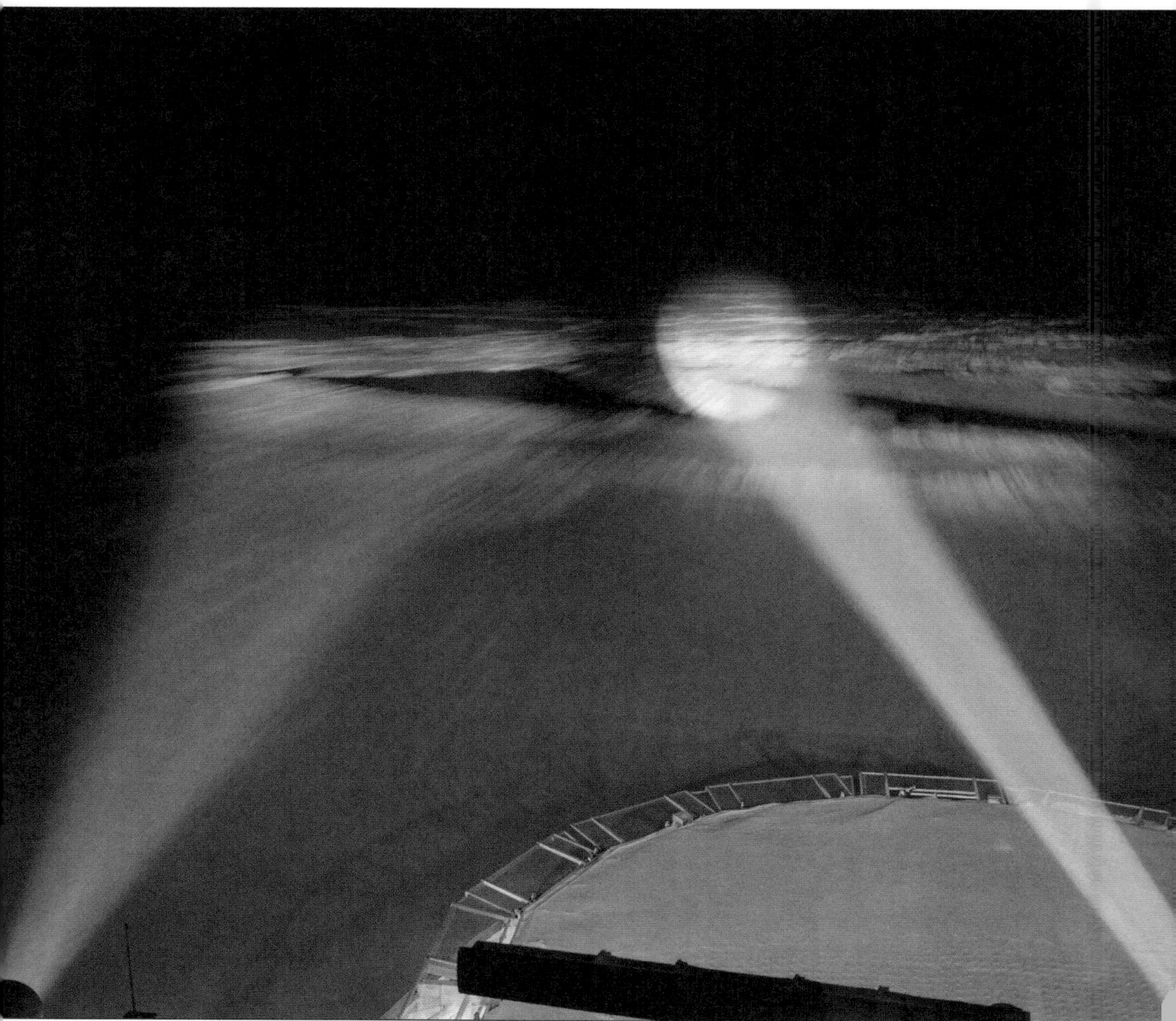

In March 2002, Mark Power joined the crew aboard two Finnish icebreakers, MSV *Kontio* and MSV *Fennica*, in the northern section of the Bay of Bothnia, which is the northernmost part of the Baltic Sea and freezes each year for up to six months. The crews carry out essential work in keeping shipping lanes open and in doing so help international cargo ships to reach Finnish ports. Finland's economy depends on year-round shipping and icebreakers can be in operation for as much as six months of the year. Ice is an obstacle to be overcome annually in the pursuit of safe waterways for sea traffic.

Power's almost monochrome image captures something of the movement of the huge icebreaker and the thrill of being aboard. In an interview about the project on Magnum Photos' website he spoke vividly of his experience : 'As the ship moved around large ports and tiny harbours I got to see a Finland that most people probably never do.'

He said that the immense silence and sense of solitude when the engines stopped, was something he had 'never known before or since'. As the viewer travels with Power into the darkness, it is possible to sense something of its almost otherworldly solitude. The image of the searchlight and vessel forging ahead into a great unknown acts as a metaphor for human endeavour and exploration. It also stands as a metaphor for photography itself, a medium whose evolution has been driven by humans' desire to confront and overcome technological and creative challenges. It is thanks to visionaries such as Power who venture into the world's most challenging environments and return to share what they have seen in the form of photographs that others have access to photographic records through which to make sense of the world.

+ PHOTOGRAPHER BIO
British, b. 1959

+ GOOGLE THESE
The Shipping Forecast (1993–96), *The Sound of Two Songs* (2004–10), *Mass* (2010–12)

+ READ THIS
Mark Power's 2014 book *Die Mauer ist Weg! (The Wall is Gone!)*, showing his photographs of the Fall of the Berlin Wall, November 1989.

+ SEE THIS
Power's website: markpower.co.uk.

Like This? Try These

- → Peter van Agtmael
- → David Fathi
- → Awoiska van der Molen

John Divola

Zuma #25

1978

The contrast between the human-made and the natural world could not be starker in this image by John Divola. From his landmark series, *Zuma* (1977–78), in which the artist photographed inside an abandoned beachfront property in southern California, the image pulls the outside in and at the same time there is a sense that the interior is clamouring to break into the expanse beyond.

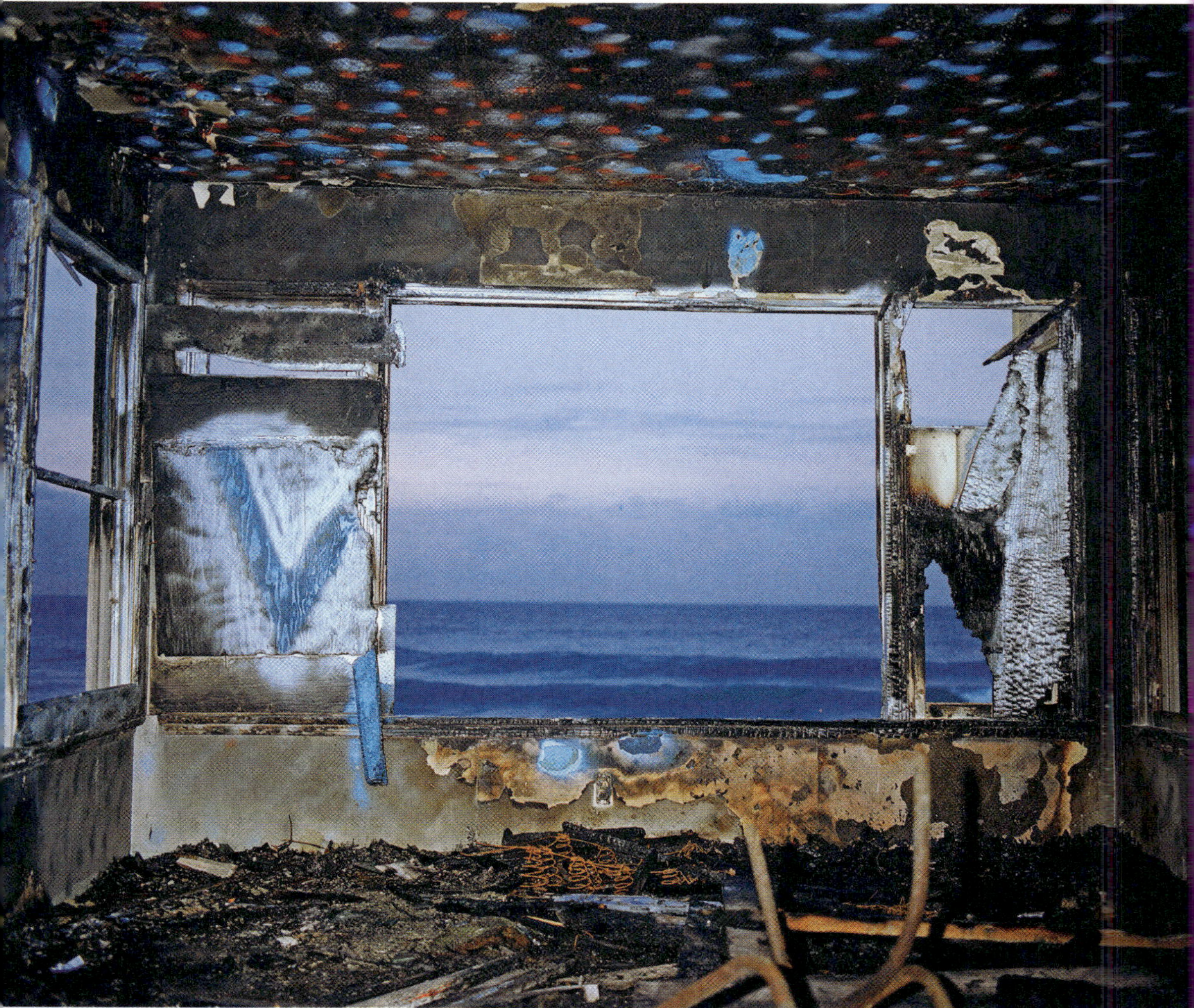

Nature and humankind have been thrust into the same space and a compelling tension, visually and environmentally, ensues. The human-made structure frames the natural world perfectly, and the viewer is left with an overwhelming feeling of something being perpetually just out of reach.

It is tempting to romanticize an image like this with its dreamy sky and gently rising and falling sea, but to try to explain it through metaphor misses the point. As Divola told the *Los Angeles Times* in 2013: 'You can't photograph the sublime, you can only traffic in the specific and its relationship to the symbolic.'

In light of his statement, the viewer should be mindful of reading too much into photographs. Nonetheless, the image asks the viewer to think about how people engage with the world and how photography might be used to do that.

Divola came across the derelict property on Zuma Beach and then spent two years observing and documenting its changing state. The building was used by the fire service for training and as such suffered from fire damage as well as vandalism. Divola also began to intervene, using spray paints to make his own mark on the building. Gradually, the site became a place where performance art, sculpture and installation coexisted and was recorded with forensic, deadpan clarity through photography. Divola is aware of the limitations of his chosen medium to truly articulate the nuances of experience and feeling, nonetheless he has said he wants his photographs to be seductive and be about 'unattainable desire'. As such, the viewer may be forgiven for using the space he has created within this image to reflect upon what the natural world means especially at a time when environmental concerns have become important for so many.

+ PHOTOGRAPHER BIO
American, b. 1949

+ GOOGLE THESE
Isolated Houses (1995–98), *Dogs Chasing My Car in the Desert* (1996–98)

+ READ THIS
'Who, What, Where, With What, Why, How and When? The Forensic Rituals of John Divola' by David Campany at davidcampany.com.

Like This? Try These

- → John MacLean
- → Richard Misrach
- → Jill Quigley

Richard Misrach

Untitled

2007

Richard Misrach's name has been synonymous with large-format colour landscape photography since the 1970s. He focuses on the American west and humankind's complex and destructive relationship with the natural world in particular.

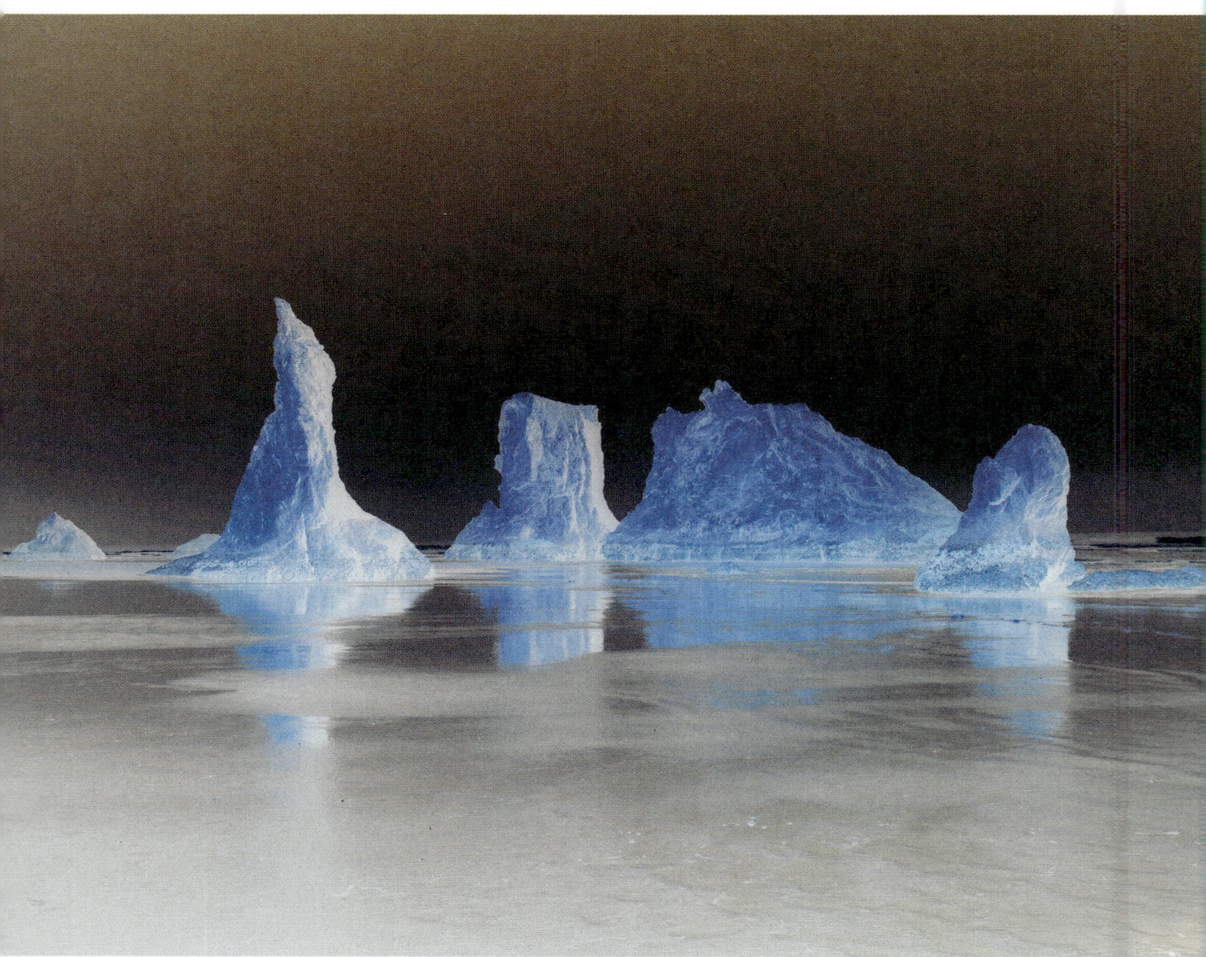

In the mid to late 2000s, Misrach made a series of large-scale works shot digitally rather than on film, reversing the colours to create what have been described as 'chromatic negatives'. The strange, eerie scenes he depicts seem almost apocalyptic and are unsettling because they teeter on the edge of familiarity. What you think you are looking at is often not what you are being shown. This photograph is a case in point: what the viewer presumes are icebergs rising from an icy sea are rock formations off the coast of Oregon. Misrach's decision not to divulge contextual information by leaving the image untitled leaves the work open to interpretation.

Like many of his photographs, it creates a sense of awe and wonder. Misrach presents a take on the landscape sublime yet at the same time there is a nagging sense of melancholy and impending doom. Beauty in Misrach's photographs is never straightforward; it is often bound up with inconvenient truths. His carefully realized photographs are reminders that there is no way to avoid the stark realities the viewer may wish to ignore, ranging from the cost to the environment of nuclear testing to the harm caused by industrial development and petrochemical production. During an interview with Aperture magazine in 1992, editor-in-chief Melissa Harris asked Misrach if he was 'aestheticizing the horrific'. He replied: 'I've come to believe that beauty can be a very powerful conveyor of difficult ideas. It engages people when they might otherwise look away.'

Misrach knows that beauty captivates, and that it has the power to motivate people to stop, look and take note. Moreover, he understands how to wield that power photographically for maximum effect and that power is on display here. By referencing the idea of rapidly disappearing icebergs in such a hauntingly beautiful way, Misrach points to the seminal issue of the moment, climate change.

+ PHOTOGRAPHER BIO
American, b. 1949

+ GOOGLE THESE
Untitled (Burning Bush #2, Arizona) (1976), *Stonehenge #4* (1976), *Untitled (Psychedelic Lance #2)* (2007), *Untitled (Reverse colour of haystack rock)* (2007)

+ WATCH THIS
'Photographer Spotlight: Richard Misrach' on the Los Angeles Review of Books YouTube channel.

Like This? Try These

- → Edward Burtynsky
- → David Maisel
- → Richard Mosse

Camille Silvy

River Scene, France

1858

This photograph of the Huisne River in France took the world by storm when it was put on display in 1858. The pastoral masterpiece is the image for which French photographer Camille Silvy is best-known.

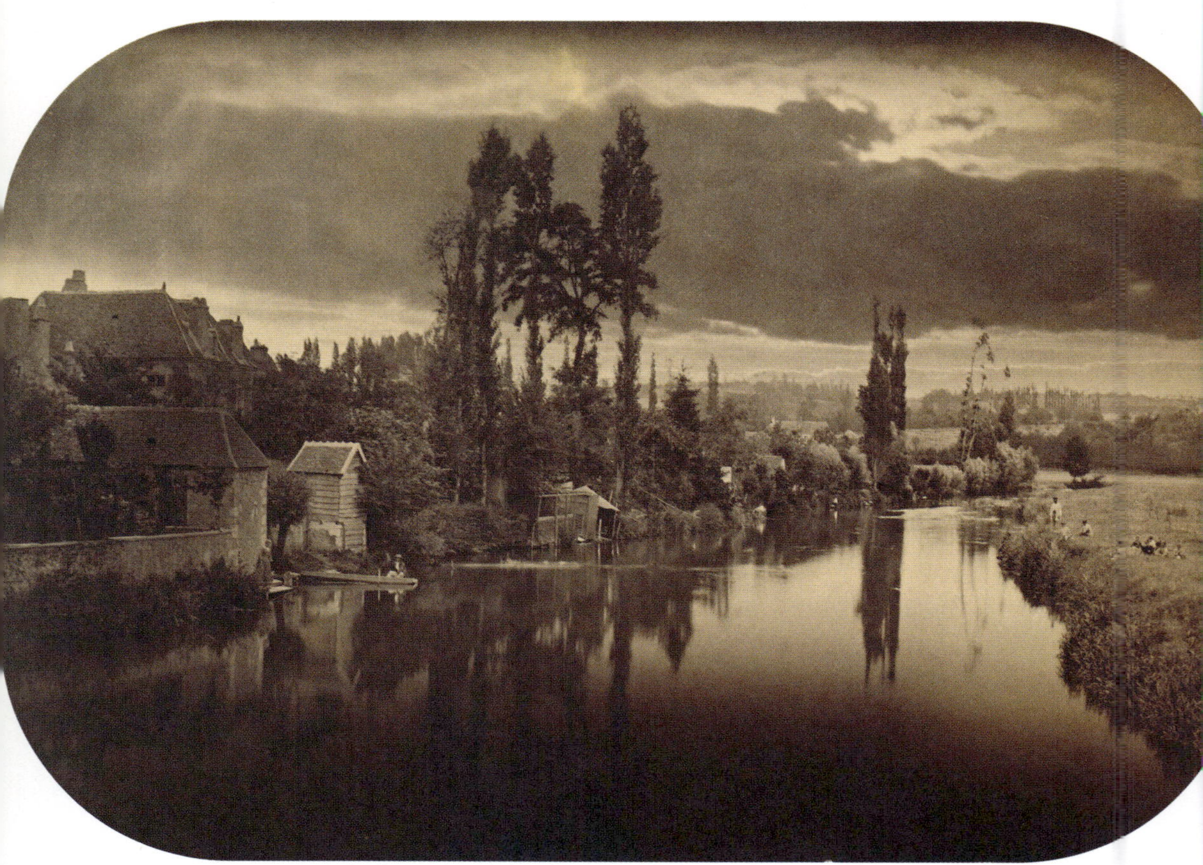

Perhaps the image's extraordinary sense of tranquillity is down to the glassy river or enigmatic sky, or maybe it is the soft shadows on the water's surface or majestic trees that stretch up to the brooding clouds above. Possibly it is the humble fields that stretch into the distance as far as the eye can see. The photograph's power could be the combination all of these elements.

When it was first shown in Edinburgh, critics praised its beauty and marvelled at the level of detail on display. As British historian Mark Haworth-Booth wrote in his book about the photograph, reviewers were quick to elevate the photograph to the realm of painting with one critic calling it 'equal' to any work by seventeenth-century Dutch landscape painter Aert van der Neer, who was known for his paintings of river scenes. Photography was in its infancy in the 1850s, and comparisons to painting were not uncommon as critics clamoured to make sense of the new medium.

Silvy took the photograph from a bridge over the river one summer's day not far from his birthplace at Nogent-le-Rotrou in northern France. He used two exposures to create his composite photograph – one for the foreground and another for the sky – which were then joined together. This technique was commonly used in photography's early period, especially in landscape photographs, to capture detail evenly across a scene where there are contrasting areas of light and dark. The join would have been disguised by hand. As contemporary photography historians have pointed out, such an approach is a reminder of the medium's inherent artifice. Although the photograph is a construction of a fabricated reality that does not distract from its breathtaking beauty. It is a photograph that is steeped in nostalgia, and should be celebrated for its unapologetic sentimentality.

+ PHOTOGRAPHER BIO
French, 1834–1910

+ GOOGLE THIS
Studies on Light: Twilight (1859)

+ READ THIS
Camille Silvy: River Scene, France (1992) by Mark Haworth-Booth.

Like This? Try These

- Henry Hamilton Bennett
- Lady Clementina Hawarden
- Gustave Le Gray

Alexander Mourant

Blue Tree

2017

+ PHOTOGRAPHER BIO
British, b. 1994

+ GOOGLE THIS
Peckham I, To Feel Its Touch, Peckham 24 (2019)

+ READ THIS
Read an interview with Alexander Mourant on the Photoworks website: photoworks.org.uk/interview-alexander-mourant.

Alexander Mourant's photograph of a cluster of trees in an ancient Japanese forest is unusual as the trees appear blue. He used a cut-to-fit piece of coloured glass from a church window attached to his camera's filter holder to achieve the startling effect so that blue appears to wash over the entire landscape.

The blue colour here is all encompassing, all consuming. You almost breathe it in, so that it captivates utterly. The experience recalls French philosopher Gaston Bachelard's observation: 'In the domain of blue air more than anywhere one feels that the world is permeable to the most indeterminate reverie.' All is obliterated with monochromatic efficiency save the spindly and feathery trees, which stand tall amid the mist. Bachelard inspired French artist Yves Klein for whom blue was famously 'the invisible becoming visible', a colour beyond dimensions. Klein in turn inspired Mourant, who uses the colour blue to play with notions of visibility. At first you see less because all is blue – indeed, blue is all you can see, it is disorientating – but as you become used to its presence you almost forget the blue is there and are drawn further into the picture. A scene previously eclipsed opens up before you as details initially overlooked become visible.

Mourant has spoken about his affinity to the colour blue and how an urge to embrace it within his work became almost overpowering. That intensity is evident here. He began to explore how blue might be used photographically in a previous project, *Aurelian* (2016–2017), a meditation on the passing of time and memory. However, in this body of work, *Aomori* (2017), which means 'blue forest' in Japanese, Mourant goes further: He ponders not only what blue might be or mean in a philosophical sense but how it might be used as a lens or a filter to look at nature itself. In photography, the colour blue and nature share a history, not least in English botanist and photographer Anna Atkins's cyanotypes, but Mourant's rendering pulls you into the realms of reverie where blue is infinite, deep and unknowable.

Like This? Try These

→ Yojiro Imasaka

→ Sam Laughlin

→ Ryan L. Moule

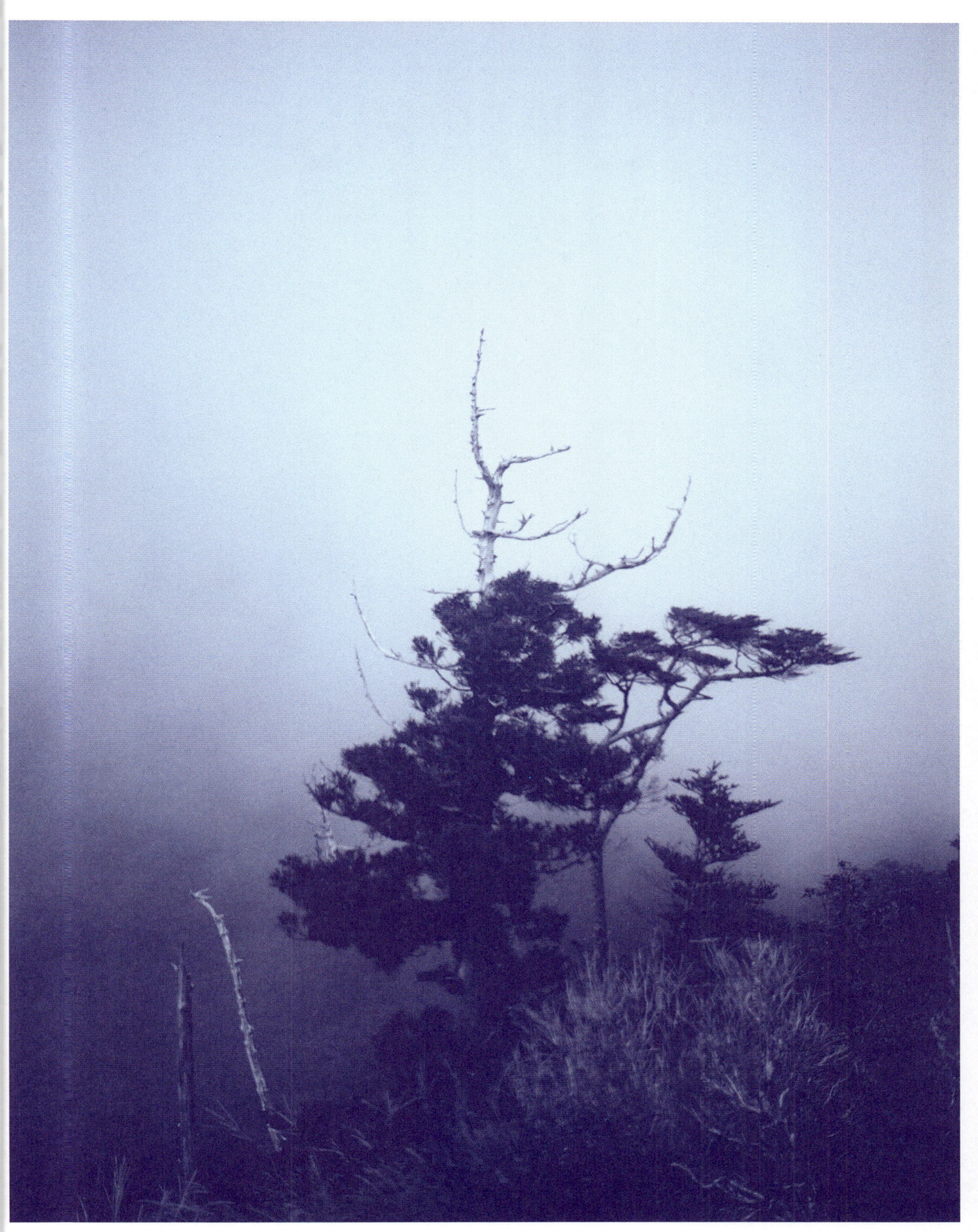

CHAPTER 10

CAPTURING WHAT THE EYE CAN'T SEE

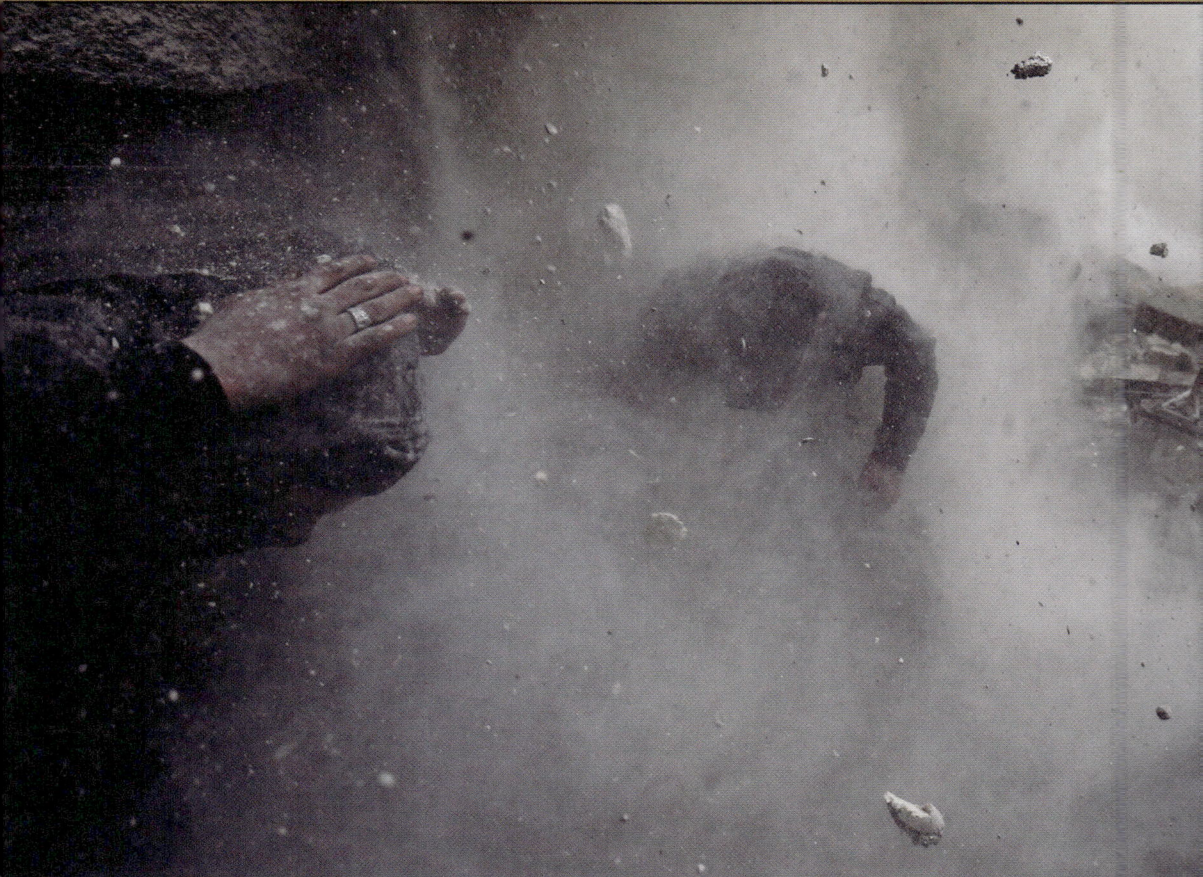

 Goran Tomasevic—Syrian Rebels Dodge Debris

Goran Tomasevic

Syrian Rebels Dodge Debris

2013

A man covers his head in an attempt to protect himself from flying debris as another runs for cover. All is chaos after a tank shell fired by the Syrian Army explodes in Damascus, Syria, taking most of a nearby wall with it.

Tomasevic's photograph is so convincing and real you can almost hear the temporary ringing in ears that follows an explosion. It puts the viewer at the heart of the action as the scattered debris seems to be hurtling straight at you. To take such a picture requires the photographer to be in the centre of the action. Serbian photographer Tomasevic is no stranger to photographing in war zones. His first experience of photographing conflict was in 1991 in his native Yugoslavia, and he has also worked in Kosovo, Afghanistan and the Palestinian Territories. On this occasion, he was with the Free Syrian Army in the Damascus neighbourhood of Ain Tarma on 30 January 2013 when the explosion happened, destroying the wall he had been using for cover. Minutes before, a rebel had been shot and killed by a sniper in front of him. Tomasevic photographed the sequence of events as the man was dragged away to die from his injuries, and he kept on shooting as a desperate situation became even more dire. The resulting series *Under Fire in Damascus* (2013), chronicles two hours of intense fighting with terrifying realness and was shortlisted for the 2014 Pulitzer Prize in the Breaking News Photography category. As a photo story, the series shows how the action unfolded, like a ghastly newsreel made up of stills.

However, this image also has a strange quality as if time has been frozen meaning it sticks in the mind – and the throat. How Tomasevic managed to capture such a moment unscathed is unfathomable. What makes his photograph so powerful is that even in the midst of an explosion he manages to retain an artistic eye to convey the immediacy of the event and draw you in. With great virtuosity honed over many years, Tomasevic captures a moment that most people will thankfully never experience and conveys the realities of war in a way few can.

+ PHOTOGRAPHER BIO
Serbian, b. 1969

+ GOOGLE THESE
US Marine Corps Assaultman Kirk Dalrymple Watching Statue of Saddam Hussein Topple in Baghdad, April 9, 2003 (2003), *A Battle Against Islamic State Fighters* (c. 2011–16)

+ SEE THIS
A gallery of Goran Tomasevic's images in 'Serbian Photographer On The Front Lines Of History' on the RadioFreeEurope/RadioLiberty website, rferl.org.

Other Compelling Photojournalists

→ Andrea Bruce

→ Tim Hetherington

→ Yuri Kozyrev

Naoya Hatakeyama

Blast #05707A

1998

Few people have witnessed an explosion in real time and fewer still will have attempted to photograph such a moment as it happens. Naoya Hatakeyama is one of the few photographers to have successfully captured this spectacle on film not once but several times.

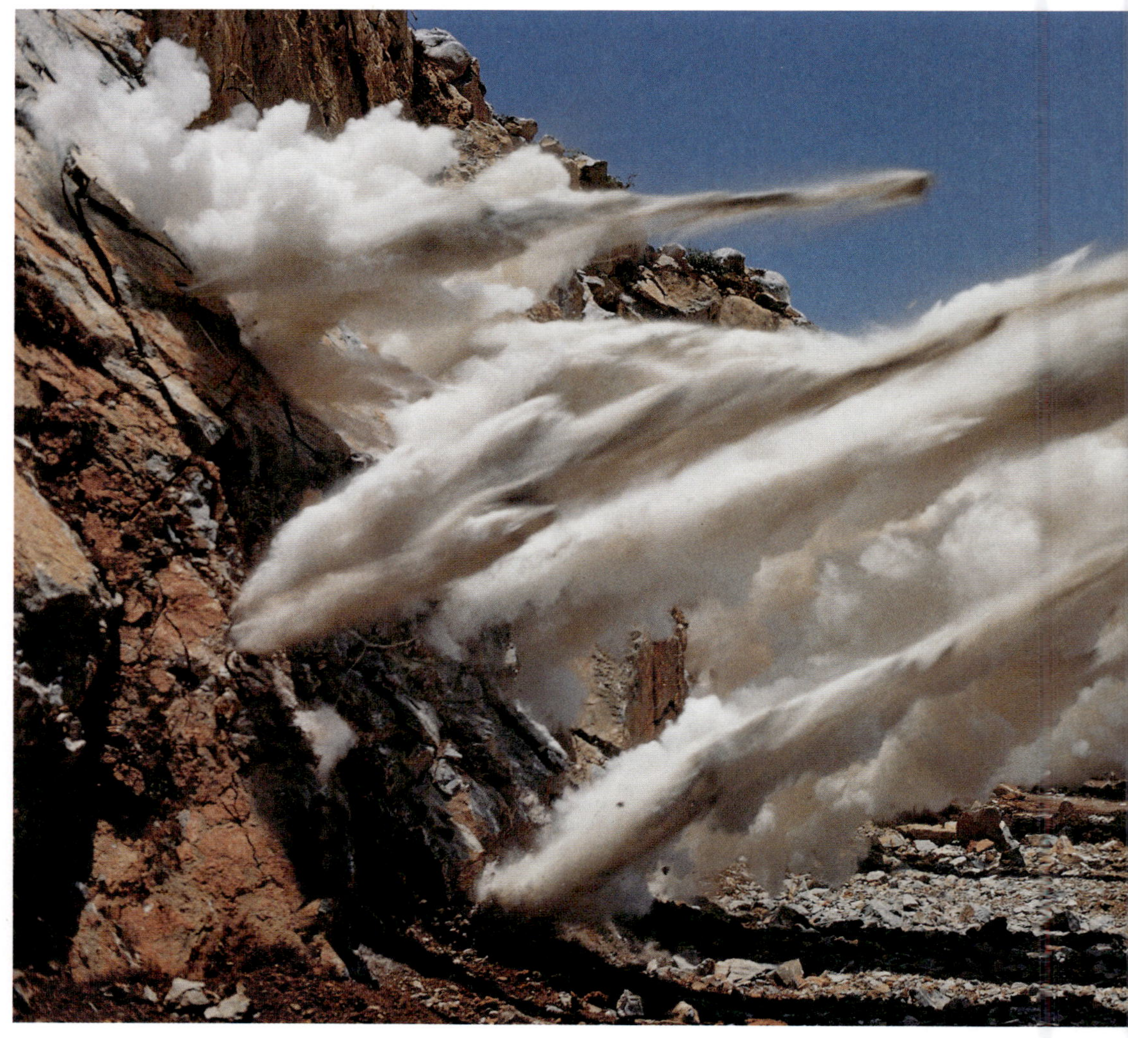

In 1995, he began a series of photographs showing controlled explosions in limestone quarries in Japan. The detonations enable the limestone, a key material used to make cement, to be extracted. Hatakeyama grew up on the north-east coast of Japan where limestone is plentiful . His father worked in a cement factory and often took him fishing at a port where quarried limestone was being loaded onto ships, so limestone played an important part in his vision of the world. After studying art at the University of Tsukuba, he photographed the quarries and factories he saw around him before turning his attention to the explosions themselves.

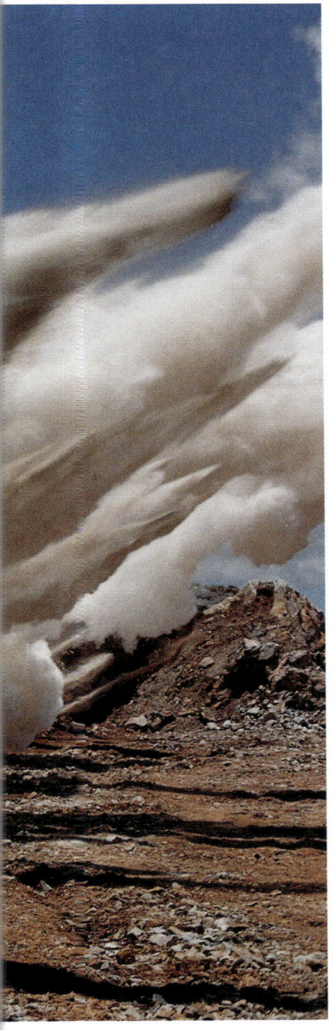

What is remarkable about Hatakeyama's Blast (1995–2008) series is that rather than photographing from a distance with a telephoto lens, Hatakeyama used a remote-control camera system and, with the help of engineers, calculated, the precise moment to trigger the shutter. Consequently, the moment of capture and moment of detonation are aligned perfectly. In doing so, Hatakeyama creates a wonderful parallel or synergy between the two events. The surge of energy and extreme force of the explosion is recorded in impressive detail. Photographs often document humanity's impact on the earth but in this image the results of human activity are explicit. The process of destruction unfolds before the viewer. Were it not for photography it would not be possible to witness such a sight slowed down and frozen in time as it is here. That the image calls to mind volcanic eruptions, a blast in a war zone or even the devastating Japanese earthquake of 2011 is testimony to its mystique.

+ PHOTOGRAPHER BIO
Japanese, b. 1958

+ GOOGLE THESE
Lime Hills (1986–90), *Underground* (1998–99)

+ READ THIS
Visit the San Francisco Museum of Modern Art website www.sfmoma.org/artist/Naoya_Hatakeyama to read an overview of Hatakeyama's work.

Like This? Try These

→ Andrea Botto

→ Harold Edgerton

→ Ori Gersht

Robert Capa

Death of a Loyalist Militiaman

1936

This is one of the most instantly recognizable but also hotly contested and widely discussed photographs in the history of photography. It was taken in September 1936, less than two months after the start of the Spanish Civil War (1936–1939).

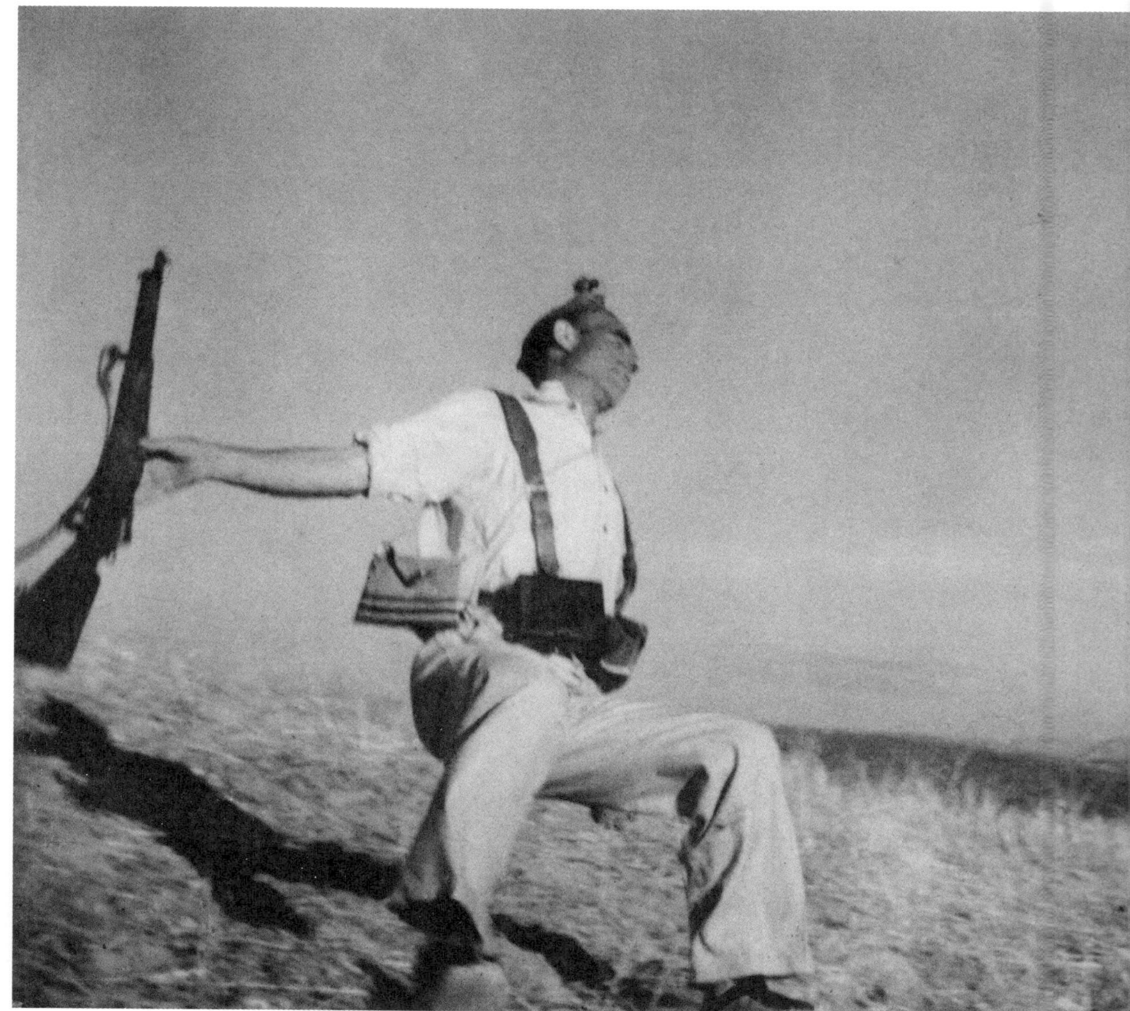

Robert Capa's photograph of a militiaman who has just been shot resonated deeply with audiences when it was first published three weeks after it was taken and it has barely been out of public consciousness since. The photograph is one of the first to show a soldier dying in action on a battlefield. It is thought that Capa took the photo of the loyalist soldier at Cerro Muriano, just north of Córdoba in southern Spain. However, disputes have raged over its veracity since the 1970s when claims were first made that Capa may have staged the photograph. Much discussion has taken place since then with fresh assertions put forward most notably by a Spanish researcher in 2009 claiming that the photograph was not taken where, when or how people thought. Some theories even contend that the soldier posed for Capa's camera and was then shot by a sniper. Capa said he had been in the trenches with Republican militiamen and took the picture by holding the camera above his head. Without a full sequence of negatives, it is impossible to corroborate any of the theories.

Supporters have vehemently defended the photograph over the years, denying claims that it was faked. But there is no doubting the power of this sober depiction of the moment of death. How rare it is to see the moment of impact, to bear witness to such a violent end, preserved through a medium with an undeniable link to the world, even if the truth it purports to tell is never black or white.

+ PHOTOGRAPHER BIO
American-Hungarian, 1913–54

+ GOOGLE THESE
Omaha Beach, Normandy, France (1944), *Death of an American Soldier, Leipzig, Germany, 18 April, 1945* (1945)

+ WATCH THIS
Cynthia Young, curator of the International Center of Photography, explains the controversy surrounding this photo in the video 'Altered Images: Cynthia Young' on Bronx Documentary Center's channel on Vimeo.

Other Compelling Photojournalists

→ Eddie Adams

→ Yevgeny Khaldei

→ Don McCullin

Richard Drew

Falling Man

2001

+ **PHOTOGRAPHER BIO**
American, b. 1946

+ **GOOGLE THESE**
Assassination of Robert F. Kennedy, Los Angeles (1968), Thomas Hoepker's photograph of New Yorkers on 11 September 2001

+ **LISTEN TO THIS**
Drew talks about *Falling Man* on the B&H Photography podcast, available at bhphotovideo.com.

+ **WATCH THIS**
Drew discusses the making of *Falling Man* in 'The Story Behind the Haunting 9/11 Photo of a Man Falling From the Twin Towers' at Time.com.

It is a photograph almost too graphic to look at. Yet just as we have an inability to resist looking over to the site of an accident when we see blue flashing lights at the roadside, it is hard not to look at Associated Press photographer Richard Drew's infamous and controversial photo taken during the attacks on New York's Twin Towers on 11 September 2001.

On the left-hand side is the North Tower and on the right, the South. The man, who is presumed to have jumped from the building, perfectly bisects the towers as he speeds towards his death. There are few photographs in history that show the death of a human as it happens. Other examples include Hungarian-American war photographer Robert Capa's photograph of a shot soldier (see page 204) and American photographer I. Russell Sorgi's photograph of Mary Margaret Miller (see page 208). These kinds of images do not happen often, which makes them more impactful when they do. It is only photography with its limitless capacity for instant capture that can record such terrible moments.

The title of Drew's photograph comes from an article written by Tom Junod published in *Esquire* in 2016, which discusses in gruesome detail the possible identity of the man. He is believed to have worked at the restaurant at the top of the North Tower. Drew says the picture is quiet and does not show blood and guts yet it has proved controversial. Perhaps it is because we do not want to be confronted with death. Somehow the photograph, solemnly poetic and undoubtedly bleak, chilling and disturbing in its quietness, gets under our skin. Its possibilities for existential discussion are limitless. Perhaps you are in the camp that questions whether Drew should have taken it or if it should have been published at all. Whatever your view, Drew was doing his job and without such photographs, as horrific as they are, our capacity to reflect upon humanity, unimaginable adversity and life itself would be woefully reduced.

Other Photographers of 9/11 Images

→ Steve McCurry

→ Gilles Peress

→ Larry Towell

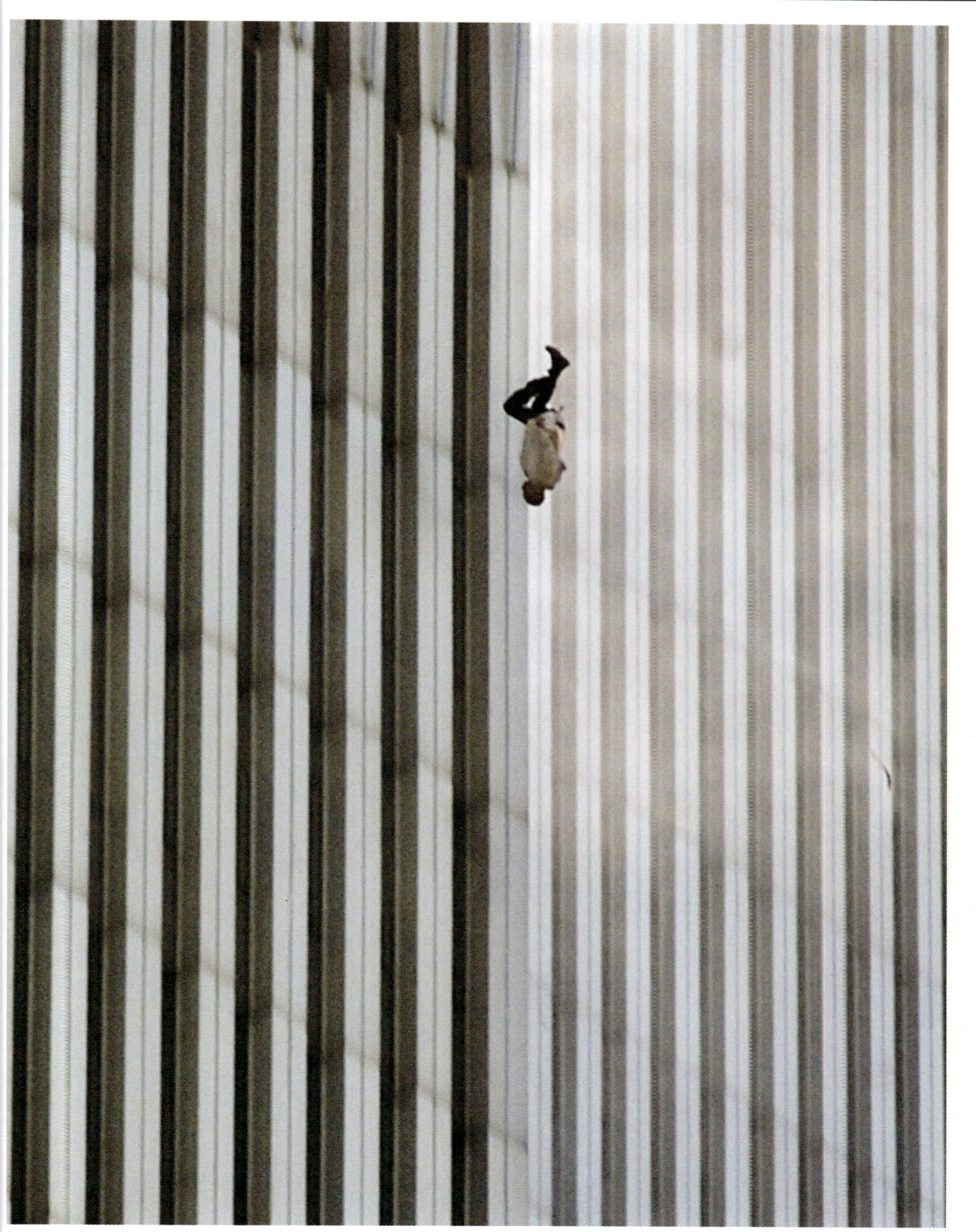

I. Russell Sorgi

Suicide, Buffalo

1942

It is debatable whether images are the product of chance or design. In the case of this haunting image it is both.

As Terence Wright discusses in his in-depth analysis of this photograph, when I. Russell Sorgi, a staff photographer with the *Buffalo Courier-Express* newspaper, spotted a blue-lit police car, he decided to investigate. What followed was something he could not have foreseen, but he did have some control over how he photographed events. The woman in his picture is thirty-five-year-old divorcee Mary Margaret Miller from Chicago who leapt from an eighth-storey ledge of the Genesee Hotel where she was staying. For Sorgi, the encounter was a photographic opportunity. Later, he wrote: 'The chance that every news photographer dreams of – to be in the right spot at the right time – fell right into my lap'.

Sorgi took a couple of exposures and then, after Miller jumped, waited for her to pass the second or third storey before releasing the shutter. The result is a picture that is as beautiful as it is tragic. She looks almost balletic and graceful as she falls, suspended between life and death. American academic Thomas Stubblefield wrote of the photographer's motivation: 'Clearly the intent was to capture the inevitability of impact, to come as close to death as possible without actually touching it'.

Sorgi,'s photograph is the perfect example of the dazzling and sometimes horrific brilliance of spot news photography. When it works, when everything comes together, this type of photography is unsurpassable. His is an image that continues to fascinate critics who delight in dissecting the image and pondering possible interpretations. Writers including Stubblefield have commented on the picture's harrowing disconnect as a result of the individual happenings – the police officer entering the building, patrons looking out from the coffee shop and falling woman – forever separated by Sorgi's camera, the obliviousness of the protagonists to what is unfolding and the tragedy encapsulated in Sorgi's image given that the police officer will always be just too late to talk the woman down. If Sorgi is an eyewitness, we are with him too, watching in vain as a woman who we know so little about brings her life to an end in the most violent way.

+ PHOTOGRAPHER BIO
American, 1912–95

+ GOOGLE THESE
The Burning Monk (1963) by Malcolm Browne, *The Most Beautiful Suicide (Evelyn McHale), Life* magazine (1947) by Robert C. Wiles

+ READ THIS
For more on this photograph see 'Case Study: I. Russell Sorgi's photograph of a suicide' in *The Photography Handbook* (1956) by Terence Wright.

Other Compelling Photojournalists

→ Alphonse Bertillon

→ Mell Kilpatrick

→ Weegee

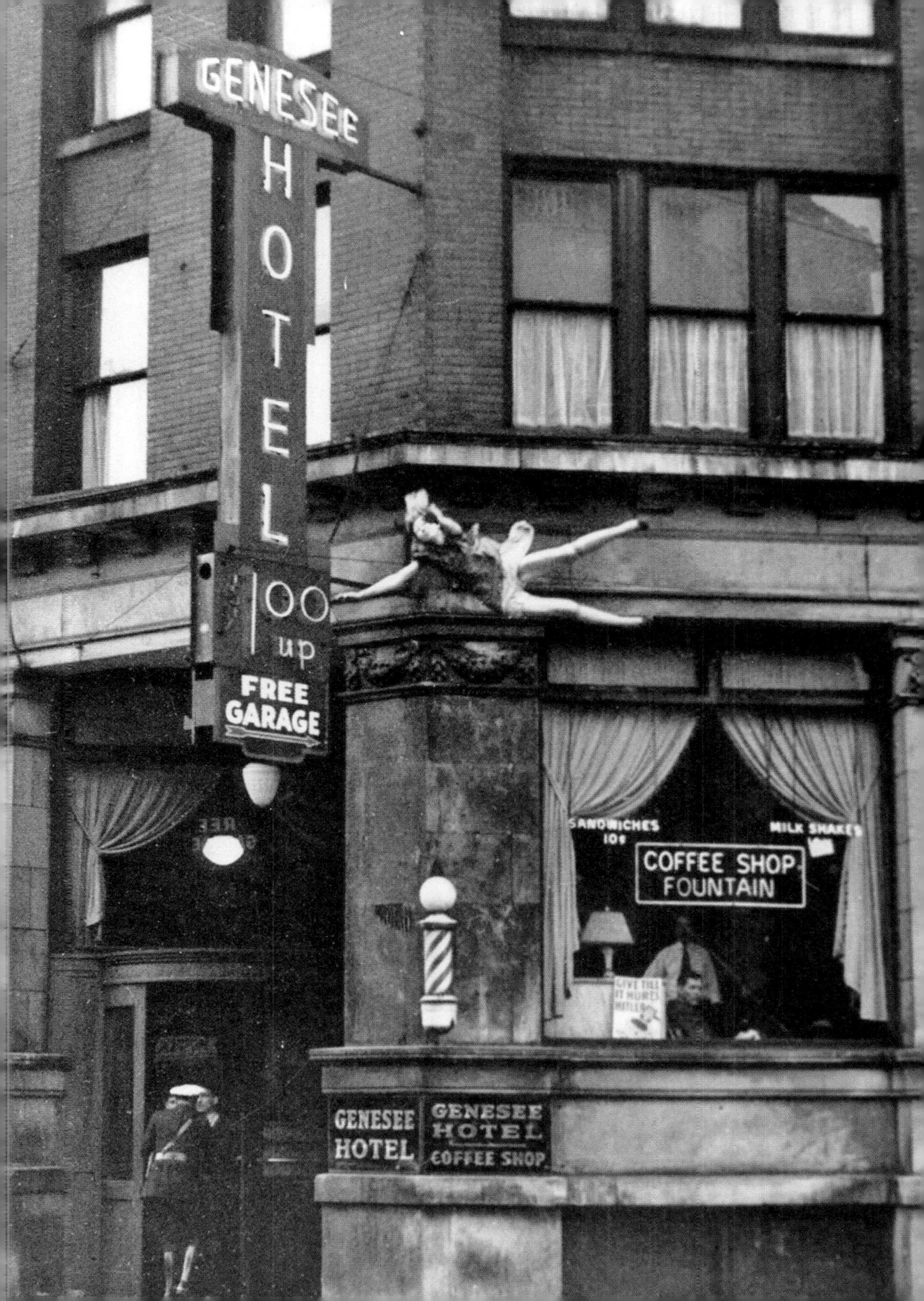

GENESEE
HOTEL
100 up
FREE GARAGE
SANDWICHES 10¢
MILK SHAKES
COFFEE SHOP FOUNTAIN
GENESEE HOTEL
GENESEE HOTEL COFFEE SHOP

Eadweard Muybridge

Plate 755, Pigeon Flying

c. 1887

Everyone has seen pigeons in the sky or scrabbling around on the ground. Fewer have seen pigeons like this. It is hard to believe that the humble pigeon could look so extraordinary, so angelic and divine.

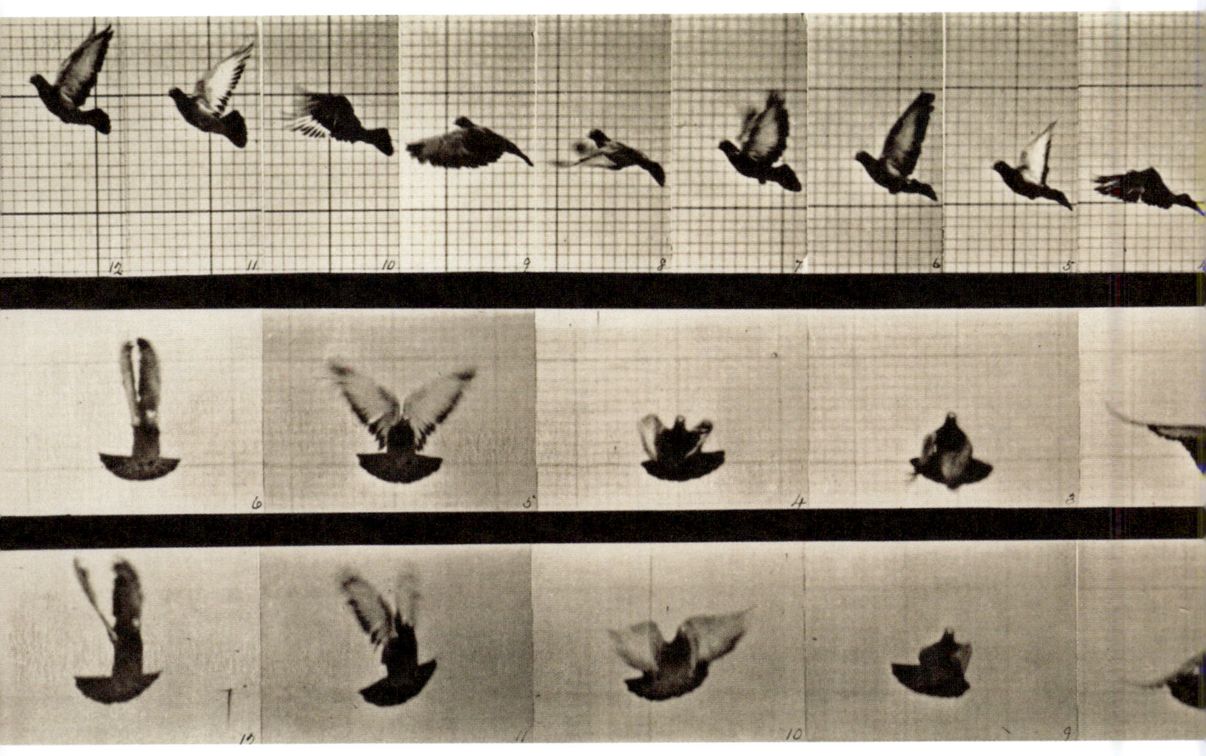

In Eadweard Muybridge's hands every animal and human he photographed became an object of fascination as he sought to show how motion works through his photography. When he was working in the late 1800s, he wowed audiences with his experiments, which showed things that had never been seen before. But even in the photography and cinema saturated world of the twenty-first century his images are as impressive as ever for their brilliant illustration of deconstructed movement. In 1877, Muybridge successfully proved that when a horse trots there is a point when all four of its feet are off the ground. He went on to make hundreds of photographic studies of other animals including cats, dogs and people. He gave lectures using a device he developed called a zoopraxiscope, which allowed him to project images in rapid succession making them appear to move, and his work is lauded as a precursor of modern cinema.

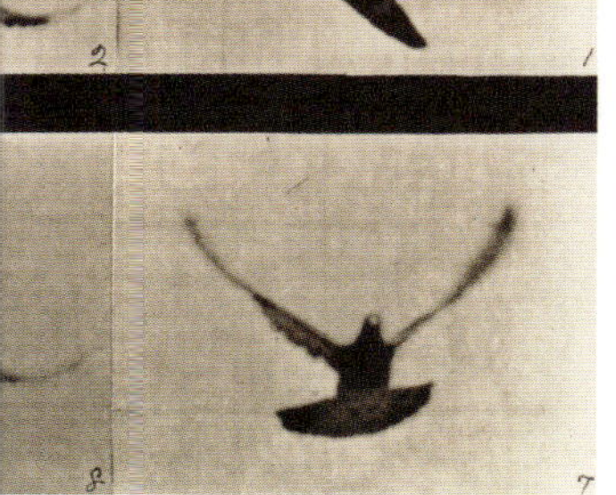

This plate, number 755, is one of almost 800 Muybridge included in his epic work, *Animal Locomotion: An Electro-photographic Investigation of Consecutive Phases of Animal Movements* (1872–1885). The majority of plates depict men and women moving in various ways from walking and running to leaping and dancing, but the animal sequences are equally insightful. Muybridge's earlier horse sequences have been widely published and they are rightly famed for what they depict. However, there is something about the movement of this pigeon, and the elegance and fluidity of motion that makes this sequence hard to tear your eyes away from. Thanks to Muybridge's pioneering efforts we are able to see precisely how animals and birds move.

+ PHOTOGRAPHER BIO
English-American, 1830–1904

+ GOOGLE THIS
Animal Locomotion: An Electro-photographic Investigation of Consecutive Phases of Animal Movements (1872–1885)

+ SEE THIS
Search 'Eadweard Muybridge' at royalacademy.org.uk to view the many works of his they hold in their collection.

+ WATCH THIS
A video on Muybridge and his groundbreaking work at sfmoma.org/artist/Eadweard_Muybridge.

+ READ THIS
Motion Studies: Time, Space and Eadweard Muybridge (2003) by Rebecca Solnit.

Like This? Try These

→ Ottomar Anschütz

→ Étienne-Jules Marey

→ Gjon Mili

Jacques Henri Lartigue

My Cousin, Bichonnade, Paris

1905

If ever there was a photograph that celebrates joie de vivre, this is it. Jacques Henri Lartigue was just eleven years old when he took this photograph of his cousin in Paris, and he would continue to make photos that tapped into twentieth-century life in France.

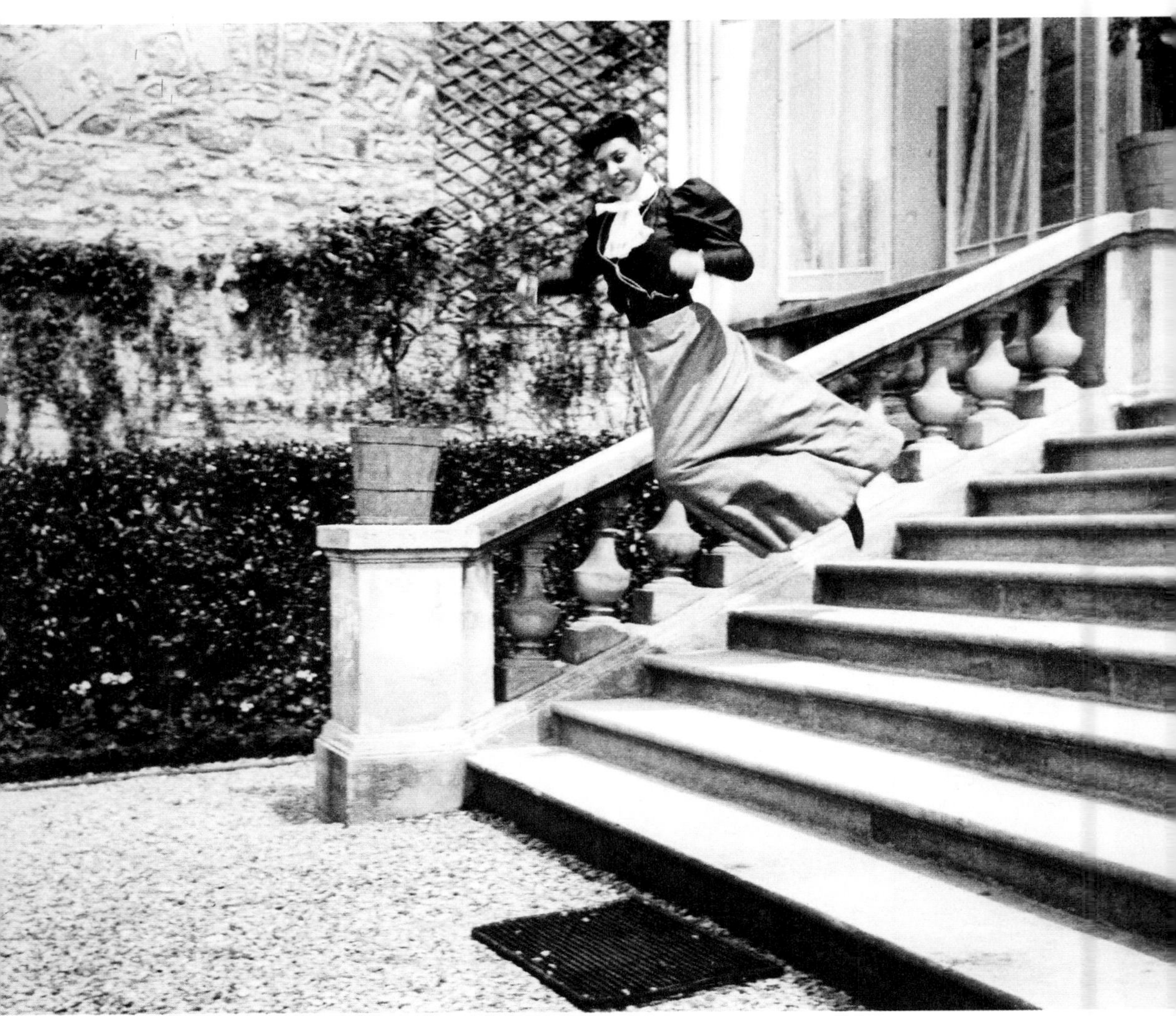

Lartigue has been called 'a gifted amateur' and had a talent for spotting moments as they happened and snapping them at lightning speed. He was a child prodigy who was given a camera at the age of seven. Highly tuned into the fashions of the day, he had an eye for details, expressions and gestures. He also had a fascination for movement that resulted in a penchant for stopping action in time.

This photograph is the most wonderful example of Lartigue's indefatigable skill in exploiting the camera's time-stopping ability and an example of how adept he was at bending photography to his will. Everything in the image comes together perfectly, from the converging lines of the staircase, the plant pots at the top and bottom of the rail to the mat, the creases on the woman's skirts, her well-positioned foot, joyful expression and hands that seem to propel her forwards. Had he clicked the shutter a fraction of a second earlier or later, the result may not have been so brilliant.

You can wonder why cousin Bichonnade was leaping and what had happened moments before and afterwards, but you can also enjoy the photograph for its light-heartedness. Lartigue's great skill lies in inviting you to enjoy this most carefree of moments and to delight in the pleasures of looking. Photography is full of mysteries and unanswerable questions but he reminds you it is OK to enjoy it for its own sake.

+ PHOTOGRAPHER BIO

French 1894–1986

+ GOOGLE THESE

Cousin Caro and Mr Plantevigne, Villerville (1906), *Avenue du Bois de Boulogne Paris, January 15, 1911* (1911)

+ READ THIS

'Snap Judgment: How Photographer Jacques Henri Lartigue Captured the Moment' by William Boyd at guardian.com.

+ READ THIS

Lartigue: The Boy and the Belle Époque (2020) by Louise Baring.

Like This? Try These

- → Eugène Atget
- → Henri Cartier-Bresson
- → André Kertész

+ PHOTOGRAPHER BIO
British, b. 1972

+ GOOGLE THESE
Our Kids are Going to Hell (2009), *God Forgotten Face* (2011)

+ READ THIS
Robin Maddock discusses *III* in an interview called 'Spot the Ball' with *British Journal of Photography*, at bjp-online.com.

+ WATCH THIS
Maddock discuss his series *Nothing We Can't Fix By Running Away* (2018) at photoworks.org.uk/listen-robin-maddock.

Like This? Try These

→ Thomas Albdorf

→ André Kertész

→ David Spero

Robin Maddock

LA/III/2012

2012

If there is such a thing as a perfectly composed photograph this might just be it. You may think it is not much to look at, but to hurry past it, to turn the page is to overlook its intrinsic poetry and fail to appreciate its aesthetic flair.

Like many great photographers before him, Robin Maddock took to the streets of California one day with his 35mm camera, loaded with black and white film. Unlike other photographers, however, he set himself the task of photographing three things: a ping-pong ball, a sheet of blank paper and splashes of milk, utilizing sunlight and shadow to sketch out his compositions.

The result is *III* (2014) a series about movement, or rather, what movement looks like when photographed. Maddock says levity and brevity link the objects, along with 'making something stop in the camera'. This is a series about stopping or stopped time. In this photograph, as in others from Maddock's conceptually-driven project, time is halted for the briefest of moments. Movement is stopped and recorded in the way that only a camera can record such a thing – as a trace, a record that proves that what we are seeing happened.

Photography scholars talk about the 'index', a type of sign characterized by its physical link to the thing it signifies, and a footprint and a shadow are two examples of the index at work. Maddock's photograph playfully espouses this idea that is so fundamental to analogue photography. He does this through the depiction of the ping-pong ball and its shadow, and the post and its shadow, which in turn simultaneously bisects the frame and anchors the photograph. The subject may just be a ping-pong ball, a post, paving stones, a wall cracks and scuffs, but in Maddock's hands these items become so much more than what we consider them to be. The repetition of dots, cracks that echo the weeds and lines that appear to be etched into the ground all add up to create a photograph that is about nothing much and everything.

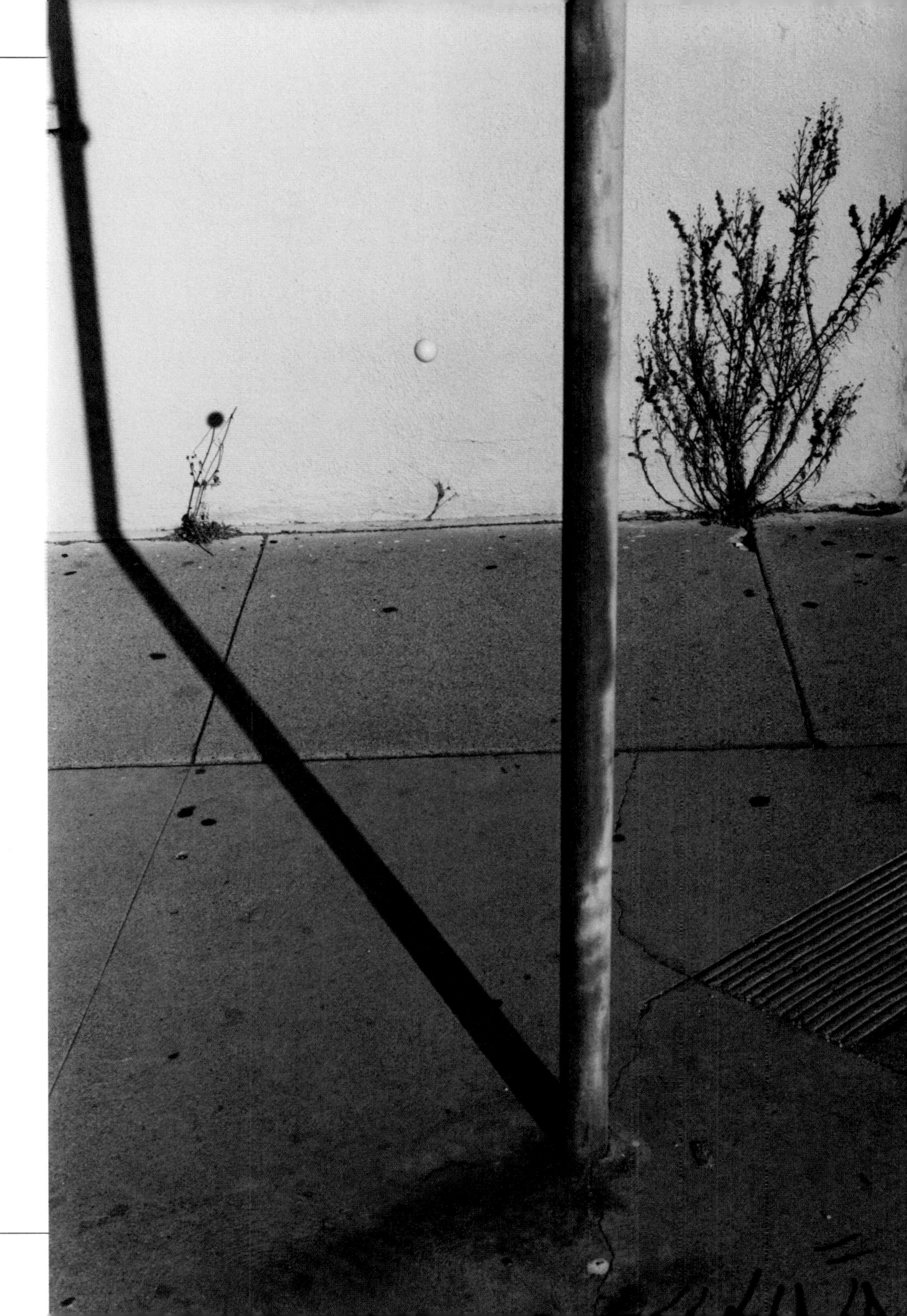

Gjon Mili

Triple Exposure of Pablo Picasso Drawing with Light

1949

Although English-American photographer Eadweard Muybridge got there first, Albanian-born photographer Gjon Mili's experiments with photography have significantly aided understanding of human movement and furthered appreciation of the medium's ability to convincingly depict and deconstruct motion.

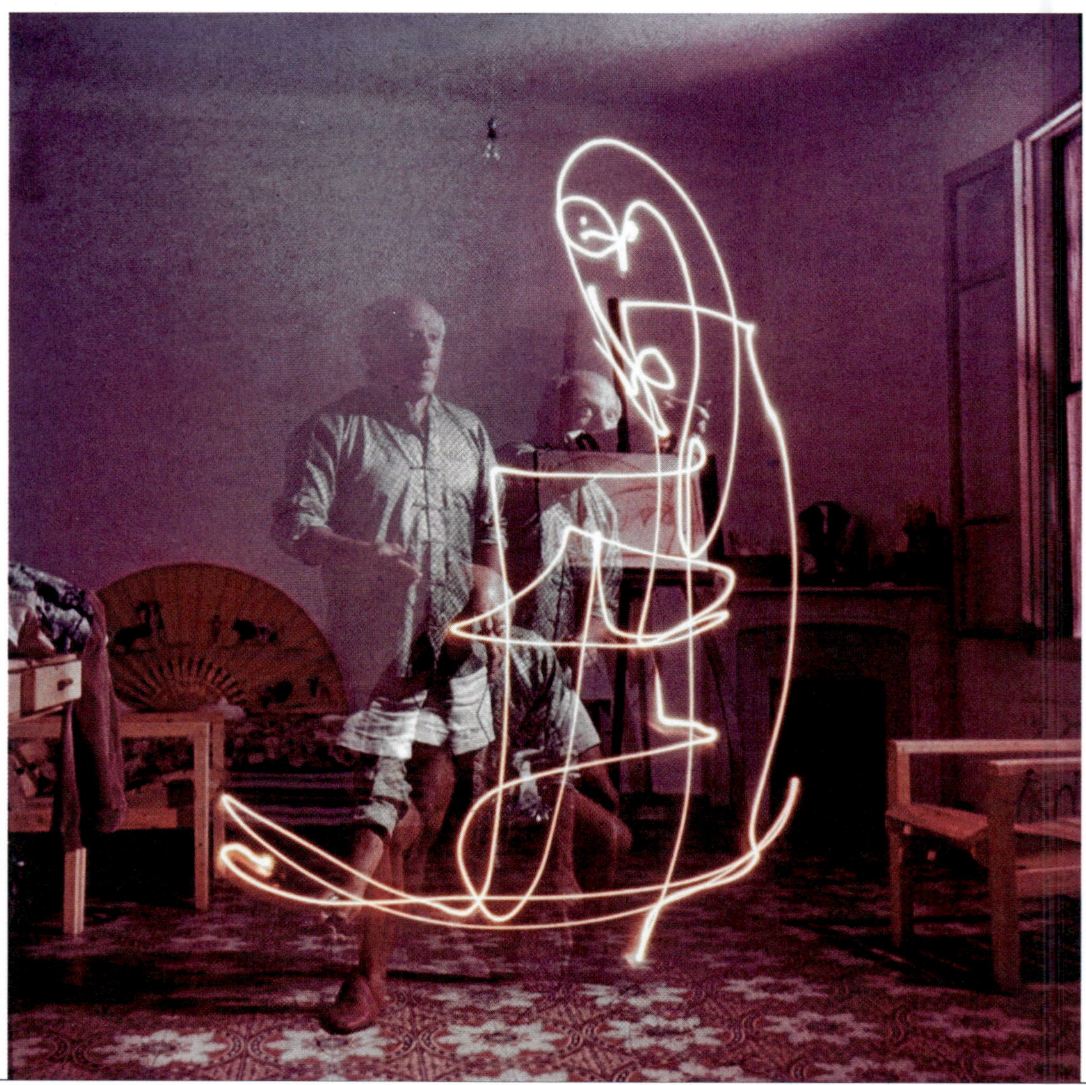

Mili trained as an electrical engineer in the United States and worked with pioneering photographer and inventor Harold Edgerton at Massachusetts Institute of Technology to develop electronic flash and stroboscopic light technologies as well as tungsten filament lights for use in colour photography. Both became known for their influential work with stop-motion photography. Mili put his knowledge and findings to work capturing dancers, musicians, sportspeople and artists for *LIFE* magazine for whom he worked from 1939 until the end of his life.

He is best known for his images that show Spanish artist Pablo Picasso drawing with light. Here, in this triple exposure, you see the maestro at work in an almost frenzied state at his home in Vallauris in the south of France. He is using a flashlight to draw in the air. Using a 1/10,000-second strobe light Mili was able to capture Picasso as he moved and the light streaks in the same image. In Mili's photograph, one of a series he made during his visit to Picasso's home in 1949, the painter, wild-eyed, appears magician-like, like a man possessed. It is almost as though he is having an out-of-body experience. The artist has drawn what looks to be a centaur or bull – two creatures that fascinated him and often appear in his paintings. It is said that Mili had shown Picasso photographs he had made of ice skaters moving in the dark. The skaters had lights embedded in their skates and cut an impressive sight as they leapt in the air and twirled, creating light trails as they went. His attention piqued, Picasso granted Mili five sessions in which the pair experimented with light and light drawing in a darkened room. No one knows what makes a creative genius tick and photography cannot provide the answer but Mili's light-streaked image comes pretty close. His strange portrait gives a glimpse of the man behind the mask with Picasso simultaneously deep in thought and in action. Such a depiction is only possible because of Mili's own creative genius and photography's light-painting capacities.

+ PHOTOGRAPHER BIO
Albanian-American, 1904–84

+ GOOGLE THESE
The Juggler Stan Cavenaugh (1941), *Stroboscopic Image of a Trick Shot by Billiards Champion Willie Hoppe* (1941), *Multiple Exposure of Dancer Alicia Alonso Doing a Pas de Bourré* (1944)

+ SEE THIS
Watch Picasso create his light drawings in a sequence of images by Gjon Mili on the Getty Images YouTube channel.

+ READ THIS
A history of light drawing at lightpaintingphotography.com.

Like This? Try These

- Étienne-Jules Marey
- Barbara Morgan
- Eadweard Muybridge

Ori Gersht

Blow Up: Untitled No. 19

Photo taken: 2007; This print: 2016

Exploding flowers are not something you see every day. Without photography, it is something you may not see at all.

Israeli photographer and video artist Ori Gersht is not the first to explore the differences between human and photographic vision – the American inventor of the electronic flash, Harold Edgerton, made history with his high-speed photographs in the mid twentieth century, but Gersht made his own take on the subject by freezing flowers with liquid nitrogen before detonating them and recording the results at a rate of 1,600 fps. His set-up included ten digital cameras connected to flash guns, calling to mind the efforts of pioneering nineteenth-century English-American photographer Eadweard Muybridge, who also used multiple cameras.

In Gersht's series of large-scale photographs *Blow Up* (2007–08), elegant floral arrangements shatter into thousands of pieces. They evoke the oeuvre of nineteenth-century French painter Henri Fantin-Latour, known for his exquisite still lifes of flowers. However, in Gersht's work, beauty is destroyed in the most violent way, underlining the tension between creation and destruction, and life and death.

Gersht has long been interested in photography's philosophical concerns, among them how the camera can reveal what the human eye cannot see. He points to German literary critic Walter Benjamin's concept of the 'optical unconscious' as an important reference, which explores how photography mediates the viewer's experience and knowledge of the world in unconscious ways. As the viewer ponders the unexpected sight of flowers blown to pieces it brings to mind the camera's powerful and unique way of depicting reality: what it presents to the viewer looks unreal, fake almost. Yet, paradoxically, it is as faithful a representation of reality as is possible. Gersht is also interested in challenging the notion of 'objective truth' in photography and the idea that a photograph is infallible. In this instance he does so by literally shattering that idea of the absolute. His image asks what a photograph is and what its relationship with reality is, begging the question about what constitutes truth. Neither Gersht nor his image provides any firm answers, but in stopping to look and think the viewer may discover nuanced realities and hitherto unknown truths.

+ PHOTOGRAPHER BIO
Israeli, b. 1967

+ GOOGLE THESE
Pomegranate (2006), *Cyclamen D03* (2018), *New Orders, Evertime 10* (2018)

+ WATCH THIS
'Artist Profile: Ori Gersht on his Still Life Series and Art Studio' on the Guggenheim Museum YouTube channel.

Like This? Try These

- → Harold Edgerton
- → Naoya Hatakeyama
- → Laura Letinsky

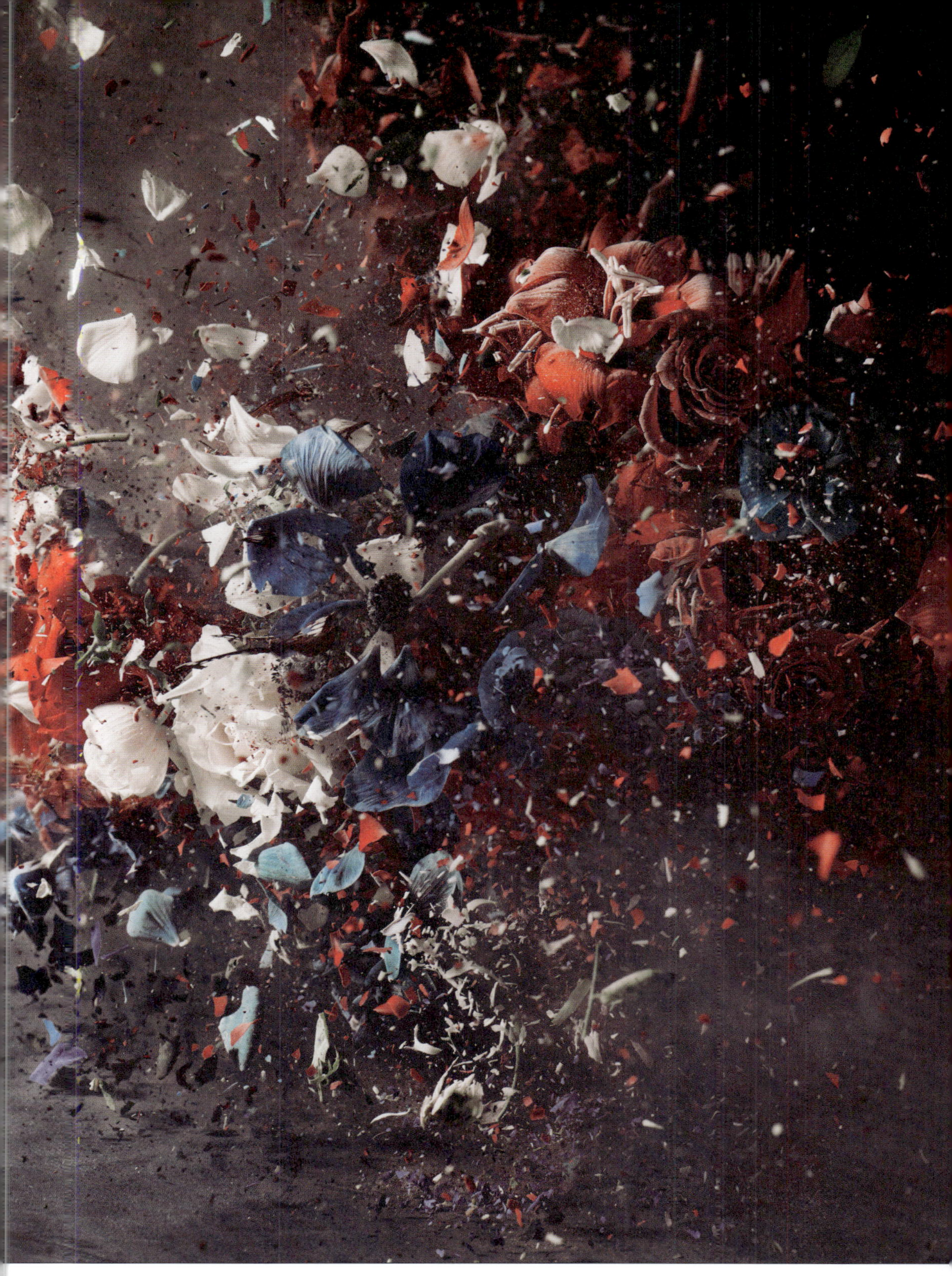

Index